Globalization and Entrepreneurship

THE MCGILL INTERNATIONAL ENTREPRENEURSHIP SERIES

Series editor: Hamid Etemad, *McGill University, Canada.*

Future titles in the series include:

Emerging Paradigms in International Entrepreneurship
Edited by Marion V. Jones and Pavlos Dimitratos

International Entrepreneurship in Small and Medium Size Enterprises
Orientation, Environment and Strategy
Hamid Etemad

Globalization and Entrepreneurship

Policy and Strategy Perspectives

Edited by

Hamid Etemad

McGill University, Canada

and

Richard Wright

University of Richmond, USA

THE MCGILL INTERNATIONAL ENTREPRENEURSHIP SERIES

Edward Elgar

Cheltenham, UK • Northampton, MA, USA

Published by
Edward Elgar Publishing Limited
Glensanda House
Montpellier Parade
Cheltenham
Glos GL50 1UA
UK

Edward Elgar Publishing, Inc.
136 West Street
Suite 202
Northampton
Massachusetts 01060
USA

A catalogue record for this book
is available from the British Library

Library of Congress Cataloguing in Publication Data
Globalization and entrepreneurship : policy and strategy perspectives / edited by Hamid Etemad, Richard Wright.
    p. cm.
  Selected papers from a conference held in Sept. 2000 at McGill University, Montreal.
  Includes bibliographical references and index.
  1. International business enterprises–Management–Congresses. 2. Small business–Management–Congresses. 3. Small business–Technological innovations–Congresses. 4. Strategic planning–Congresses. 5. Entrepreneurship–Congresses. 6. Globalization–Congresses. I. Etemad, Hamid. II. Wright, Richard W.

HD62.4 .G553 2003
658'.049–dc21   2002192762

ISBN 1 84376 024 X

Printed and bound in Great Britain by MPG Books Ltd, Bodmin, Cornwall

Contents

v

PART 3 EMERGING DIMENSIONS OF MANAGEMENT POLICY

Figures

Tables

Contributors

Alam, Quamrul, La Trobe University, Australia

Brenner, Gabrielle A., University of Montreal, Canada

Brown, Peter, Dunedin City Council, New Zealand

Bryer, Philip, Nanzan University, Japan

Chulikavit, Kittinoot, Maejo University, US

Dahab, Sônia, Universidade Nova de Lisboa and Universidade Federal da Bahía, Portugal

Dana, Leo-Paul, University of Canterbury, New Zealand

Esperança, José Paulo, Instituto Superior de Ciências do Trabalho e da Empresa and Universidade Católica Portuguesa, Portugal

Etemad, Hamid, McGill University, Canada

Filion, Louis Jacques, University of Montreal, Canada

Korot, Len, Technology Incubator, US

Lituchy, Terri R., Cal Poly State University, US

Manalova, Tatiana S., Boston University, US

McNaughton, Rod, University of Waterloo, Canada

Menzies, Teresa V., Brock University, Canada

Michaelas, Nicos, Manchester Business School, UK

Pacher, John, La Trobe University, Australia

Poutziouris, Panikkos, Manchester Business School, UK

Reavley, Martha A., University of Windsor, Canada

Rose, Jerman, Washington State University, US

Soufani, Khaled, Concordia University, Canada

Tovstiga, George, ABB Business Services, Switzerland

Wright, Richard, University of Richmond, US

Preface

On the surface, the activities of small or entrepreneurial businesses and those of multinational enterprises seem highly divergent. Until recently, they have in fact operated in largely separate realms, each in its own competitive space, and each with characteristics markedly different from those of the other. However, globalization has begun to dismantle the barriers that traditionally segregated local business opportunities and local firms from their international counterparts. Local markets are becoming integral parts of broader, global markets. Consequently, internationally oriented entrepreneurs can now view a much broader range of opportunities and competitive modes, unrestricted by national boundaries. In this integrating global environment, entrepreneurs and emerging businesses face both new opportunities, and formidable new challenges.

One result of the breakdown of the lines of demarcation, that formerly segregated these disparate fields of management, is the emergence of a new subfield of research – *international entrepreneurship*. To explore and develop this emerging area of research, a pioneering, three-day conference was held in September 2000 at McGill University, in Montreal, Canada, under the joint auspices of McGill's Business and Management Research Centre, and the Dobson Centre for Entrepreneurial Studies. The conference brought together leading scholars from international business, and from small business/entrepreneurship, to stimulate integration of research in what had previously been widely divergent fields.

Selected papers were subjected to a rigorous process of peer review and comments. Each was revised extensively to incorporate and to reflect the perspectives of other disciplines. The final product is a series of leading-edge research papers presented in this volume, as well as in two other publications.[1]

The authors acknowledge with special gratitude McGill's Dobson Centre for Entrepreneurial Studies and its director, Peter Johnson, for their sustained support of these pioneering conferences, especially the inaugural one in September 1998, which have generated these and other leading-edge contributions to the emerging field of international entrepreneurship. We thank the many contributing authors, both for their helpful feedback to other authors, and for their patience in revising – sometimes repeatedly – their own contributions. Finally, we commend the foresight of Edward

Elgar Publishing and its Acquisition Editor, Alan M. Sturmer, for recognizing the importance of international entrepreneurship by its prominent publication of research in this emerging field. *The McGill International Entrepreneurship series* from Edward Elgar, which includes this book, is a culmination of that foresight.[2]

It is clear that as globalization proceeds apace, entrepreneurs and small businesses will play a more prominent role in the global business arena. In this increasingly interconnected world, it is ever more important that we learn from each other – both across cultures and across academic disciplines. The works in this collection provide a wealth of new insights on both traditional and emerging aspects of SME internationalization, from a variety of national perspectives and from a variety of disciplines. We hope that they will provide valuable insights for business leaders, policy formulator, and academics alike in understanding and coping with our rapidly changing world.

Hamid Etemad
Richard Wright

Montreal, December 2001

NOTES

1. Other papers emanating from the 2000 McGill conference have appeared in special issues of *Journal of International Management*, Vol. 7, No. 3 (Fall 2001); and in *Small Business Economics* (2002, forthcoming). Both collections are under the guest editorship of Hamid Etemad and Richard W. Wright.
2. A companion volume in the Elgar series, entitled *International Entrepreneurship in Small and Medium Size Enterprises: Orientation, Environment and Strategy* (forthcoming), edited by Hamid Etemad, will also house a collection of papers from the conference.

PART 1

The Internationalization Process

1. Globalization and entrepreneurship

Hamid Etemad and Richard Wright

INTRODUCTION

The global business environment is changing dramatically. Traditionally, competition in international markets has been the realm of large companies, while smaller businesses remained local or regional in scope. However, the removal of government-imposed barriers that segregated and protected domestic markets and recent technological advances in manufacturing, transportation and telecommunications allows even the smallest firms access to customers, suppliers and collaborators around the world. Economic growth and innovation, both domestically and internationally, are fuelled increasingly by small companies and/or entrepreneurial enterprises. These trends will impact profoundly on management strategies, on public policies, and on the daily lives of all people.

This volume focuses on the phenomenon of globalization, and specifically its relevance to and impact on small and medium-sized enterprises (SMEs) and entrepreneurship. The collective writings and insights presented in this book, by authors from around the world, shed new light on prevailing research topics, as well as challenging certain aspects of the received literature. Consider, for example, the unresolved issues surrounding the internationalization process. It seemed initially that theories of incremental internationalization or 'stage models', put forth by Bilkey and Tesar (1977), Cavusgil (1984), Cavusgil and Nevin (1981), Johanson and Vahlne (1990 and 1992) and others, which advocated experiential growth in international markets from a small, domestic operation through progressively fuller and riskier international operations organizations, would be more applicable to SMEs than the 'internationalization theory of MNEs' as articulated by Buckley and Casson (1976), Hymer (1976), Dunning (1980 and 1988), and others. The research findings presented in this volume suggest that while parts of each theory can help to explain parts of the SME internationalization phenomenon, none can adequately explain all aspects of the process. There is a need for new insights and new perspectives, which this book strives to provide.

Globalization of the business environment may have changed the implicit assumptions of both schools of thought. Markets are becoming much more competitive than ever before, exposing SMEs – both at home and abroad – to greater competitive risk. But these risks are largely industry-specific, and they exist even at home, due largely to liberalization of environments and deregulation of markets. To compete successfully in today's business arena, firms must be globally competitive, even if they do not compete directly in foreign markets. Internationalizing enterprises no longer need to gain incremental experience through their own gradual, progressive presence in international markets in order to become globally competitive, as the 'stage' theories suggest. On the one hand, many SMEs already experience world-scale industry-specific competition in their domestic markets; and on the other, improved communication has removed many barriers to knowledge acquisition at home. Learning and experiencing by proxy are increasingly feasible. Location-specific barriers no longer need impede internationalization as they once did.

While the fast pace of technological change has helped to harmonize many aspects of international operations – hence reducing some of the risks associated with diversity – it also imposes a temporal regime of its own, forcing firms, both large and small, to move rapidly into international markets. Several chapters of this book provide insights into this quickening pace, which is prompting many SMEs to internationalize at rates unforeseen by conventional theories.

As SMEs face a growing intensity of industry-specific competitiveness at home, they may either 'internationalize' at home by outsourcing to other firms with international coverage, or they may venture out of the home market, often in alliance with other local enterprises facing similar competitive conditions. Through such alliances, SMEs can avoid many of the location-specific risks due to 'foreignness' (Hymer, 1976) and inadequate knowledge of the foreign operating environment, as their local partners may compensate for these shortcomings. As a result, SMEs can leverage their competitive and comparative advantages to internationalize rapidly, often sharing technological and information infrastructures with other like-minded firms. Research findings reported in this book provide insights into how integration and coordination of such informational and technological support systems can successfully mitigate against adversity. Localized public policies, embodied in various forms of networking and cluster facilitation, may serve not only to strengthen local enterprises; they can also reduce the risks of technology transfer from afar to these dense pockets of globally oriented activities. The dynamics of SME internationalization now focus more on the commonalities of firms rather than on the differences. The contributors to this book provide new insights into how SMEs can leverage advantage through commonalities, or mutual benefits, shared with others based in different parts of the world – often regardless of size – to establish a meaningful presence in international markets.

THE INTERNATIONALIZATION PROCESS

The opening section of this book explores alternative routes by which small firms can achieve international presence. The three chapters that follow the overview focus on traditional models of SME internationalization: exporting; integrated partnership with large firms through contract manufacturing; and foreign direct investment.

The first of these, Chapter 2, examines what traditionally has been the most common route of internationalization for small firms: exporting. Panikkos Poutziouris, Khaled Soufani and Nicos Michaelas discuss the findings of their recent empirical study of the determinants of successful exporting of 4,345 SMEs, drawn from a rich base of 110,000 British-based companies from ten broad sectors, over a period of eight years. This database yields some 25,000 cross-sectional firm-year data points, far more than in most previous studies. Other research databases of this size have generally excluded small firms; thus very little is known about them. All of the companies studied here are unlisted, independent, privately held companies with fewer than 250 employees. Using multivariate statistical techniques and panel data analysis, the authors regress export intensity against a number of demographic, business and financial factors, including the firm's age, size, degree of operating risk, asset structure, financial leverage, technological intensity, growth rate, profitability, business location and industry sector and the state of the economy.

While many previous studies have examined the factors influencing export intensity on a cross-sectional basis, the significance of the research reported here is in its simultaneous analysis of several variables in a very large sample size; the extended period over which the sample firms were studied; and its specific focus on SMEs. The findings reported confirm some previous research findings, based on much smaller and industry-specific examples, but they also contradict others. For example, the negative association the authors found between age of the firm and export intensity implies that time is not a critical factor in export growth. The finding lends support to the recent rapid globalization phenomenon, commonly known as 'born global', but it does not support the concept of expansion over time through experiential learning, as posited by the 'stage' theories of internationalization. Their findings also reinforce earlier evidence that export growth is positively correlated with firm size.

Another interesting finding of this study is the highly significant and negative impact of 'financial gearing' (ratio of total debt to total assets): SMEs with higher export intensity were found to have lower debt-to-asset ratios than non-exporters. Either these firms are more profitable (financing growth from retained earnings), or they leverage their assets more effectively than firms with lower export intensity, which may imply that exporting firms are better managed than their non-exporting counterparts. Yet another significant finding is that 'exporting firms tend to have a lower investment in intangible assets' than do non-exporters. One explanation may be that SMEs – especially younger SMEs – are failing to leverage their intangible assets (such as technology, brand equity, and human assets) effectively. The authors report that 89 firms in their sample had 'no intangible assets recorded in their balance sheet'. Taken to its logical conclusion, this appears to be a significant oversight by SMEs, with far-reaching implications: investment in intangible assets, especially in brand equity, can potentially help to propel the globalization of SMEs just as it has for larger, multinational firms.

In Chapter 3, two researchers from Portugal, Sônia Dahab and José Paulo Esperança, focus on another route by which smaller firms increasingly achieve global efficiencies and market access: integrated outsourcing. They explain that large firms have a growing propensity to rely on various forms of external partnerships for elements of their value chains, instead of investing in their own vertical integration. In contrast to more conventional outsourcing where relatively short-term production-cost considerations play a major role in fostering external purchasing, integrated outsourcing leads to a much closer integration between the client and supplier firms' production lines and delivery systems. Dahab and Esperança review the management implications of vertical integration versus outsourcing decisions by large firms. They illustrate, with two case examples, how synergistic, integrated outsourcing arrangements can provide SMEs with opportunities both to achieve new efficiencies and to 'piggyback' on larger firms to enter foreign markets. By piggybacking, firms can establish their own foreign presence and acquire their own country-specific knowledge swiftly and without the risk and investment normally required.

The literature on international marketing distinguishes between *direct* and *indirect* exporting. In conventional, 'direct' exporting, a firm takes direct management of its exporting process: it adopts the higher risk–reward structure of export markets, learns about the export market, collects information about the market behavior of competitors and establishes its own presence in the local market. In contrast, SMEs involved in 'indirect' exporting – usually by serving as arm's-length suppliers to larger, international firms – are sheltered from dealing with the market directly by piggybacking on a larger firm's presence in the foreign marketplace. But, as a result, they are deprived of all the information, experience and learning benefits of direct exporting. However, *integrated outsourcing*, as Dahab and Esperança describe, provides a new type of arrangement whereby the smaller firm can gain the efficiencies of world-scale production by integrating directly into the value chain of the large firm, thus gaining indirectly some of the experiential aspects of internationalization through the larger firm. The concept of integrated outsourcing, taken to its logical extension, can consume many of the conventional market entry modes and potentially become a network of integrated outsourcing of all functions, each located in a different part of the world, serving global markets. This may, for example, include local distribution arrangements (exporting), local production facilities (outsourcing), and partial local investment and acquisition (equity joint ventures), as well as fully owned green-field operations.

Traditionally most small firms have achieved international presence either by exporting to foreign markets (Chapter 2), or by entering into supplier relationships with larger, international firms (Chapter 3). However, an increasing number of small companies establish affiliates abroad and thus emerge and compete as small multinationals. The drivers of foreign direct investment (FDI) by SMEs differ significantly from those influencing exporting, and they appear also to be highly industry-specific. While the size limitation of the domestic market may be a key driver of exporting, drivers such as market disequilibria, government-imposed distortions, or market structure imperfections influence foreign direct investment.

In Chapter 4, Tatiana S. Manalova addresses the question of what industry structural and competitive forces determine foreign direct investment by SMEs. She first reviews theoretical perspectives on the small multinational, from various disciplines. She then develops a model of industry structural and competitive influences on FDI by SMEs. The model captures the impact of six supply-side structural forces: scale economies, R&D scale, advertising scale, capital scale, industry age and industry growth; two demand-side structural forces: market demand and market size; and four competitive forces: oligopolistic rivalry, mimetic isomorphism, strategic networks, and community influences. She operationalizes her model by formulating 12 propositions on the directional impact of these forces, and discusses the theoretical and practical implications of the framework.

FACILITATING SMALL-FIRM INTERNATIONALIZATION

The second section of this book focuses on different kinds of systems – both formal and informal – which may enable or facilitate the internationalization of small firms. The first two chapters provide examples of how governments can help and/or hinder small-firm internationalization, while the two following chapters illustrate how entrepreneurs can create their own social support systems to enhance growth and internationalization.

Manalova (Chapter 4) demonstrated that 'global industries' need not be *terra incognita* for small companies. Public policies, both at home and abroad, impact substantially on the modes of SME internationalization. While hostile domestic (home) conditions can *force* companies to venture out, conducive domestic policies and conditions can *propel* SMEs to evaluate global supply, demand, competition and industry conditions in various potential host countries before favoring one mode of internationalization and one host country over another. The competitiveness of supply conditions, related industries, demand conditions, and fiscal and technological infrastructures at home can all enhance the global competitiveness of a country's SMEs, whether they decide in favor of growth strategies based on staying at home or venturing abroad. When they are competitive at home, they become excellent candidates to supply other, internationalized SMEs, or larger firms. Should they decide to venture into international markets, the likelihood of their success is correspondingly high.

Conducive environments are usually virtuous, self-reinforcing cycles, as, for example, they attract globally competitive FDI with more advanced technologies, logistics and strategies. In contrast, when environments are adverse, the reverse cycle may operate: local enterprises, including SMEs, are not empowered to internationalize; nor is globally competitive FDI attracted. As a direct result, enterprises in such environments may be less well equipped to compete globally than their counterparts in more conducive environments.

Part 2 of the book opens with an overview of the challenges and opportunities facing Australian SMEs by two Australian-based scholars, Quamrul Alam and John Pacher. Their essay points to the ambiguity of Australia's business environment. Despite well-intentioned public policies, the authors identify a host of problems which impede the successful internationalization of Australian-based SMEs: lack of strategic direction, outdated export strategy, inadequate managerial expertise, inefficient use of information technology, and the general absence of an innovation-driven culture. Australia's traditional dependence on inbound FDI to enhance domestic competitiveness is also rendered less effective, as multinational enterprises (MNEs) consider more conducive environments located elsewhere for their subsidiary operations. Relatively less competitive Australian SMEs suffer further from lack of exposure to foreign exchange transactions, and from inadequate cultivation of overseas markets and relationships with foreign companies. According to Alam and Pacher, the lack of a well-defined industrial policy, coupled with low labor productivity, causes Australian SMEs to lose out on all fronts. They are neither competitive enough to outsource at home for other SMEs or MNEs (see Dahab and Esperança, Chapter 3) nor capable of venturing into the international markets on their own by exporting (see Poutziouris, Soufani and Michaelas, Chapter 2) or by FDI (see Manalova, Chapter 4).

Among the policy recommendations proposed by Alam and Pacher is the encouragement of government-assisted cluster development programs for Australian SMEs. Localized, industry-specific assistance programs, as opposed to national industrial policies based on the Australian model, may be more effective in creating environmentally conducive conditions for SMEs. Chapter 6 focuses on the concept and the practical implementation of such programs. Peter Brown and Rod McNaughton first review and synthesize the literature on geographical co-location. Then they examine cluster development programs initiated in New Zealand, informed by data gathered from interviews with executives of 27 firms actively engaged in an electronics cluster in Christchurch.

This chapter highlights important aspects of public policy toward SMEs. Although the industrial cluster policy of the New Zealand government seems conceptually sound, the authors feel that its implementation is less effective than it could be. Data from their research indicate that there is a significant gap between policy development and the specific needs of firms within the cluster. Firms within the Christchurch electronic cluster made a clear call for services from government agencies in response to their needs, including access to applied research, promotional activities, market development, and dissemination of market information; but many of the managers involved felt that these needs were inadequately met. This chapter is rich in practical insights, both in identifying strengths and weaknesses in the implementation of the Christchurch cluster, and in addressing the broader implications relevant to public policy and SME management with regard to localized and industry-specific clusters, wherever they may be located.

While governmental policies can be instrumental in creating conditions for firms to exploit networking and relation-related advantages through industrial clusters, as Chapter 6 illustrates, firms can also establish their own networks, and draw network-related advantages from them, even in the absence of governmental initiatives. Prominent examples are ethnic and social networks. The following two chapters consider aspects of informal networking by SMEs.

Ethnic networks have long been recognized as vital to the success of many ethnic entrepreneurs. However, relatively little emphasis has been placed specifically on this important phenomenon as an internationalization engine for SMEs. In Chapter 7, Teresa V. Menzies, Gabrielle A.

Brenner and Louis Jacques Filion present and discuss the findings of their comprehensive, multidisciplinary review of the literature on ethnic minority entrepreneurship, social capital and networks. They begin with a brief outline of some major theories in the field; then they summarize the findings and conclusions of 80 studies on ethnic minority entrepreneurship conducted between 1988 and 1999 in Europe, North America and Asia. The review finds strong use of ethnic social capital, including co-ethnic labor, markets and sources of finance. They present strong evidence of the existence and use of 'dense' co-ethnic networks, many of them transnational and integral to international entrepreneurship. They found, however, that a few ethnic groups did not make use of their ethnic resources and lacked dense networks, relying instead on informal family networks. The authors conclude their chapter by framing their findings as tentative propositions that can act as a guide for further discussion, as research questions for empirical studies, and as potential steps in theory building.

Still another important phenomenon in international entrepreneurship is the growing role of women entrepreneurs, many in business firms which are international or even 'born global'. Even in business-friendly environments, such as Japan, women are often treated by society as subordinate to their male counterparts. Women entrepreneurs are thus exposed to the double jeopardy of gender discrimination and small firm size. To understand better the role of women who own small businesses in other cultures, Terri R. Lituchy, Philip Bryer and Martha A. Reavley (Chapter 8) conducted structured interviews with women entrepreneurs in the Czech Republic and Japan. They sought to understand why women forge ahead on their own as entrepreneurs, despite the barriers of glass ceilings and other forms of gender-related discrimination in the workplace. They open by discussing three common models of entrepreneurship. They find that the women interviewed faced many of the same challenges and difficulties as women entrepreneurs in North America: delegating and managing people, for example, were important concerns for all interviewed. Specific regional problems, which the authors identified, include the poor cash-flow management skills of the Czech women (which, they feel, can be explained by the long dominance of a Communist economic system in that country prior to 1989). In Japan the lack of business skills training and the absence of role models hindered women from developing entrepreneurial skills. This chapter provides original and highly useful insights into the crucially important role of women as potential and actual international entrepreneurs in the developing and industrialized world alike.

EMERGING DIMENSIONS OF MANAGEMENT POLICY

The evolution of entrepreneurship combined with globalization of the business environment has created new opportunities and given rise to new managerial challenges. The rapidly evolving technology- and information-intensive environment, for example, requires new techniques both for protecting intellectual property and for exploiting it globally. Likewise, conducting international business through the World-Wide Web by e-commerce is pushing many traditional concepts beyond their boundaries, requiring a re-examination of accepted practices of the past. The final section of this book elaborates on new tools and emerging developments in managing the internationalization of SMEs. The first chapter focuses on knowledge management; the second on the role and management of e-commerce in small-firm internationalization; and the third on managing inter-firm relationships.

The premise underlying the research of Leo-Paul Dana, Len Korot and George Tovstiga, reported in Chapter 9, is that high-technology, knowledge-intensive organizations are the vanguard of a new, networked, global economy that is rapidly overriding national and cultural boundaries. To test this premise, they studied knowledge management practices of 69 small, knowledge-intensive firms located in three diverse areas: the Silicon Valley in California, the Netherlands, and Singapore. Employing a so-called Knowledge Practices Survey, they were able to establish a momentary 'fingerprint' of the cultural and practical profiles of each organization's practices and processes relating to how knowledge is dealt with in the firm. Their research provides evidence that knowledge management practices and cultural beliefs, values and behavioral norms of innovative entrepreneurial firms are more akin than dissimilar, regardless of the national context. They found that knowledge-related practices of 'Network Age' firms in all three regions exhibit common features such as: (1) experimentation is actively encouraged; (2) knowledge is collectively shared; and (3) decision making is collective. They found, further, that leading-edge firms have a flexible and self-adapting structure, possessing the ability to evolve and thrive amid continuous and unpredictable change.

The conclusions of this chapter suggest that although each region has its own culture, there is also an inter-continental innovation culture among leading-edge firms – which the authors call 'techno-culture' – that transcends national boundaries. The chapter concludes by identifying significant gaps between perceived importance and current practice regarding knowledge management in each of the regions.

The leveraging of information and technology by internationalizing

SMEs is embodied in electronic commerce. Chapter 10 focuses on the prospects and problems of e-commerce by internationalizing SMEs in developing countries. Kittinoot Chulikavit and Jerman Rose conducted in-depth
interviews and developed case studies of four small Thai firms, each of
which has attempted to use e-commerce within the past five years to expand
its markets internationally. Two of the firms were relatively successful in
their use of e-commerce to internationalize, while the other two were not.
In their analysis, Chulikavit and Rose identify and discuss two factors
which appeared critical in determining the success or failure of e-commerce
in the firms they studied. The first factor involved the degree of complexity and customization of the firm's products. The second was the role of
management's experience with and commitment to e-commerce, including
not only an understanding of how e-commerce works and its costs and
benefits, but also international skills and experience required to achieve
success, including English-language competence, understanding of cultural differences, and international marketing skills. The authors conclude by
synthesizing their own findings with those of other researchers to develop
a conceptual framework and specific hypotheses, to guide future research
into this important emerging area of SME internationalization.

The research findings reported in this book emphasize repeatedly that, in
today's integrating business environment, small firms must be globally
competitive to survive, even if they do not compete directly in foreign
markets. But very few small firms are equipped to achieve these efficiencies
on their own. Increasingly, small firms are relying on collaborative linkages
with other firms to complement their limited internal resources. SMEs may
establish symbiotic relationships with larger MNEs through such forms as
integrated outsourcing (described in by Dahab and Esperança in Chapter
3) in order to increase their mutual competitiveness. As well, they can
network with other small firms, either in formal clusters (see Brown and
McNaughton in Chapter 6), or through informal social networks (see
Menzies, Brenner and Filion in Chapter 7, and Lituchy, Bryer and Reavely
in Chapter 8) to accomplish similar objectives.

In the concluding chapter, Hamid Etemad elaborates on the role and
management of relationships in the internationalization of SMEs. He
emphasizes, first, that collaborative international business networks are not
new: relationships have always been the essence of international business.
Indeed, the parent–subsidiary structure of the traditional MNE is, in effect,
a collaborative network of organizations, held together through shared
ownership and hierarchical control. While the subsidiary is highly dependent on the MNE's network, especially in the early stages of its life cycle in
a foreign environment, Etemad finds that their relations evolve with time.
The initial relations, based on a uni-directional dependence of the subsidi-

ary on the MNE's system, may change to one of interdependence and even reverse themselves when a subsidiary begins to become globally competitive. But even in such large established companies, the traditional management structure, based on formal ownership and control, is waning, as firms focus more on developing their own core competencies within the context of a globally competitive value chain and outsource other elements of value elsewhere to deliver higher value to the entire network. Newer modes of internationalization, based on networks of partnerships and alliances, are also emerging. The conventional models of managing relationships by virtue of hierarchy and ownership are being replaced by partnership-based arrangements, in which size is largely immaterial.

Etemad first suggests that the new partnership-based arrangements portray characteristics of *symbiosis* and *synergy*, in which a partner strives to deliver higher value to its network of partners. He then illustrates, with specific case examples, the shift from traditional forms of collaboration to newer forms of collaboration in which stability and control emanate from interdependence and mutuality of benefit. The author argues that this represents a new competitive paradigm, in which the unit of competition is no longer the individual firm but, rather, networks of firms collaborating for increased global competitiveness based on mutual benefit. SMEs can develop their own capabilities and competencies for generating higher common benefits to be shared with others based in different parts of the world – often regardless of size – thereby establishing a meaningful presence in international markets. The key to successful internationalization of SMEs no longer lies just in their internal resources and management capabilities, but increasingly in the ability of SME managers to understand their relative position in relation to the network with which they have established interdependence, and to manage such inter-firm relationships to generate globally competitive value chains. Etemad suggests that such demanding and evolving objectives can be achieved through *relation-based management* of constituent enterprises, often of different sizes and in different locations. This is the challenge facing internationalizing SMEs.

REFERENCES

Bilkey, Warren J. and George Tesar (1977), 'The export behavior of smaller sized Wisconsin manufacturing firms', *Journal of International Business Studies*, 8 (1): 93–8.

Buckley, Peter J. and Mark Casson (1976), *The Future of the Multinational Enterprise*. London: Macmillan.

Cavusgil, S. Tamer (1984), 'Differences among exporting firms based on their degree of internationalization', *Journal of Business Research*, 12 (2): 195–208.

Cavusgil, S. Tamer and R.J. Nevin (1981), 'International determinants of export marketing behavior', *Journal of Marketing Research*, 28: 114–19.

Dunning, John H. (1980), 'Toward an eclectic theory of international production: empirical tests', *Journal of International Business Studies*, 11(1): 9–31.

Dunning, John H. (1988), 'The eclectic paradigm of international production: a restatement and some possible extensions', *Journal of International Business Studies*, 19(1): 1–31.

Hymer, Stephan (1976), *International Operations of National Firms: A Study of Direct Foreign Investment.* Cambridge, MA: MIT Press.

Johanson, Jan and Jan-Erik Vahlne (1990), 'The mechanism of internationalization', *International Marketing Review*, 7(4): 11–24.

Johanson, Jan and Jan-Erik Vahlne (1992), 'Management of foreign market entry', *Scandinavian International Business Review*, 1(3): 9–27.

2. On the determinants of exporting: UK evidence

Panikkos Poutziouris, Khaled Soufani and Nicos Michaelas

INTRODUCTION

The post-industrial development of the UK economy has been clearly associated with the sustainable performance of internationally competitive industries involving both small and large enterprises that operate in the production, distribution and services sectors. According to industrial statistics, export growth has been the main driving force behind the recovery in UK production output in the early 1990s, and, recognizing this, government often calls for a more strategic approach to fostering the export performance throughout the economy (HM Government, 1994). The characteristics of larger, exporting firms have been well documented in the literature. For such firms it is observed that exporting enhances business growth potential (i.e. through economies of scale and scope), accelerates technological and marketing innovations, diversifies business risk and improves company financial performance (Terpstra and Sarathy, 1994 and Bradley, 1995). However, even though it has been noted that an increase in the number of actively exporting small and medium-sized enterprises (SMEs) would make a larger contribution to job creation, stimulate economic growth, and improve the national balance of payments (Verhoeven, 1988; Samiee and Walters, 1990), little study has been done on which SMEs successfully internationalize and why.

Increases in local competition between enterprises, irrespective of their scales of operation, result in additional pressures to seek new markets for their products, which can be found by internationalizing, that is, by launching their entrepreneurial activities beyond their local or national boundaries. An important mode of internationalization for SMEs – exporting – is considered by many to be instrumental in ensuring their survival and growth (D'Souza and McDougall, 1989; Edmunds and Khoury, 1986). Despite the availability of overseas market niches, SMEs appear to be far from realizing their export growth potential. SMEs often find the pursuit of lengthy internationalization strategies outside of their planning horizon and beyond their organizational and entrepreneurial capabilities. Along with other factors, such hurdles have led specialists in industry, government and academia to conclude the existence of an 'export gap' for SMEs (Bannock and Daly, 1994). The primary aim of this investigation is to extend empirical work on exporting SMEs by establishing a profile of the export-oriented small-scale venture, thereby informing debate about optimal SME exporting strategies so that this gap in the literature may be bridged.

THEORETICAL FRAMEWORK

Theories of international business identify factors that explain why businesses, large or small, internationalize. A frequently made assumption is that internationally oriented businesses are experienced, are well established in the market place (operating nation-wide or enjoying domination in a loyal local niche), are well endowed by financial resources and human capital, and are able to adopt a strategic approach to the management of risk and uncertainty. This is the dominant stream in the theoretical literature, covering the economics and diversification of relatively large multinational enterprises (MNEs), their development and their strategies. The other stream of studies looks at the internationalization of small and medium-sized enterprises (Dichtl *et al.*, 1984).

As exporting is an important mode of internationalizing, there have been many studies on the organizational determinants of exporting. These studies examined the structural and behavioural parameters within the organization that have a facilitating or inhibiting effect on various aspects of its export behaviour, such as export propensity, development and performance (Olson and Wiedersheim-Paul, 1978). Also, many of these studies were confined to manufacturing companies because of the significant contribution to economic activity and the dominant position in international trade that these firms enjoy (World Bank, 1995). Additionally, some studies have looked at organizational factors in the agricultural sector (Aksoy and Kaynak, 1994), service companies (Edvadsson *et al.*, 1993), and retail institutions (Salmon and Tordjman, 1989); these sectors were subject to separate investigation due to idiosyncratic export behaviour patterns (Leonidou, 1998). Again, the emphasis in this work was on larger enterprises.

Studies of the international activities of SMEs have been conducted primarily in the field of international marketing, focusing on the motives for exporting, differences between (passive and active) exporters vis-à-vis non-exporters, and market factors leading to export success rather than organizational factors. In this study, we use the general framework set up in the extensive literature review conducted by Leonidou (1998). In his research, exporting-related studies were categorized along conceptual, methodological and empirical dimensions so that the examination of the relationships between organizational factors and the different aspects of export behaviour could be unified. Leonidou (1998) classifies organizational determinants of exporting into four broad categories, as follows:

- *company demographics*: location, age of the firm, size, business ties and business activity;
- *operating elements*: product characteristics, domestic expansion, and operating capacity;
- *enterprise resources*: marketing capabilities, financial resources, human resources, technological background, research and development;
- *corporate objectives*: business growth, profitability, and stability.

Based on the above theoretical framework and on the information available in our database, discussed below, we work with a subset of these variables, detailed below.

Business Age

With regard to the relationship between exporting and business age, researchers have very conflicting views. A number of studies have found that younger firms are more inclined to export as this can be one strategy for them to increase sales and achieve growth (Lee and Brasch, 1978; Czinkota and Ursic, 1983). This is particularly true for new high-technology firms that enter the global arena even before the finalization of the prototype product (Brush, 1995). The opposite view contends that more established companies resort to exports as a way to capitalize on their business experience and exit the saturated home market (Welch and Wiedersheim-Paul, 1980; Cambridge Small Business Research Centre, 1992). In the case of SMEs, we hypothesize that older, more established ventures will have the financial and human capital to reinvent their product life cycle overseas and to 'break out' from national and often local niches. Thus our first hypothesis is:

H1: Age of the company is positively related to export intensity.

Business Size

Company size, measured in terms of the number of employees, turnover, or value of total assets, constitutes one of the most important factors stimulating export performance (Reid, 1982; Rynning and Andersen, 1994). As Leonidou (1998) summarizes, the export orientation of large enterprises is positively related to the presence of human capital, resource base, economies of scale and risk propensity. Large enterprises tend to have more competent, dynamic and open-minded management who appreciate the usefulness of exporting and thus perform foreign marketing tasks effectively (Tookey, 1964; Bilkey and Tesar, 1977; Abdel-Malek, 1978). Additionally, large firms have access to more and better marketing, financial, technical expertise and engineering resources which can support and sustain export functions (Abdel-Malek, 1978; Cavusgil, 1980; Garnier, 1982; Cavusgil and Naor, 1987; Calof, 1994; Tyebjee, 1994). Moreover, larger firms have economies of scale in production and marketing which facilitate easier access to foreign markets (Hirsch and Adar, 1974; Samiee and Walters, 1990). Not surprisingly, given their resource base and market power, large enterprises tend to be more risk-tolerant and adventurous in the market and can afford to make wrong moves (Bonaccorsi, 1992; Calof, 1994). Thus, our next hypothesis is:

H2: Company size measured by turnover is positively related to export intensity.

Operating Risk

A firm operating in overseas markets is exposed to high levels of risk and uncertainty, as it has to deal with the fluctuations and uncertainties under-pinning the economic climate of more than one country. Such high levels of risk and uncertainty may lead to high fluctuations in returns and hinder export initiation and expansion (Wiedersheim-Paul *et al.*, 1978). These firms are more risk-tolerant due to their easier access to information sources, and because of their organizational capability and resource base that can alleviate operating risk and thus can endure the impact of less than optimal international business strategy (Bonaccorsi, 1992; Calof, 1994). The higher the reliance of firms on overseas markets for the sale of their products or services, the higher their exposure to overseas market uncer-tainties. Under such circumstances we could expect export-oriented firms to face higher fluctuations in their returns (operating risk), reflecting the fluctuations in the international economic climate. Based on these argu-ments, we propose the following hypothesis:

H3: Operating risk is positively related to export intensity.

Asset Structure

Access to finance enables investment in fixed assets (i.e. production equipment, research development function etc.), working capital (i.e. raw material) and labour force (Colaiacovo, 1982), which are important factors for export involvement. Furthermore, financial resources can assist firms to invest in the development of export marketing programmes (i.e. market research, product adaptation, pricing policies, distribution and inventory systems, promotion and advertising etc.) that can initiate and stimulate export performance. To overcome financial constraints, SMEs tend to minimize the ratio of fixed assets to total assets by leasing machinery and equipment in overseas markets (i.e. sell and leaseback techniques). This strategy is adopted to unlock finance from long-term investment, and invest it in more 'close to the market' activities, accommodating an increase in working capital requirements (Chittenden *et al.*, 1998; Michaelas *et al.*, 1999). Therefore, our next hypothesis is:

H4: Asset structure is negatively related to export intensity.

Financial Leverage: Gearing

The ability of the firm to command short-term and long-term debt for financing its long-term operations and working capital requirements can also be considered an important financial element influencing export. Small firms at the early stages of internationalization may have more difficulties in obtaining the necessary funds for exporting (Bilkey and Tesar, 1977). This may be because they are entering new territories and may be regarded as more risky by financiers (Bank of England, 1998). High levels of debt may inhibit firms from pursuing exporting as the risk of conducting such operations will be greater than in the domestic market, consequently negatively affecting their ability to service debt. Therefore, using gearing as a notion of financial leverage, measured by the ratio of debt to total assets, we hypothesize:

H5: Gearing is negatively related to export intensity.

Technological Intensity: Research and Development Expenditures

New, technology-based, small firms are very different from their mainstream counterparts in the product/service sectors, as they are often at the forefront of technological change and innovation. The development of the business and product life cycle of new, technology-based firms involves disproportionately high 'front-end' investment in research and development, particularly during their gestation period (Oakey, 1995). Moreover, technologically sophisticated small firms are identified as having extremely high growth potential in domestic and overseas markets. It is imperative for their survival and for their emergence from the gestation period (often characterized by failure to make any profits) to target export niches in their emerging markets.

Research and development is emphasized as a prerequisite to successful exporting, particularly regarding business performance in foreign markets (Ong and Pearson, 1982). Investment in a state-of-the-art technological base and in human capital will enable innovative activities, which subsequently might increase the firm's competitiveness in the international markets (Kirpalani and MacIntosh, 1980; Ong and Pearson, 1982). Moreover, high R&D expenditures also reflect the commitment of management to invest in innovative capacity, central to the development and adaptation of products to the specific requirements of foreign customers (McGuiness and Little, 1981). The product design and quality were seen to influence business export behaviour (Cavusgil and Naor, 1987), especially when products were technologically superior (Albaum *et al.*, 1994) and patented (Brooks and Rosson, 1982). Thus our next hypothesis is:

> *H6: R&D expenditure is positively related to export intensity.*

Business Growth

The corporate objectives relating to the growth of firms, among other performance parameters, such as profitability, were also seen to influence export behaviour (Albaum *et al.*, 1994). This is because expansion into overseas markets offers firms the opportunity to increase sales and turnover through market development, hence leading to production and organizational growth. Consequently, the stronger the company's motivation to grow, the greater is the likelihood that these firms will explore exporting as a supplement to any strategy for corporate expansion (Wiedersheim-Paul *et al.*, 1978). We propose the following:

> *H7: Firms pursuing growth-oriented objectives are more likely to have higher export intensity.*

Profitability

The profitability-based objective of the business can be an element in considering export activation. Despite the fact that exporting involves higher risks and costs than domestic business, foreign markets might contribute profitable alternatives for many companies (Simpson and Kujawa, 1974; Roy and Simpson, 1981). Consequently, firms guided primarily by profit objectives are more likely to adopt exporting in order to capture the benefits of 'breaking out' from traditional local markets into overseas market niches. The next hypothesis is:

H8: Profitability is positively related to export intensity.

Business Location

It was argued that firms located near information centres or national boundaries are more exposed to export stimuli and thus more likely to engage in foreign business activity (Olson and Wiedersheim-Paul, 1978). Exporting is also facilitated by the proximity of firms to any transportation infrastructure of the home country, such as air, sea, or railway, that can improve the cost-effectiveness of exports (Wiedersheim-Paul *et al.*, 1978). More recently, Westhead (1997) found no relation between rural business location and export intensity in new firms. However, not many studies considered the relation of location of the firm – in assisted or non-assisted areas – to export performance. Assisted areas are also known as development areas, where firms tend to receive support and incentives to (re-)locate in a geographical location that lacks positive economic externalities (such as infrastructure); this may encourage export development.

H9: Firms located in assisted areas are more likely to achieve higher export intensity than those in non-assisted (metropolitan) areas.

Industry Type

Another key variable in the internationalization process of the firm is the product or service offered by the enterprise. The nature of the industry to which the firm belongs is hypothesized to facilitate or inhibit export intensity (Leonidou, 1998). Miesenbock (1988) notes that whenever industries were distinguished, the analysts found differences in export behaviour (Cannon and Willis, 1983; Garnier, 1982; Kedia and Chokar, 1985; Hirsch and Lev, 1974). We look at the manufacturing industry mainly because of its significant contribution to economic activity and the dominant position in international trade that these firms enjoy. Thus our next hypothesis is:

H10: Firms in the manufacturing industry are more likely to achieve higher export intensity.

State of the Economy (Time Factor)

Firms can face variations in their sales due to seasonal, cyclical or other temporal effects, which can prompt them to spread their distribution of sales in order to insulate business performance from such potential disruptions (Wiedersheim-Paul *et al.*, 1978). For instance, unfavourable interest rate and/or exchange rate movements and other macro-economic trends might affect sales and profits and ultimately export intensity. It has been asserted that firms guided by stability objectives tend to be more cautious and less aggressive in exporting than companies led by growth and profit objectives (McConnel, 1979). Here, we can argue that the export intensity of small firms is sensitive to temporary macro-economic changes. This leads to our following hypothesis:

H11: Export intensity varies over time and over different economic cycles.

Export development has been the focus of substantial research (Leonidou and Katsikeas, 1996). It has been argued that the progress of the firm along the internationalization path is an evolutionary and sequential one, consisting of several identifiable and distinct stages (Bilkey and Tesar, 1977; Czinkota and Ursic, 1983). The availability of corporate resources was seen as important in determining the progress in export development (Welch and Luostarinen, 1988). Some researchers (e.g., Katsikeas and Piercy, 1993) argued that the demographics of the organization have an impact on export initiation, development and sustenance. Finally, it was also argued that there are other dimensions which will affect export behaviour such as export planning (Samiee and Walters, 1990), foreign market expansion (Reid, 1982), and international marketing strategy (Lim *et al.*, 1993). Given the nature of our database, it is not possible in our study to test for these characteristics, However, future research may be able to provide information on these issues, which we do not address here.

DATA AND VARIABLES

The methodology involves a multivariate statistical analysis of an extensive panel database of UK-based SMEs (unlisted, independent, privately held limited companies with fewer than 250 employees) over a period of eight years (1990–97), from all the sectors of the economy. The panel character of the data permits the use of statistical techniques that can limit bias and ensure robust results. All data used in this study were gathered from the

Lotus OneSource Database[1] of UK private companies. A total of 4,345 firms that satisfied the definitional and data requirements for the research were randomly selected. In an attempt to make the database as representative of the UK's SME sector as possible, we selected firms from all the different sectors of the economy. We ensured that the number of firms selected from each sector was representative of the real size of the sector, based on the 1995 Department of Trade and Industry statistics.

As discussed earlier, the firm and market characteristics of interest are age, size, operating risk, asset structure, gearing, R&D expenditure, growth and profitability. In addition, the regression model is extended to consider the dependence of export intensity with certain dummy variables representing business location, and industry sector and (time) state of economic conditions.

The data utilized consisted of the profit and loss accounts and balance sheets for the 4,345 sample for the period covering 1990–97, except in the case of firms that were less than ten years old, in which case data for all available years were collected. It should be noted here that the data on sample firms are provided on CD-ROM and are based on the audited accounts submitted to the UK Companies House. As some variables require three years of data, the first year for which we have panel data analysis is 1990, giving us a total of 24,400 cases. Thus, the data do not have a complete panel character since, for some firms, less than eight years' worth of information is available. However, this was inevitable, as we wanted to include younger firms in the analysis: one of our hypotheses specifically involves the effect of business age on export intensity. A descriptive analysis of the database is offered in Table 2.1.

All firms in the sample are small, unlisted, independent private limited companies, with less than 250 employees. No pretence is made that the sample is representative in any ultimate sense. It includes only surviving small limited companies. Nevertheless, simply because surviving small firms comprise a material component of the economy, their behaviours have inherent importance.

Estimation of Dependent and Explanatory Variables

All the variables used in the study are based on book values. Because there is a large variation in the size of firms, a direct comparison of these variables is impossible. To standardize our measures, we use size-related

---

[1] Lotus OneSource is a database of 110,000 UK companies and it is based on the audited accounts submitted to Companies House by the companies. In the UK companies are required by law to submit audited accounts to Companies House every financial year.

Table 2.1   Panel database: number of firms

Year	Sector										
	1	2	3	4	5	6	7	8	9	10	All
1997	146	811	414	1283	121	278	161	826	112	193	4345
1996	143	791	408	1255	117	272	153	789	104	177	4209
1995	130	695	352	1125	107	239	141	682	86	164	3721
1994	118	610	305	992	91	212	122	587	75	141	3253
1993	111	546	263	879	78	182	101	499	66	124	2849
1992	91	467	207	766	64	156	75	341	55	88	2310
1991	81	414	180	677	52	126	65	269	49	76	1989
1990	72	371	159	588	46	110	58	213	42	65	1724
All	893	4707	2291	7569	681	1581	883	4214	598	1038	24400

Note: Where: Sector 1: agriculture, forestry and mining; Sector 2: manufacturing; Sector 3: construction, Sector 4: wholesale and retail trade; Sector 5: hotels and restaurants; Sector 6: transport and communication; Sector 7: finance; Sector 8: business services; Sector 9: education, health and social work; and Sector 10: other.

denominators and compute ratios. Thus, where appropriate, we deflate the variables by total assets or sales turnover.

- EXPORT INTENSITY = Ratio of exports to sales turnover.
- LOCATION = Sample firms are classified as developed areas, inter-mediate areas, and non-assisted areas, where developed areas receive the higher government assistance, while intermediate areas receive less assistance than developed areas. Non-assisted areas are metro-politan areas that receive no government assistance.
- AGE = Age of the firm since date of incorporation.
- SIZE = Sales turnover.
- RISK = Operating risk is defined as the coefficient of variation in profitability during 1990–97.
- ASSET STRUCTURE = Ratio of fixed assets to total assets.
- GEARING = Total debt to total assets, where total debt includes short-term and long-term debt finance. Short-term debt is defined as the portion of the company's total debt repayable within one year. This includes bank overdraft, the current portion of bank loans, and other current liabilities. Long-term debt is the total company's debt due for repayment beyond one year. This includes: long-term bank loans and other long-term liabilities repayable beyond one year (i.e. directors' loans, hire purchase and leasing obligations).
- R&D EXPENDITURE = The ratio of intangible assets to total

assets. Intangible assets include: research and development expenditure, trademarks, patents and copyrights.

- GROWTH = Percentage increase in turnover in last three years.
- PROFITABILITY = Ratio of pre-tax profits to total assets.

A summary of the descriptive statistics of the different dependent and explanatory variables described above as well as a correlation matrix is offered in Tables 2.2 and 2.3.

Table 2.2   Means (and standard deviations) of dependent and explanatory variables

		1990	1991	1992	1993	1994	1995	1996	1997
Export Intensity	Mean	0.104	0.100	0.095	0.101	0.098	0.100	0.105	0.099
	S.D.	0.218	0.218	0.217	0.225	0.223	0.225	0.229	0.222
Age of Firm	Mean	26.6	25.2	24.2	23.1	21.8	20.6	19.6	19.1
	S.D.	17.7	17.5	17.5	17.9	17.7	17.5	17.3	17.3
Size of Firm	Mean	4986	5172	5029	5050	4850	4781	5173	5500
	S.D.	57645	58502	65264	67473	64331	60706	61623	62998
Risk	Mean	0.088	0.096	0.098	0.099	0.101	0.101	0.100	0.100
	S.D.	0.113	0.150	0.168	0.167	0.167	0.164	0.162	0.162
Asset Structure	Mean	0.297	0.299	0.302	0.305	0.295	0.287	0.284	0.286
	S.D.	0.252	0.254	0.259	0.274	0.272	0.272	0.274	0.276
Financial Leverage	Mean	0.426	0.439	0.430	0.417	0.408	0.414	0.427	0.424
	S.D.	0.251	0.275	0.275	0.281	0.273	0.266	0.261	0.263
R&D Expenditure	Mean	0.007	0.007	0.008	0.008	0.009	0.010	0.010	0.010
	S.D.	0.043	0.041	0.044	0.046	0.049	0.054	0.053	0.054
Growth	Mean	0.403	0.258	0.186	0.262	0.402	0.457	0.417	0.414
	S.D.	0.834	0.737	0.784	0.989	1.223	1.230	1.070	1.195
Profitability	Mean	0.044	0.034	0.032	0.050	0.068	0.069	0.065	0.067
	S.D.	0.253	0.267	0.212	0.345	0.227	0.287	0.290	0.312

METHOD

Explanatory data have been drawn primarily from the observable financial data (income and balance sheets) of UK-based SMEs; indeed, this is one of the novelties of our study. Moreover, we utilize panel data analysis to examine empirically the hypotheses formulated above. Hsiao (1985) points out that panel data sets for economic research possess several major advantages over conventional cross-sectional or time-series data sets. First, panel data usually provide a large number of data-points, increasing the degrees

Table 2.3 *Correlation matrix*

No.	Variable	Statistics	Pearson correlation coefficient								
			1	2	3	4	5	6	7	8	9
1	Export Intensity	Pearson Correlation	1.000								
		Sig. (2-tailed)	.								
2	Age of Firm	Pearson Correlation	−0.016	1.000							
		Sig. (2-tailed)	0.083	.							
3	Size of Firm	Pearson Correlation	0.067	0.010	1.000						
		Sig. (2-tailed)	0.000	0.099	.						
4	Risk	Pearson Correlation	0.047	−0.101	−0.023	1.000					
		Sig. (2-tailed)	0.000	0.000	0.000	.					
5	Asset Structure	Pearson Correlation	−0.160	0.158	−0.032	−0.081	1.000				
		Sig. (2-tailed)	0.000	0.000	0.000	0.000	.				
6	Financial Leverage	Pearson Correlation	−0.067	−0.217	−0.010	0.184	0.124	1.000			
		Sig. (2-tailed)	0.000	0.000	0.099	0.000	0.000	.			
7	R&D Expenditure	Pearson Correlation	−0.025	−0.097	−0.004	0.029	−0.031	0.066	1.000		
		Sig. (2-tailed)	0.005	0.000	0.494	0.000	0.000	0.000	.		
8	Growth	Pearson Correlation	0.034	−0.146	−0.008	0.103	−0.075	0.085	0.029	1.000	
		Sig. (2-tailed)	0.002	0.000	0.271	0.000	0.000	0.000	0.000	.	
9	Profitability	Pearson Correlation	0.022	−0.006	−0.003	−0.229	−0.019	−0.199	−0.013	0.108	1.000
		Sig. (2-tailed)	0.017	0.316	0.612	0.000	0.002	0.000	0.036	0.000	.

of freedom and reducing the collinearity among explanatory variables, hence improving the efficiency of econometric estimates (Hsiao, 1985). Furthermore, panel data are better able to study the dynamics of adjustment and to identify and measure effects that are simply not detectable in pure cross-sections or pure time-series data.

The panel character of our data permits the use of variable-intercept models that introduce firm-type (industry) and/or time-specific effects into the regression equations that reduce or avoid the omitted variables bias (Hsiao, 1985). One common issue that arises with variable-intercept model estimation is whether the individual effects are to be thought of as 'fixed-effects' or 'random effects'. Hsiao (1985) points out that when inferences are made about a population of effects, of which those in the data are considered to be a random sample, then the effects should be considered random. Our data cover all ten industries of the UK economy, so the industries examined cannot be considered a small sample of a much larger population of industries. In this case, a fixed-effects model would be more appropriate than a random-effects one. As such, the hypotheses formulated above are tested by including the different explanatory variables in a least squares dummy variable (LSDV) model that is based on the fixed-effects assumption. Thus, for all but the first time period (1990), as well as for all but the first industry (Industry 1), a separate dummy variable is included in the regression equations (seven time and nine industry dummy variables), replacing the intercept. The dummy variables will capture the firm-type (industry) and time-specific effects of the omitted as well as the included variables.

RESULTS AND IMPLICATIONS

Table 2.4 presents the results from the LSDV model which regresses export intensity against the variables in the hypotheses formulated in the section above.

Business Age (H1): The regression coefficient of the age variable is negative, indicating an inverse relationship between age and export intensity. However, the relationship is not significant, and as a result we can conclude that export intensity is not highly associated with the age of the firm. Based on this observation, we reject H1. As discussed above, age may have a two-way effect on export intensity. Young (especially high-tech) firms may be looking at exporting as a growth strategy, hence a negative relationship between age and export intensity (Lee and Brasch, 1978; Czinkota and Ursic, 1983). On the other hand, more experienced and established firms may be more likely to export, trying to break out of saturated home

Table 2.4   Estimated least squares dummy variable (LSDV) regression coefficients

Variable	Coefficient (B)	Standard Error	t-statistic	Significance
Age of firm	-5.4×10^{-5}	0.000	-0.396	0.692
Size of firm	2.6×10^{-6}	0.000	8.337	0.000
Risk	0.172	0.022	7.853	0.000
Asset Structure	-0.123	0.011	-11.035	0.000
Financial Leverage	-0.035	0.010	-3.399	0.001
R&D Expenditure	-0.210	0.053	-3.953	0.000
Growth	0.007	0.002	3.051	0.002
Profitability	-0.003	0.003	-0.989	0.323
Dummy Variables				
Development Area	-0.034	0.011	-3.257	0.001
Intermediate Area	-0.010	0.009	-1.107	0.268
Industry 1	0.132	0.010	13.638	0.000
Industry 2	-0.020	0.011	-1.743	0.081
Industry 3	0.102	0.009	10.982	0.000
Industry 4	0.047	0.019	2.540	0.011
Industry 5	0.070	0.013	5.400	0.000
Industry 6	0.074	0.018	4.084	0.000
Industry 7	0.045	0.011	4.048	0.000
Industry 8	0.058	0.020	2.932	0.003
Industry 9	0.076	0.016	4.784	0.000
Year 1991	0.046	0.012	3.778	0.000
Year 1992	0.048	0.011	4.240	0.000
Year 1993	0.052	0.011	4.732	0.000
Year 1994	0.048	0.011	4.482	0.000
Year 1995	0.050	0.010	4.853	0.000
Year 1996	0.053	0.010	5.358	0.000
Year 1997	0.046	0.010	4.757	0.000
Adjusted $R^2 = 0.231$			F-Statistic $= 99.493$**	

Note: ** Statistically different from zero at a 10% level of significance.

markets, hence a positive relationship between age and export intensity (Welch and Wiedersheim-Paul, 1980). Thus, the insignificant regression coefficient of the age variable, presented in Table 2.4, may reflect these two opposite effects of age on export intensity. For managerial and policy implications, it is fair to argue that the age of the SME may not be an important determinant of the ability and willingness to export and that other factors may have a stronger impact.

Business Size (H2): From the regression coefficient of the size variable (total assets), we can observe the existence of scale effects on the export intensity of sample firms. The positive relationship between the size of the firm and exporting indicates that the bigger the firm, the more likely it is for it to engage in exporting. This provides strong support for H2. A positive relationship between size and export intensity is also reported by Abdel-Malek (1978), Cavusgil (1980), Garnier (1982), Calof (1994) and Tyebjee (1994). As Leonidou (1998) summarizes, larger firms have more competent export-oriented management, they have the necessary resources to support export programmes, enjoy economies of scale and can be more competitive in overseas markets, and are more risk-tolerant than smaller counterparts. The managerial and policy implications here relate to the ways to achieve growth rates in turnover for small businesses in the domestic market that will enhance the financial position through cash flow, and then explore the international market by exporting.

Operating Risk (H3): Our results indicate that small firms which exhibit higher export intensity ratios are also likely to exhibit higher operating risk ratios (variation in profitability). The observed positive relationship between risk and export intensity provides support for H3. The performance of firms involved in exporting programmes will largely reflect the uncertainties characterizing overseas markets. As the economic conditions in overseas markets fluctuate, so too will the profits of active exporting firms targeting and servicing diverse markets. Firms that are willing to take more risk exposure can be good candidates to internationalize their business operations by exporting.

Asset Structure (H4): As shown in Table 2.4, the regression coefficient of the asset structure shows that the ratio is negative and statistically significant. This suggests that exporting firms rely on lower ratios of fixed assets to total assets. It could be argued that exporting firms appear to be under-capitalized compared to their less export-oriented counterparts. This can be due to the notion that many firms resort to leasing their equipment, thus reducing the need to finance investment in long-term fixed assets. The implication here is that export-oriented firms release valuable financial resources that can be used for the development of export marketing programmes. Therefore, H4 is therefore accepted.

Financial Gearing (H5): With respect to financial leverage (gearing), our results indicate a negative and significant relationship between the total debt ratio and export performance. This finding supports H5. It could be argued, therefore, that small exporters are financially constrained compared with their non-exporting counterparts. As pointed out by the Bank of England (1998), finance providers often regard the risks associated with lending to exporters as greater than those involved in lending to firms selling only in the domestic market due to the type of receivable. As a result, many exporters may find it difficult to obtain sufficient finance and will have to rely on lower gearing ratios. There is a managerial implication here and that is for the firm to search for alternative financing options both domestically and internationally that bolster the working capital position by improving cash flow; this can be explored in the working of the factoring and invoice discounting industry.

R&D Expenditure (H6): The statistical analysis of the relationship of the research and development variable (intangible assets to total assets) and exporting paradoxically established that exporting firms tend to have lower investment in intangible assets. This is a contradiction to our hypothesis, so we reject H6. This can be due to the fact that SMEs tend not to capitalize on their investment in intangible assets. This informal approach to the treatment of investment in intangible assets is underlined by the systemic failure of smaller companies to register and successfully defend patents etc. Just over 89 per cent of our sample firms have no intangible assets recorded in their balance sheet.

Business Growth (H7): The results establish a positive relationship between growth and export intensity, indicating that exporting firms are more likely to sell in the international market as a strategic option to achieve growth. H7 is accepted. The results support the arguments reported by Wiedersheim-Paul *et al.* (1978) in which they stated that expansion into overseas markets offers firms the opportunity to increase sales and turnover, hence leading to organizational growth.

Business Profitability (H8): The regression coefficient of the profitability variable is negative, indicating an inverse relationship between profits and export intensity. However, the relationship is not significant, and therefore we can conclude that export intensity is not highly associated with profitability. We reject H8. Our findings are in contrast to the arguments reported by Simpson and Kujawa (1974) and Roy and Simpson (1981).

Business Location (H9): As Table 2.4 demonstrates, the regression coefficient of the development area dummy is negative and statistically significant, indicating that firms located in assisted areas (development areas) are less likely to engage in exporting programmes compared to businesses located in developed metropolitan areas. Development areas may lack infrastructure systems that can link firms to international markets and firms within this area do not benefit from agglomeration economies, i.e., networking, supplier links, knowledge transfer etc. Therefore we accept H9. Firms located in intermediate areas are also likely to exhibit lower export intensity ratios than businesses located in developed areas, but the relationship is not statistically significant.

Business Sector (H10): Our results also suggest that industry type is related to export intensity. Table 2.4 shows that eight out of the nine industry dummy coefficients are significantly different from zero at the 5 per cent level of significance, indicating that industry type exhibits an effect on the export intensity of small firms. As can be seen in Figure 2.1, export intensity is as high as 13.7 per cent and 12.9 per cent in manufacturing and finance industries respectively, and as low as 0.4 per cent and 0.6 per cent in the hotels/restaurants and construction industries respectively. Based on these findings, we accept H10. These findings are in agreement with Leonidou (1998) and Wiedersheim-Paul *et al.* (1978), who found evidence supporting an association between export intensity and sectoral activity. Not surprisingly, manufacturing firms and trading companies are more prolific in exporting.

State of the Economy (H11): Finally, the time dummies included in the regression model to capture the effect of time (or economic climate) on the

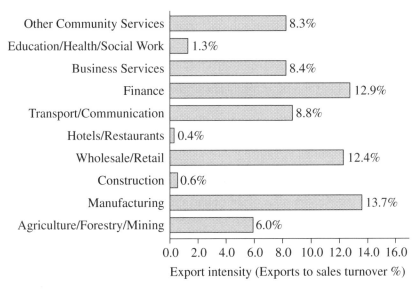

Figure 2.1   Export intensity across sectors

export intensity of small firms are all statistically significant. This suggests that there are significant time effects on the export intensity of sample firms. Evidently, volume of exports will be largely affected by the economic conditions in the overseas markets. We could therefore expect export intensity to fluctuate over business economic cycles. In Figure 2.2, we plot the coefficients of the seven time dummy variables obtained in the regression model against the years to which they refer (right axis). On the left axis of Figure 2.2 we plot the sterling effective exchange rate during the period examined (effective exchange rate is indexed on 1990, where base year 1990 = 100).

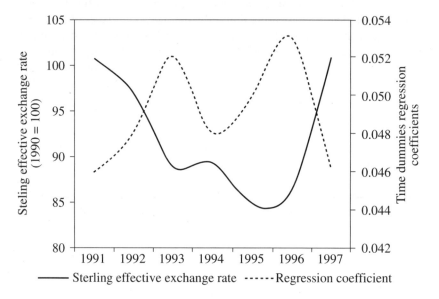

Figure 2.2   Coefficients of time dummy variables

Figure 2.2 shows that there is a distinct pattern in the values of the coefficients on the time dummy variables. This pattern exhibits a negative relationship with the sterling effective exchange rate. We can see that as the value of the pound decreases, making exports cheaper in overseas markets, export intensity appears to be increasing relative to other years. On the other hand, increases in the value of the pound appear to have a negative effect on export volumes. We can therefore conclude that there are significant time effects on the export intensity of smaller firms. Exporting volumes will be largely determined by the broader economic conditions in the marketplace. The economic climate in domestic and overseas markets will determine exchange rates and hence prices, which will, in turn, affect exporting volumes between different trading countries. We therefore accept H11.

Given the above results and discussion we can argue that there are a number of potential policy and managerial implications that arise from the empirical findings. More established companies (in terms of their product and service and their domestic marketplace) may find it easier to engage in export activities because they can capitalize on their business experience and have access to financial and managerial support. This argument can also be extended to larger SMEs with substantial annual turnover; these companies can have access to more and better marketing, financial and technical expertise, which can support and possibly sustain their export functions. Therefore, it is recommendable for older and larger SMEs to explore export markets more aggressively. With regard to younger and smaller SMEs, they can search for policy incentives provided by the government to stimulate export in order to bolster their marketing and financial positions. This includes acquiring subsidies to attend international fairs and exhibitions, financial export guarantees, and human resource development. It is important to note that firms seeking export markets have a higher exposure to risk than those concentrating on domestic markets. Therefore, it is advisable that SMEs explore the different strategies available for risk management, especially financial risk, by seeking advice on foreign exchange hedging, collection of accounts receivables, letters of credit, and international factoring and invoice discounting.

The findings in this chapter with regard to asset structure and financial leverage indicate that exporting companies rely on lower ratios of fixed assets and are not financially constrained. This has important financial implications for firms wanting to engage in exporting. It may be beneficial for SMEs to minimize the ratio of fixed assets to total assets by leasing machinery and equipment in order to unlock finance from long-term investment and utilize the financial resources in export marketing programmes, product development, human resources, and research. In addition to this it is crucial that firms seeking export should reduce their debt exposure as a way of managing their cash-flow situation and bolstering their working capital.

Small firms can achieve higher growth rates by exporting to international markets. Successful entry into overseas market increases sales and turnover; consequently, the policies that would facilitate entry into new markets can foster and promote growth rates of SMEs. The government can provide incentives and information about the potentials of overseas markets by informing SMEs about international commercial fairs, availability of financial resources, and export guarantees.

This chapter shows that the business location can play an important role in increasing export intensity. Therefore, firms seeking export markets may find it useful to locate their production operation close to the export market or even in areas that are assisted by government grants and subsidies.

CONCLUSIONS

This chapter revisited some of the existing literature and proposed new hypotheses with regard to firm determinants on exporting by looking at the financial statements of a sizeable panel data with ten years of observations and 4,345 firms representing 24,400 cases. The size and financial nature of the database, in addition to the statistical method adopted, can be considered as the most important contribution of the chapter. The results from this study of the determinants of exporting in SMEs suggest that there is considerable evidence, within the UK SME and micro-enterprising sector, for a relationship between the certain demographic variables and export development. In summary, *the profile of export-active SMEs is sizeable in established, production-based companies (but also trading and finance-related activities)*. It has also emerged that the *primum operandi* motives for the activation and development of an exporting function are related to growth. Exporting remains a risky business and there is scope for a more export-related support mechanism seeking to help SMEs overcome the barriers to export development.

This study has attempted to offer a diagnosis of the financial profile of export-active firms. The charting of an export-oriented business strategy will depend on the prevailing business climate (macro- and micro-economic conditions, stage of industry and technological development, state of output and input markets etc.) but also on the resource base of the organization.

We contemplate a further development of this empirical investigation to a more longitudinal-based one in order to establish the development pattern of SME export champions. The aim is to develop a more holistic diagnostic model that will also incorporate quantitative variables (e.g. market position, competitiveness, alternative measurements of research and development etc., environmental factors (cost of transportation, supplier chain, networking), and more behavioural variables such as human capital, management structure, objective/motivations etc.

In addition, there is scope to examine the experience of such firms in terms of performance, growth constraints, internal (personal, familial and behavioural) and external (market-based) triggers of growth. Also of interest is to identify the policy measures required to alleviate supply-side gaps (e.g. finance, managerial/skills, technological etc.) in order to bolster SME export development strategies.

Policy makers, scholars and other enterprise development agents with an interest in SME development must recognize that there is a need for more inter-disciplinary investigations, with the (ambitious) aim to develop not only diagnostics but also *prognostics* that can ascertain whether firms have the *propensity and entrepreneurial aspirations* to pursue export growth. In addition to industrial and (inter-) organizational dynamics and small business matters, it is imperative that the increasingly complex behavioural dynamics of SMEs are also addressed. Since the great majority of SMEs are owner-managed, it can be argued that smaller enterprises do not always pursue their growth objectives by internationalization but rather by concentrating on their domestic or local market.

REFERENCES

Abdel-Malek, T. (1978), 'Export marketing orientation in small firms', *American Journal of Small Business*, 3(1): 25–34.

Aksoy, S. and E. Kaynak (1994), 'Export behaviour of fresh produce marketers: towards coordination with general theory of exporting', *International Marketing Review*, 11(2): 16–32.

Albaum, G. *et al.* (1994), *International Marketing and Export Management*, Harlow: Addison-Wesley.

Bank of England (1998), *Smaller Exporter*, London.

Bannock, G. and M. Daly (1994), *Small Business Statistics*, London: Paul Chapman Publishing.

Bilkey, W.J. and G. Tesar (1977), 'The export behaviour of smaller-sized Wisconsin manufacturing firms', *Journal of International Business Studies*, 8(1): 93–8.

Bonaccorsi A. (1992), 'On the relationship between firm size and export intensity', *Journal of International Business Studies*, 23: 605–35.

Bradley, F. (1995) *International Marketing Strategy* (second edition), Harlow: Prentice-Hall International (U.K.) Ltd.

Brooks, M.R. and P.J. Rosson (1982), 'A study of export behaviour of small and medium sized manufacturing firms in three Canadian Provinces', in M.R. Czinkota and G. Tesar (eds), *Export Management: An International Context*, New York: Praeger Publishers.

Brush, C. (1995) *International Entrepreneurship*, New York: Garland Publishing.

Calof, J.L. (1994), 'The relationship between firm size and export behaviour revisited', *Journal of International Business Studies*, 25(2): 367–87.

Cambridge Small Business Research Centre (1992), *The State of British Enterprise: Growth, Innovation and Competitive Advantage in Small and Medium-sized Firms*, Cambridge: Small Business Research Centre, Department of Applied Economics, University of Cambridge.

Cannon, T. and M. Willis (1983), 'The smaller firm in overseas trade', *European Small Business Journal*, 1: 45–55.

Cavusgil, S.T. (1980), 'On the internationalisation process of firms', *European Research*, November, pp. 273–81.

Cavusgil, S.T. and J. Naor (1987), 'Firm and management characteristics as discriminators of export marketing activity', *Journal of Business Research*, 15: 221–35.

Chittenden, F., P. Poutziouris and N. Michaelas (1998), 'Financial management and working capital practices in UK SMEs', a European Regional Development Fund Publication (supported by NatWest Bank and KPMG).

Colaiacovo, J.L. (1982), 'Export development in Latin America', in M.R. Czinkota and G. Tesar (eds), *Export Policy: A Global Assessment*, New York: Praeger Publishers, pp. 102–11.

Czinkota, M.R and M. Ursic (1983) 'Impact of growth expansion on smaller firms', *International Marketing Review*, 1(2): 26–33.

Dichtl, E. *et al.* (1984), 'The export decision of small and medium-sized firms: A review', *Management International Review*, 24(2): 49–60.

D'Souza, D.E. and P.P. McDougall (1989), 'Third world joint venturing: a strategic option for the smaller firm', *Entrepreneurship Theory and Practice*, 14: 19–33.

Edmunds, S.E. and S.J. Khoury (1986), 'Exports: a necessary ingredient in the growth of small business firms', *Journal of Small Business Management*, 24: 54–65.

Edvadsson, B., L. Edvinsson and H. Nysrtrom (1993), 'Internationalisation of service companies', *Service Industrial Journal*, 13(1): 80–97.

Garnier, G. (1982), 'Comparative export behaviour of small firms in printing and electronic industries', in M.R. Czinkota and G. Tesar (eds), *Export Management: An International Context*, New York: Praeger Publishers, pp. 113–31.

Hirsch, S. and Z. Adar (1974), 'Firm size and export performance', *World Development*, 2(7): 41–6.

Hirsch, S. and B. Lev (1974), 'Sales stabilisation through export diversification', *Review of Economics and Statistics*, 8: 270–77.

HM Government (1994), *Competitiveness Helping Business to Win*, Cmnd 2563, London: HMSO, p. 87.

Hsiao, C. (1985), 'Benefits and limitations of panel data', *Econometric Reviews*, 4: 121–74.

Katsikeas, C.S and N.F. Piercy (1993), 'Long-term export stimuli and firm characteristics in a European LDC', *Journal of International Marketing*, 1(3): 23–47.

Kedia, B. and J. Chokar (1985), 'Factors inhibiting export performance of firms: An empirical investigation', *Management International Review*, 26(4): 33–43.

Kirpalani, V.H. and N.B. MacIntosh (1980), 'Internal marketing effectiveness of technology-oriented small firms', *Journal of International Business Studies*, 11: 81–90.

Lee, W. and J.J. Brasch (1978), 'The adoption of export as an innovative strategy', *Journal of International Business Studies*, Spring/Summer, 91–109.

Leonidou, L. (1998), 'Organisational determinants of exporting: conceptual, methodological and empirical insights', *Management International Review*, Special Issue, pp. 7–52.

Leondinou, L. and C.S. Katsikeas (1996), 'The export development process: an integrative review of empirical models', *Journal of International Business Studies*, 27(3): 517–51.

Lim, J.S., T. Sharkey and K. Kim (1993), 'Determinants of international marketing strategy', *Management International Review*, 33(2): 103–20.

McConnel, J.E. (1979), 'The export decision: an empirical study of firm behavior', *Economic Geography*, 5(3): 171–83.

McGuiness, N.W. and B. Little (1981), 'The impact of R&D spending on the foreign sale of new Canadian industrial products', *Research Policy*, 10: 78–98.

Michaelas, N., F. Chittenden and P. Poutziouris (1999), 'Financial policy and capital structure choice in UK, SMEs: empirical evidence from company panel data', *Small Business Economics*, 12: 113–30.

Miesenbock, K.J. (1988), 'Small businesses and exporting: a literature review', *International Small Business Journal*, 6: 42–61.

Oakey, R. (1995), *High Technology New Firms: Variable Barriers to Growth*, London: Paul Chapman Publishing.

Olson, H. and F. Wiedersheim-Paul (1978), 'Factors affecting the pre-export behaviour of non-exporting firms', in M. Ghertman and J. Leontiades, (eds), *European Research in International Business*, Amsterdam: North Holland, pp. 283–305.

Ong, C.H. and A.W. Pearson (1982), 'The impact of technical characteristics on export activity: a study of small and medium-sized UK electronic firms', *R&D Management*, 12: 189–96.

Reid, S.D. (1982), 'The impact of size on export behaviour in small firms', in M.R. Czinkota and G. Tesar (eds), *Export Management: An International Context*, New York: Praeger Publishers: pp. 18–38.

Roy, D.A. and C.L. Simpson (1981) 'Export attitudes of business executives in the smaller manufacturing firm', *Journal of Small Business Management*, 19(2): 16–22.

Rynning, M and O. Andersen (1984), 'Structural and behavioural predictors of export adoption: a Norwegian study'; *Journal of International Marketing*, 2(1): 73–85.

Salmon, W. and J. Tordjman (1989) 'The Internationalisation of retailing', *International Journal of Retailing*, 4(2): 3–16.

Samiee, S. and P.G.P. Walters (1990), 'Influence of firm size on export planning and performance', *Journal of Business Research*, 20: 235–48.

Samuels, J., S. Greenfield and H. Mpuka (1992), 'Exporting and the smaller firm', *International Small Business Journal*, 10: 24–36.

Simpson, C.L. and D. Kujawa (1974), 'The export decision process: an empirical inquiry', *Journal of International Business Studies*, Spring, 107–17.

Terpstra, V. and R. Sarathy (1994), *International Marketing*, sixth edition, Fort Worth, TX: The Dryden Press.

Tookey, D.A. (1964), 'Factors associated with success in exporting', *The Journal of Management Studies*, 1(1): 48–66.

Tyebjee, T.T. (1994), 'Internationalization of high-tech firms: initial vs. extended involvement', *Journal of Global Marketing*, 7(4): 59–81.

Verhoeven, W. (1988), 'The export performance of small and medium-sized enterprises in the Netherlands', *International Small Business Journal*, 6: 20–33.

Welch, L.S. and R. Luostarinen (1988), 'Internationalization: evolution of a concept', *Journal of General Management*, 14, winter: 24–55.

Welch, L.S. and F. Wiedersheim-Paul (1980), 'Initial exports – a marketing failure?' *The Journal of Management Studies*, 17(4): 334–44.

Westhead, P. (1997), 'Exporting and non-exporting small firms in Great Britain – A matched pairs comparison', *International Journal of Entrepreneurial Behaviour and Research*, 1(2): 6–36.

Wiedersheim-Paul, F., H. Olson and L.S. Welch (1978), 'Pre-export activity: the first step in internationalization', *Journal of International Business Studies*, Spring/Summer, 47–48.

World Bank (1995), *World Tables*, Washington, DC: The Johns Hopkins University Press.

3. Integrated outsourcing: a tool for the foreign expansion of small-business suppliers

Sônia Dahab and José Paulo Esperança

INTRODUCTION

The 'make-or-buy decision' is a classical issue in management textbooks from such diverse fields as accounting, business strategy and corporate finance. However, the professional manager is usually restricted to the somewhat trivial suggestion of acting in whatever manner minimizes costs. Not only is cost difficult to calculate, but there is also a significant intertemporal dimension as an investment decision tends to be associated with the 'make' choice. Quite often, some level of investment is also required from the supplier, in the context of the 'buy' decision.

The growing prominence of this topic in the research of the 1990s demonstrates that the answer to the 'make-or-buy' question is far from settled. It is also a fascinating topic from the researcher's perspective, given the deep implications for understanding the nature and boundaries of the firm in the context of the markets versus hierarchies dichotomy (Williamson, 1975).

From the corporate manager's perspective, a revolution is in the making. A prime example is the sheer shift from manufacturing to buying found in such industries as car parts and packages. Data from *The Carmaker* (July 1997) show that the production of metal cans by companies in the American food industry has declined from 54 per cent in 1985 to a paltry 19 per cent in 1996. An article in the 5 September 2000 issue of *The Economist* tells of a significant transformation in the car industry. Pioneered in Brazil, outsourcing goes beyond the most advanced of previous practices by further externalization and the physical proximity of suppliers and assembly plants:

> [The Brazilian] Chrysler's factory . . . has outsourced much of the work that would normally be done on an American assembly line. Dana Corporation, which is based in Ohio, has set up its own plant just a mile down the road, where it can build the Dakota's 'rolling chassis', the basic framework on which body

and engine are mounted. The chassis arrives at Chrysler's plant with wires and hoses already in place – even the tires are mounted and balanced. (*The Economist*, 5 September 2000 p. 62)

The first choice to be made is between 'make', a form of internalization leading to backward vertical integration, and 'buy', showing a preference for a market mechanism. Making or *in*sourcing should be selected if the activity belongs to a company's 'core competencies'. This path then enables the firm to obtain cheaper, better and more timely goods (Quinn and Hilmer, 1994, p. 48). When these conditions are not met, the alternative 'buy' should be selected. According to the literature on core competencies, buying is a sort of 'default option'.

However, the 'make-or-buy decision' is not the only choice confronting manufacturers. There are also several intermediate models such as: 'concurrent making and buying', and buying partially unfinished goods, which are then completed internally to ensure better quality control. The decision to buy brings with it other necessary choices. A crucial one concerns the stability of the prospective commercial relationship. A firm may try to solidify its bargaining power vis-à-vis its suppliers by purchasing off-the-shelf goods from alternative suppliers (Porter, 1980). Kappor and Gupta (1997) presented an even more radical view in support of 'aggressive sourcing':

> If a buyer's objective is to minimize cost (at any chosen level of quality or value), that objective is, to some degree, at odds with the interests of suppliers. . . . The supplier is likely to resent and resist with as much sales and marketing savvy and muscle as possible. . . . Knowledge of and a willingness to use free-market competition is the strongest weapon available to the buyer. (p. 27)

It has been advocated by a large number of authors that long-term partnerships – in which a buyer commits to a long-term relationship with a supplier – bring significant benefits to both parties (Venkatsen, 1992; Kumar, 1996; Dyer *et al.*, 1998; Dana *et al.*, 2000; Dana 2000). This view is consistent with the transaction costs explanation of market failure (Williamson, 1971; 1975). However, pure market mechanisms are not the most efficient transaction organizing mode in the context of high transaction costs because of: (i) small numbers – there is a reduced number of potential suppliers; (ii) asset specificity – customized items required by a buyer; (iii) opportunism – the potential for one party in the transaction to benefit illegitimately at the expense of the other. Strong transaction costs explain why pure market mechanisms are not the most efficient choice. In the extreme case of very high transaction costs vertical integration (the make decision) becomes the most efficient mode. However, there are also intermediate contractual arrangements. If the levels of customization, or asset specificity, are not very significant, stable, arm's-length relationships become more efficient. With larger levels of customization that require shared knowledge, such as between car manufacturers and fabricators of car components, strategic partnerships then become the most efficient mode. Figure 3.1 summarizes the sourcing alternatives available to firms:

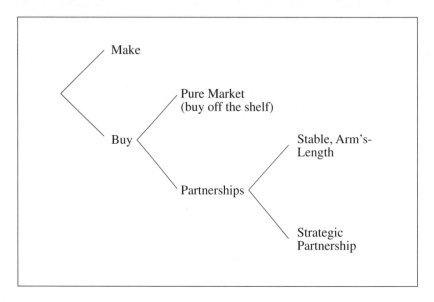

Figure 3.1   Sourcing alternatives

The Japanese *keiretsu*, with their extensive networking of supplier–customer relationships, are an example of strategic partnerships. The speed with which Japanese car manufacturers can introduce new models is related to the extensive exchange of knowledge and information among affiliate members. Both governance mechanisms and a long-term view reduce the potential for opportunism, such as disclosing relevant information to competitors.

Dyer *et al.* (1998, p. 58) summarize the arguments in favor of strategic partnerships:

– share more information and are better at coordinating interdependent tasks;
– invest in dedicated or relation-specific assets which lower costs, improve quality and speed product development; and
– rely on trust to govern the relationship, a highly efficient governance mechanism that minimizes transaction costs.

Strategic partnerships involve a high interdependence between supplier and buyer. Under this type of sourcing there is a loss of flexibility compared to the arm's-length, stable relationships and an even larger loss when a firm engages in off-the-shelf buying. However, high levels of asset specificity may require joint development and, in some cases, exclusivity contracts. Advertising is an interesting example. Advertising agencies usually serve no more than one firm in a given industry because their clients are afraid that the knowledge obtained through the joint design of these campaigns could leak to their competitors if they were served by the same agency (Esperança, 1993). Mergers of advertising agencies have led to the loss of important accounts.

More substantial transaction costs can also lead to partial or full ownership of the supplying unit – a preference for the make solution. Quinn and Hilmer (1994, p. 50) underscore the point that ownership or vertical integration is the best approach when flexibility needs are low and control needs are high. Figure 3.2 presents the expected relationship between transaction costs and sourcing mode. Examples of transacted goods are given in italics.

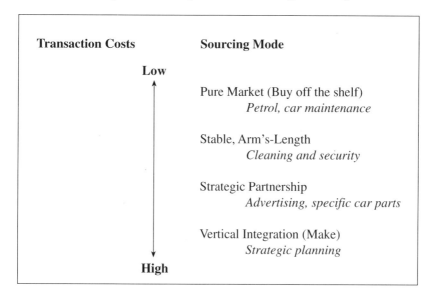

Figure 3.2   Transaction costs' impact on sourcing

This chapter focuses on a specific type of strategic partnership – integrated outsourcing. In this format, a typical case of quasi-vertical integration, the supplier's facilities are located within the client's plant. As the technological and production interactions are so intense, the supplying unit is an integrated production unit in every way except that an independent firm owns it. We explore the trends leading to the creation of new internal boundaries and business units from the perspective of transaction cost economics, business strategy and the dynamic capabilities of the firm.

By contrast with more conventional outsourcing, integrated outsourcing leads to a much closer integration between the client firm's production line and the supplier's delivery system. Typically, it takes the form of a quasi-vertical integration, in which the supplier's plant, located within the client firm's facilities, produces at a pace which practically mirrors the pace of the client's own production line. Thus, any problems associated with irregular ordering and seasonality will be met almost instantly by the highly integrated supplier, which can reduce intermediate inventories accordingly.

Such integration is particularly efficient in the plastic-based packaging business because the transportation costs of very light, cheap but voluminous empty bottles add enormously to the final cost. Unlike glass and tin, the minimum efficient scale for plastic tends to be low, thus allowing for the installation of efficient small 'factories'.

These emerging characteristics of firm organizations can be considered a managerial response to the new imperatives of an environment characterized by four major tendencies:

- Accelerating technological change and obsolescence, which require faster depreciation of capital and know-how investments. Firms are then driven to allocate a larger part of their financial and human resources to innovation and to avoid rediscoveries.
- Diffusion of information technology, which promotes organizational flexibility and new forms of co-ordination and monitoring external links.
- Competitive pressures to maintain company profitability, forcing firms to reduce slack capacity, costs and inventories, and to avoid making investments that are not strictly related to their core capabilities.
- Intense worldwide competition, creating a strong incentive to look for partners abroad that can help selling in foreign markets or share the risk of a new product.

This chapter is structured as follows. The second section discusses the theoretical arguments that lead firms to vertical integration rather than looking for outside sources. It concludes that most of the theoretical framework was based on static arguments against or in favor of vertical integration. The next section focuses on the arguments based on collaboration and the dynamic capabilities of the firm in an attempt to explain why some companies select integrated outsourcing as a strategic choice. The fourth section delves into the applicability of these theoretical arguments in case studies which are based on a set of interviews with the managers of the packaging firms and several of their client firms. The last section summarizes the main conclusions and suggests paths for future research.

VERTICAL INTEGRATION VERSUS OUTSOURCING

Theoretical arguments in business strategy and transaction costs economics indicate that there is a substantial incentive for firms to integrate vertically. This body of literature suggests that the incentives for vertical integration depend on the type of production involved, the extent of transaction costs, the amount of specialized assets, the degree of market power at each stage of production, the distinctiveness of activities, and the amount of uncertainty concerning prices and costs. Vertical integration can also increase profits through higher prices by creating barriers to entry (Bain, 1956), allowing price discrimination (Stiegler, 1951), or providing a firm with power over buyers and suppliers (Porter, 1980).

On the other hand, the usefulness of vertical integration strategies has come under attack in the strategic literature. Vertical integration is said to raise costs for several reasons. Mobility and exit barriers may increase strategic inflexibility that traps firms into keeping obsolescent technologies and strategies (Harrigan, 1985a, b). Managerial inefficiencies may also develop because vertical integration creates complex problems of control and co-ordination among highly interdependent activities (D'Aveni and Ilinitch, 1992). Underutilized capacity can also increase costs in some stages of production because through-put is unbalanced if technological factors force firms to build plants of differing scale at adjacent stages of production (Harrigan, 1983a, b). And finally, vertical integration may force firms to forgo purchasing at low prices in the open market (Quinn *et al.*, 1990).

Still other authors argue that vertical integration may be adopted as a strategy for reasons other than efficiency. For example, vertical integration may be adopted to reduce interdependencies with their exchange partners (Pfeffer and Salanick, 1978).

Focusing on managerial aspects, a growing amount of literature considers that even if the internalization of exchanges reduces certain transaction costs, vertical integration requires an organization's hierarchy to become responsible for internally transferring goods that were formerly sold on open markets. Thus the savings from reduced selling costs may be partially or totally offset by the increased overhead associated with the bureaucracy responsible for augmented internal co-ordination (D'Aveni and Ravenscraft, 1994).

The cost of implementing vertical integration can also be substantial, because it increases the size of the organization. The expanded size then enlarges the distance between subordinates and their ultimate superiors, causing increased communication distortion (Mahoney, 1992). As firms integrate vertically and away from their core business, they are also likely to become involved in tasks that they do not have the knowledge and skills to manage efficiently. Controlling these new operations and communication losses may require new expenditures, and subsequently more administrative overhead, again raising production costs (Harrigan, 1985b).

Vertical integration may also raise production and overhead costs for several other reasons. Managerial inefficiencies can develop because vertical integration creates complex problems of control and co-ordination among highly interdependent production activities (D'Aveni and Ilinitch, 1992). Moreover, the loss of market pressures for efficiency suggests that the internal organization could be more costly than the market mechanism (Williamson, 1975). The lack of direct competitive pressure on cost of intermediate inputs can encourage increasing levels of organizational slack (Cyert and March, 1963). Average production costs may be increased by underused capacity at some production stage because production lines may be unbalanced if technological factors force firms to build different-scaled plants for adjacent stages of production (Harrigan, 1983b).

Despite the substantial theoretical justification for expecting economies/diseconomies of vertical integration, there still is a need for further study to test and to specify the extent of this strategy in a more dynamic framework. Harrigan (1983b) suggests that the proper use of vertical integration changes as industries evolve and as the focus of firms shifts to different business sectors. He argues that the presence (or absence) of certain environmental characteristics should mitigate (or enhance) the use of vertical integration. From his point of view, the economic advantages of vertical integration will be transitory because industry structures (and relationships among firms) are not static. Since most industries become settings for volatile competition at some point in their evolution, strategists must recognize that the long-term benefits of vertical integration are often primarily those of intelligence gathering or quality control. The arguments developed by Harrigan (1983b) explicitly recognize that firms: (1) may control vertical relationships without owning fully adjacent business units, (2) may (or may not) perform a variety of integrated activities at a particular stage of processing, or (3) may engage in many (or few) stages of processing in the production chain from ultra raw materials to the final consumption. These possibilities were not aspects of the old image of vertically integrated business units, whereby units were assumed to be 100 per cent owned, to be (probably) physically interconnected, and to supply 100 per cent of a firm's needs for a particular good or service. Harrigan suggests instead that firms may adjust the dimensions of their vertical integration strategies to suit competitive or corporate needs. Vertical integration needs not be the same under all circumstances in order to be effective. Managers can fine-tune their uses in accordance with changing strategic needs.

Working from a similar perspective, Porter (1990) introduces the concept of 'value chain' in which a firm is defined by its activities – each distinct in its technical and strategic content – which are co-ordinated among themselves by specific links. The configuration of the value chain depends upon the type of physical and geographical integration among the activities. Both co-ordination and configuration of the value chain will influence the firm's competitive advantages. The specific configuration will be influenced greatly by the competitive forces of the industry, whereas co-ordination depends on the internal capabilities of the firm. Although Porter's analysis of vertical integration is similar to Harrigan's arguments, his more inclusive analysis is, undoubtedly, more operational. It captures empirical specificity, and evaluates the impact of the internalization/externalization of activities on the strategies of various firms. Besides, it is a useful tool to analyze firm-internationalization strategies through the geographical configuration of value chains and the co-ordinating links that are maintained with headquarters.

Finally, the nature of synergy must be reconsidered. Synergy does not exist between strategic business units (SBUs) or activities unless executives consciously enforce policies causing them to: (1) communicate, (2) share inputs, outputs, R&D, or other useful attributes and capabilities, and/or (3) co-operate in some other useful manner. If a firm's management systems are weak, it can create situations in which vertical integration becomes a mobility barrier. If a company does not have the internal mechanisms that balance the needs of SBU autonomy and corporate strategy, it will exacerbate their problems with vertical integration. Although, as Williamson (1975) suggested, firms may integrate to escape external costs associated with market transactions, there are costs to managing transfers across internal boundaries as well. If firms are unwilling or unable to bear these management costs, they may prefer to use outside markets.

At the other extreme, the literature on outsourcing considers that if supplier markets were totally reliable and efficient, rational companies would outsource everything except those special activities in which they could achieve a unique competitive edge, that is, their core competencies. Since the markets for most suppliers are imperfect, they encompass some risks for both buyer and seller with respect to price, quality, timing or other key dimensions. Moreover, outsourcing entails transaction costs – searching, contracting, controlling and recontracting – that at times may exceed the organization costs of having the activity directly under management's in-house control.

In addition, Stuckey and White (1993) noted three types of 'asset specificity' that commonly create market imperfections which call for controlled sourcing solutions rather than relying solely on efficient markets. These characteristics are: site specificity, where sellers have located costly fixed assets in close proximity to the buyer, thus minimizing transportation and inventory costs; technical specificity, where one or both parties must invest in equipment that can be used only by the parties in conjunction with each other and has low value in alternative uses; and human capital specificity, where employees must develop in-depth skills that are specific to a particular buyer or customer relationship.

To address these difficulties, Quinn and Hilmer (1994) consider that managers should focus on three key aspects about any activity considered for outsourcing. First there is the potential to obtain competitive advantage in this activity, taking into account transaction costs. The second point encompasses the potential vulnerability that could arise from market failure if the activity is outsourced. The third aspect delves into what can be done to alleviate vulnerability in structuring arrangements with suppliers which provide appropriate controls yet, at the same time, furnish the necessary flexibility in the area of demand.

The authors conclude that in selecting a sourcing strategy for a particular segment of their business, firms have a wide range of control options. Where there is a high potential for competitive edge and vulnerability, tight control is indicated. At the opposite end, the ancillary non-core activities require loose control. The practice and law of partnerships/strategic alliances are rapidly developing new ways to deal with common control issues. Specific procedures are established that permit direct involvement in limited stages of a partner's activity without incurring the costs of ownership arrangements or the loss of control inherent to arm's-length transactions. Within this framework, there is a constant trade-off between flexibility and control. The main objective of outsourcing contracts is to have the supplier assume certain risks and investments as demand fluctuates, because, to optimize costs, the buying company may want to maintain a constant capacity. Nevertheless, the company should keep a minimum capability to internalize this activity if it is strategic to its business.

INTEGRATED OUTSOURCING

The above theoretical arguments show that the ability of a firm to manage external resources is often a major determinant of its capacity to expand rapidly or to respond effectively to sudden changes in the environment. At present, many firms have a growing propensity to rely on various forms of external partnerships instead of investing in their own physical plants. They choose this option to allow for a more profitable allocation of their human and financial resources. This resource reinvestment permits these firms to maximize their know-how and goodwill, while saving time in implementing strategic moves, as well as retaining their organization's flexibility. Growing uncertainty and change in both downstream and upstream markets also leading firms to avoid heavy investments in areas they do not regard as being part of their core business.

According to Barreyre (1988), a partnership is a co-operative behavior towards outside organizations which provides the potential required. Such a policy is fully applied in a firm when the managers, as well as taking into account the short-term advantages of subcontracting, for instance, also adopt a strategic view and look at the long-term profits and risks for both parties in the transaction. Through such an approach to commercial relations these managers see suppliers, subcontractors or franchisees as *partners* with whom opportunities should be found to develop synergistic efforts for mutual profit. Sometimes this attitude involves long-term agreements (on such items as price revisions, orders and patent rights) when productivity and innovation are expected from investments in plant, quality control and occasionally joint R&D. Such links (which do not exclude one-off transactions elsewhere) create a genuine community of interests, in other words a *solidarity* between the supplier and his partners (Barreyre and Bouche, 1982).

Well-known Japanese examples, among others, give us reasons to think that a company may combine productivity and security (for example: just in time and zero-defect quality) with a reduction of assets thanks to good subcontracting management. Furthermore, in many cases, flexibility is not incompatible with dependability. As for the economies of information, the same kind of hypothesis could be formulated: with the new technologies of transportation, telecommunications and information processing, it is often easier to communicate, and therefore to negotiate, with outside partners than within a large organization.

There are many kinds of business contracts which may result from a partnership decision: purchase contracts of standard or specific inputs and/or services; subcontracting; authorized dealer contracts; agency contracts; franchising; buyer commissions; proxy agreements; carrier contracts; licensing; and other organizational arrangements such as integrated outsourcing.

According to Teece and Pisano (1994), an expanded paradigm is needed to explain how competitive advantage is gained and held by firms. The authors argue that winners in the global marketplace are firms which have demonstrated timely responsiveness and rapid and flexible product innovation, along with the management capability to co-ordinate effectively and to redeploy internal and external competencies. Their paper also argues that the competitive advantages of firms originate from dynamic capabilities rooted in high-performance routines operating inside the firm, embedded in the firm's processes, and conditioned by its history.

Firms distinguish themselves from market transactions because they possess the competencies/capabilities to organize activities that otherwise could not be accomplished under co-ordination through the price system. As pointed out by Kogut and Zander (1992), the very essence of capabilities/competencies is that they cannot be assembled through markets. As Harrigan (1985b) wrote, although contracts matter, a firm's internal organization requires other co-ordinating mechanisms to exercise its competencies/capabilities.

The learning literature distinguishes itself from the previous contributions by considering that '. . . even more important than integration is learning. Learning is a process by which repetition and experimentation enable tasks to be performed better and more quickly and new production opportunities to be identified' (Teece and Pisano, 1994, p. 544).

Learning has several characteristics that may explain why firms strategically elect integrated outsourcing. First, learning involves organizational, as well as individual, skills because it is a process that is intrinsically social and collective, requires joint efforts, and possesses common codes of co-ordination and co-ordinated search procedures. Second, the organizational knowledge generated by such routines results in new patterns of activities, in 'new routines', or in a new logic of organization. Third, most of the learning process is tacit and difficult to codify, as pointed out by Nelson and Winter (1982).

To be strategic, a capability must be critical to a user need (so that there are customers), unique (so that the products/services produced can be priced without too much regard to competition), and difficult to replicate (so that profits will not be lost to competitors). Accordingly, any asset or entity which is homogeneous and can be bought and sold at an established price cannot be all that strategic.

As Teece and Pisano (1994, p. 541) stress, the key feature of distinctive competencies and capabilities is that there is no market for them, except possibly through that of business units or corporate control. Therefore, '. . . competencies and capabilities are intriguing assets as they typically must be built because they can not be bought'.

Teece and Pisano argue that the strategic dimension of an enterprise includes its managerial and organizational processes, its present position, and the technological paths available to it. Nelson and Winter (1982) refer to managerial and organizational processes as a firm's routines, or current practice and learning. By positioning, Teece and Pisano understand the current endowment of technology and intellectual property, as well as the firm's customer base and upstream relationship with the supplier. Path is defined as the strategic alternatives available to the firm, and the attractiveness of opportunities which lie ahead. They focus their analysis on asset structures for which no ready market exists, as these are the only assets of strategic interest.

A firm's processes and positions collectively encompass its capabilities or competencies. A hierarchy of competencies/capabilities ought to be recognized, as some competencies may be on the factory floor, in R&D labs, in executives' suites, and some in the way activities are integrated. A difficult-to-imitate competence/capability can be considered a distinctive competence.

Furthermore, Nelson and Winter (1982) deduced that they found significant firm-level differences in co-ordination routines and that these differences seem to have persisted for a long time. They suggest, then, that routines related to co-ordination are firm-specific in nature, and are difficult to imitate because organizational processes often display high levels of coherence which require systematic changes throughout the organization and among inter-organizational linkages.

For all these reasons, legal contracts are hardly complete instruments to assure learning among partners and cannot be substituted for a constant exchange of information. The concept of dynamic capability, suggested by Teece and Pisano (1994), requires the interaction of learning and co-ordination, opening the possibility to understand the need for forms of co-operation, including integrated outsourcing, as a mechanism to maximize the potential for inter-organizational learning and the dynamic/cumulative process of building competitive advantages.

INTEGRATED OUTSOURCING IN THE PACKAGING INDUSTRY

Outsourcing continues to play a growing role in the packaging industry, regardless of the type of materials employed. In the glass sector, market mechanisms tend to prevail, including 'off-the-shelf' purchasing, because of higher unit costs, higher minimum efficient scale, and bearable, relative transport costs. In metal boxes, organizational arrangements are more diverse.

One interesting case is COLEP, a tin packages manufacturer, which evolved in a similar fashion to Dana and Chrysler. In 1974, Portugal offered contradictory business conditions: political change, with the implementation of a democratic regime, led to strong demands for higher salaries which in turn increased the available income of a large share of the population. However, the political situation was unstable and unlikely to attract new, direct foreign investment. Johnson Wax, an American multinational, decided to find a local manufacturer instead of creating a new factory because it was unwilling to take a high political risk. This agreement led COLEP, a small can maker, to integrate vertically as a contract filler. Johnson Wax, as Chrysler is doing now with Dana, was outsourcing a totally manufactured component. Indeed it went even further than Chrysler, which built an assembly plant, albeit a small one, in Brazil. Johnson Wax was controlling only the two ends of its activity: conception of new products, including research and development; and marketing, including the selection of the retail network. COLEP was given the formula and complete expertise to take care of the entire manufacturing and packaging of several aerosols for Johnson Wax. This co-operative relationship still exists and has been strengthened by COLEP's 1993 purchase of a Johnson Wax plant located outside Madrid. This purchase meant a further technology transfer which benefited COLEP. An obvious threat to this model of co-operation is the potential for COLEP to become a full-fledged competitor of Johnson Wax, creating its own brands of the same products currently marketed by its partner. The duration of the partnership shows the importance of trust (as suggested by Kumar, 1996) and the value estimated by both parties to the future cash flows originated by their co-operation. These two firms provide an interesting example of partnership, based on a strong interaction and the sharing of technology, as well as complete separation of manufacturing and marketing.

A different, but equally close, form of partnership was created by Logoplaste, a plastic package manufacturer which currently owns approximately thirty 'factories' located inside its clients' facilities. Each factory is a small unit made up of a plastic filling machine and a small team of four to ten direct employees. The raw material is made of small plastic pieces (PET, generally) which are expanded through heating and mould injection, and finally achieve the shape of a plastic bottle. Standard sizes most often used are 33 centiliters and 1.5 liters. Logoplaste's work takes place at the very beginning of the clients' production lines. Given the volume of the 'expanded' empty bottles, intermediate inventories are kept low. Therefore, any breakdown or other interruption at Logoplaste's units would stop the client firm's production. On the other hand, seasonal and other variations of the production level must be met by Logoplaste's units. There are very high levels of integration with full customization of both production schedules and end products, as many clients require specific designs for the package they use.

For about twenty-five years, the company focused on domestic expansion, until there were virtually no more such opportunities. The client firms are mineral water, yogurt and soft drinks producers. Besides domestic organizations, Logoplaste counts important multinationals among its customers. In 1997 Logoplaste was seventeenth among European producers with a total turnover of US$45 million, 25 per cent of which came from foreign markets, mainly Brazil.

Logoplaste is a family-owned company. Its transformation was triggered by external factors. The current owners and managers were operating a relatively large plastic manufacturing operation which was taken over by the workers after the fall of the old dictatorship in 1974. Lacking financial resources, Logoplaste started creating small factories, capable of supplying the specific needs of its client firms, all of which belonged to the food and drink industry. The company expanded by creating a new factory approximately every year. As it consolidated its experience and reputation, further expansion became easier. Moreover, counting many affiliates of large multinational corporations as domestic customers, the firm could count on firm-specific knowledge and reputation to enter foreign markets, thus overcoming its lack of country-specific knowledge.

In the early 1990s Logoplaste started expanding to a familiar foreign market – Spain – and later ventured into a psychologically close, but geographically distant, market – Brazil. Reputation and close links with multinational clients eased the access to clients based outside Portugal. Logopaste's clients are listed in Table 3.1.

Logoplaste's customers include a number of multinational companies, among them Nestlé, Coca-Cola and Danone. Given that these multinationals are predominantly decentralized and may be classified as polycentric or multidomestic, there has been no central decision to take Logoplaste on as a global partner. Therefore, the company must be selected locally, often in competition with much larger package makers.

Although Spain has been a 'natural' expansion path given the geographical proximity, Brazil is a totally different case. Logoplaste entered the Brazilian market after a tourist trip there by its CEO, who made business contacts upon appointments he set up locally after consulting the telephone book. The partnership with Danone was extremely important as the Brazilian affiliate enjoyed a significant presence in the local market. Logoplaste estimates a 40 per cent market share of the Brazilian market for refrigerated milk products.

Most new deals survive for a long period, suggesting both a good

Table 3.1   Logoplaste's clients

PORTUGAL	
Yoplait	Milk products
Nestlé	Food products
Água do Luso	Mineral water
Água Vitalis	Mineral water
Água do Cruzeiro	Mineral water
Danone	Milk products
Coca-Cola	Soft drinks
Vítor Guedes	Food products
Unilever	Food products
Longa Vida	Milk products
Mimosa	Milk products
Nutrinveste	Milk products
Nutrinveste	Milk products
Santo Domingo – Bavaria	Beer
SPAIN	
Água Sierra de Jaen	Mineral water
Fuenpak	Soft drinks
Soc. Carbonica Vasco Catalana	Soft drinks
Nestlé	Food products
Coca-Cola	Soft drinks
BRAZIL	
Danone – Poços de Caldas	Milk products
Danone – Fortaleza	Milk products
Nestlé	Food products
FRANCE	
Nestlé	Food products

Source: Logoplaste, Internal report (1999).

understanding and high switching costs among partners. However, four Logoplaste deals have failed. L'Oréal set up a factory supplied by an integrated Logoplaste plant, but later closed the Portuguese facilities when Portugal joined the European Economic Community and import tariffs were eliminated. Alcatel also abandoned local production because of successful competition from East Asia. Finally, partnerships with a Portuguese pharmaceutical company and a Spanish organization were discontinued when the clients failed to make regular payments.

The organization structure of Logoplaste is complex as all the 'plants' report both to 'Production Management' and to the other functional units. Each plant is more than just a profit center as it enjoys a legal identity as a separate firm, wholly owned by the parent company Logoplaste. All functional areas 'sell' their services to the local plants and their accounts are open to scrutiny by the client firm. A simplified organizational chart is shown in Figure 3.3.

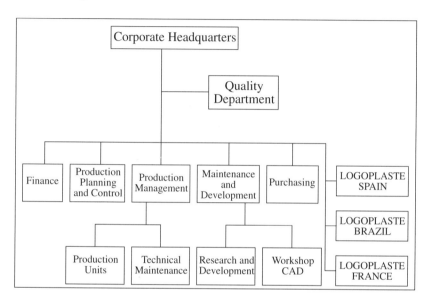

Source: Logoplaste, Internal Report (1997).

Figure 3.3   Simplified organizational chart of Logoplaste in Portugal

Although the operational core is located in Portugal, the structure is replicated in the foreign locations. This system ensures that local expertise can bring a quick solution to production breakdowns or to requirements concerning changing production schedules and product innovation. In 1996 Logoplaste obtained ISO 9001 certification. An internal information and control network – *Standard Process Control* – with intranet data transmission was created next.

Transportation costs of empty plastic bottles are so high that external purchase is possible only if a potential supplier is located near the client firm. Estimates made by Logoplaste suggest that *integrated outsourcing* is 5–7 per cent cheaper than *outsourcing.* It also facilitates customization. However, internal production for Logoplaste's clients could be a viable alternative to the present form of integrated outsourcing. The benefits accrued to the customers which use Logoplaste can be summarized as follows:

- Economic savings in the acquisition of raw material – as Logoplaste must meet the demand of a large number of individual plants it has a substantial bargaining position;
- Specialization in purchasing equipment, recruitment and training personnel – a firm with a lot of experience is better able to purchase highly customized machines efficiently;
- Product customization – technical expertise with plastic moulds facilitates the introduction of new packages, designed in co-operation with the clients' marketing departments. Logoplaste also undertakes economic feasibility studies on behalf of its customers.

The contracts signed by Logoplaste and its client partners include specifications of activity levels, product characteristics, package-cost structure and contract duration. However, the activity levels are either the consequence of exogenous factors or the outcome of the client's marketing efforts. Specified prices will be increased if the production levels fail to meet the defined target or decreased if production is higher than expected. This model reduces the risk to Logoplaste.

From a dynamics perspective, we found that new clients came from a variety of organizational arrangements. They may have been vertically integrated, having owned a package-making facility which was subsequently sold and adapted by Logoplaste. Other possibilities include being externally supplied by an independent package maker or creating an integrated outsourcing scheme from the beginning, in the case of a new plant. The last scenario was not too common in the past, however, as Logoplaste had to fight for operating clients. Logoplaste managers have stated that they were equally successful in overcoming both prospective client situations – pure buying and pure making.

Both Logoplaste and COLEP provide an interesting lesson concerning the apparently rising swing from pure market and pure hierarchy to an intermediate mode of market mechanisms arranged through partnerships. Indeed, firms are willing to give up a part of their control over their products in a trade-off for partial loss of risk. This evolution is pictured in Figure 3.4.

Although through different modes, of which integrated outsourcing is a rich case, strategic partnerships seem a stable state, with more entries than exits. Indeed, both the examples of COLEP and Logoplaste show that this mode can be superior to the alternatives of either higher integration or lower integration.

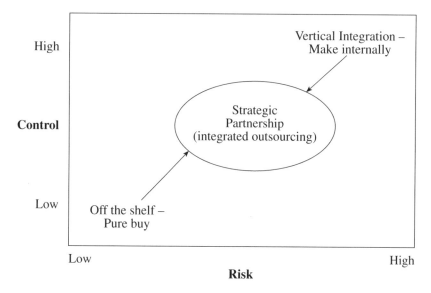

Figure 3.4   Impact of risk versus control trade-off on organizational form

CONCLUSION

The boundaries of firms are permanently shifting. While the management fad of downsizing and concentration on the core business persists, the period studied set the stage for a bigger wave of mergers and acquisitions than ever before. Under these apparently contradictory patterns, firms have evolved in ways which can only be explained through theory-based research.

Although based on a limited set of cases, this study provides interesting insights into the new features of transactions among firms.

- In an uncertain world there is value associated with flexibility (Buckley and Casson, 1988) which enhances the potential for new organizational and co-operative forms.
- Strategic partnerships, including integrated outsourcing, are taking precedence over both more hierarchical and more market-based mechanisms.
- By contrast with other types of partnerships, such as joint ventures (see Gomes-Casseres, 1988, for a study of joint-venture mortality), strategic partnerships last for a very long time unless the activity of the client firms is discontinued or becomes economically unfeasible for reasons external to the partnership.

- Integrated outsourcing tends to expand to other locations, including different nations, even within the framework of multidomestic clients. This forum creates opportunities for the internationalization of the suppliers.
- An opportunity for expansion, even overseas, is created for small firms given the small, minimally efficient scale of some types of integrated outsourcing.
- Political risk and other limitations inherent in small and poor countries render integrated outsourcing particularly suitable as a strategy to be adopted by enterprises. Even large MNEs, such as Chrysler, prefer to commit smaller resources in new risky ventures if they can find suitable partners locally.

This field requires further work. Although transaction costs theory provides an appropriate foundation for defining and testing the hypotheses associated with the economic determinants of integrated outsourcing versus alternative modes, it does require a larger, more encompassing database.

Moreover, the two cases covered in this study suggest the existence of different co-operation rules. COLEP and Johnson Wax suggest the existence of what one can call a monogamic relationship, precluding the possibility of co-operation in a defined market with each partner's competitors. By contrast, Logoplaste serves many competing firms, creating a polygamic relationship, which does not seem to upset previous clients or preclude the addition of new ones. The reasons for this seeming paradox could be Logoplaste's non-involvement with any of its client's sensitive technological assets and its reputation for maintaining absolute confidentiality. The advertising field is one example of the worldwide sensitivity and co-operation needed to work with the competitors of a current client. By studying the determinants of mono versus polygamic partnerships, new light should be shed on the definition of the boundaries of a firm.

REFERENCES

Bain, J.S. (1956), *Barriers to New Competition*, Cambridge, MA: Harvard University Press.

Barreyre, P.Y. (1988), 'The concept of "impartition" policies: a different approach to vertical integration strategies', *Strategic Management Journal*, 9: 507–20.

Barreyre, P.Y. and M. Bouche (1982), 'Pour une compétitivité fondée sur la solidarité entre les firmes: les politiques d'impartition', *Revue Française de Gestion*, 37: 8–17.

Buckley, P. and M. Casson (1998), 'Models of the multinational enterprise', *Journal of International Business Studies*, 29 (1): 21–44.

Cyert, R.M. and March J.G. (1963), *A behavioral theory of the firm*, Englewood Cliffs, NJ: Princeton-Hall.

Dana, Leo-Paul (ed.) (2000), *Global Marketing Cooperation and Networks*, New York: Haworth Press.

Dana, Leo-Paul, H. Etemad and R.W. Wright (2000), 'The global reach of symbiotic networks,' in Leo-Paul Dana (ed.), *Global Marketing Cooperation and Networks*, New York: Haworth Press, pp. 1–16.

D'Aveni, R.A. and A.V. Ilinitch (1992), 'Complex patterns of vertical integration in the forest industry: systematic and bankruptcy risk', *Academy of Management Journal*, 35: 596–625.

D'Aveni, R.A. and D.J. Ravenscraft (1994), 'Economies of integration versus bureaucracy costs: does vertical integration improve performance?' *Academy of Management Journal*, 37 (5): 1167–206.

Dyer, J.H., D.S. Cho and W. Chu (1998), 'Strategic supplier segmentation: the next "best practice" in supply chain management', *California Management Review*, 40 (2): 57–77.

Esperança, J.P. (1993), 'Modes of foreign entry by service multinationals', *Proceedings of the 19th Annual Conference of the European International Business Association*.

Gomes-Casseres, B. (1988), 'Joint venture cycles: the evolution of ownership strategies of U.S. MNEs, 1945–75', in F.J. Contractor and P. Lorange (eds), *Cooperative Strategies in the International Business*, Lexington, MA: Lexington Books.

Harrigan, K.R. (1983a), 'Vertical integration and corporate strategy', *Academy of Management Journal*, 70 (4): 397–425.

Harrigan, K.R. (1983b), *Strategies for vertical integration*', Lexington, MA: D.C. Heath.

Harrigan, K.R. (1985a), 'Exit barriers and vertical integration', *Academy of Management Journal*, 28: 686–97.

Harrigan, K.R. (1985b), 'Strategies and intrafirm transfers and outside sourcing', *Academy of Management Journal*, 28: 914–25.

Kappor, V. and A. Gupta (1997), 'Aggressive sourcing: a free-market approach', *Sloan Management Review*, Fall, 21–31.

Kogut, I. and U. Zander (1992), 'Knowledge of the firm, combinative capabilities, and the replication of technology', *Organization Science*, 24: 38–59.

Kumar, N. (1996), 'The power of trust in manufacturer–retailer relationships', *Harvard Business Review*, November–December: 92–106.

Mahoney, G.J. (1992), 'The choice of organizational form', *Strategic Management Journal*, 13: 559–84.

Nelson, R.R. and S.G. Winter (1982), *An evolutionary theory on economic change*. Cambridge, MA: Harvard University Press.

Pfeffer, J. and G.R. Salanick (1978), *The External Control of Organizations: A Resource Dependence Perspective*, New York: Harper & Row.

Porter, M.E. (1980), *Competitive Strategy: Techniques for Analysing Industry and Competitors*, New York: Free Press.

Porter, M. (1990), 'The competitive advantage of nations', *Harvard Business Review*, March–April: 73–93.

Quinn, J.B., T.L. Doorley and P.C. Paquette (1990), 'Technology in services: rethinking strategic focus', *Sloan Management Review*, Winter: 79–87.

Quinn, J.B. and F.G. Hilmer (1994), 'Strategic outsourcing', *Sloan Management Review*, Summer: 43–55.

Stiegler, G.J. (1951), 'The division of labour is limited by the extent of the market', *Journal of Political Economy*, 59 (3): 185–93.

Stuckey, J. and D. White (1993), 'When and when not vertically integrate', *Sloan Management Review*, Spring: 71–83.

Teece, D. and G. Pisano (1994), 'The dynamic capabilities of the firm: an introduction', *Industrial and Corporate Change*, 3 (3): 537–57.

Venkatsan, R. (1992), 'Strategic sourcing: to make or not to make', *Harvard Business Review*, November–December: 98–107.

Williamson, O.E. (1971), 'The vertical integration of production: market failure considerations', *American Economic Review*, 61: 112–23.

Williamson, O.E. (1975), *Markets and Hierarchies*, New York: Free Press.

4. Small multinationals in global competition: an industry perspective

Tatiana S. Manalova[*]

INTRODUCTION

Small and medium-sized enterprises (SMEs) have become increasingly dynamic international participants. In Europe, they account for up to a third of France and Sweden's exports and for over 50 per cent of Italy and Ireland's exports (OECD, 1997). Even in the USA, where small businesses have traditionally been oriented towards the domestic market, 97 per cent of all 1999 exporters were small businesses, and the number of small business exporters tripled between 1987 and 1997 (SBA, 2000).

Not only are SMEs active exporters, but they also undertake direct investment in foreign countries (Fujita, 1995a, 1995b). Small foreign investors establish production, sales, service, R&D or other affiliates abroad, joining global competition as small multinationals. There are more than 235,000 small multinational corporations in the OECD countries alone and this number is expected to grow continually (OECD, 1997; Fujita, 1998).

Of particular interest to this study is the observation that foreign direct investment by SMEs tends to be clustered in several industries, such as computers and associated peripherals, software, industrial electronics, and medical technology (Oviatt and McDougall, 1997; Knight and Cavusgil, 1997). Since SMEs enter global competition in increasing numbers, yet are not uniformly distributed across industries, it follows that some inherent industry structural and competitive characteristics favor the emergence of small multinationals. Hence the research question guiding this study is: *What industry structural and competitive forces determine foreign direct investment by small and medium-sized enterprises?*

Globalization has been touted as the order of the day and many small-business managers contemplate taking advantage of global market

* The author wishes to thank Dr Hamid Etemad, Dr Richard W. Wright, two anonymous reviewers and the participants in the Second Biennial Conference on International Entrepreneurship: Researching New Frontiers (Montreal, Canada, 23–25 September 2000) for their insightful comments on previous drafts of this paper.

opportunities. Global expansion in unfavorable industry environments, however, can be risky and costly, given the resource constraints of small companies (Hirsch and Adar, 1974). Similarly, for business development agencies worldwide which seek to encourage the international involvement of the small-business sector, 'across the board' export promotion policies may turn out to be misdirected. Therefore, the industry-level effects on foreign direct investment by SMEs have relevant managerial and public policy implications.

To understand industry-level effects on foreign direct investment by SMEs, I turned to existing theories of the multinational enterprise, but could not find an adequate explanation. Traditional international business theories, such as the monopolistic advantage theory (Hymer, 1976), or the oligopolistic reaction theory (Knickerbocker, 1973) conceptualize foreign direct investment as the exclusive domain of large, resource-rich companies. These theories treat foreign direct investment by small, resource-poor companies as an aberration. Internationalization process, or evolutionary theories (Johanson and Vahlne, 1977; Cavusgil, 1980), on the other hand, focus on the firm-specific determinants of internationalization, but they do not explain why foreign direct investment by small companies should occur in some industries and not in others. Finally, recent work on international new ventures (McDougall *et al.*, 1994; Oviatt and McDougall, 1997) provides theoretical perspectives on 'born global' companies, or 'infant multinationals', but is not directed at understanding why and how 'born domestic' small enterprises become 'global'. Thus a critical gap appears in our understanding of the industry-level drivers of foreign direct investment by small and medium-sized enterprises.

This study seeks to address this gap by developing a theoretical framework and advancing propositions on the effect of the industry-level drivers of foreign direct investment by small and medium-sized enterprises. It is organized as follows. First, theoretical perspectives on the small multinational from international business research, theories of internationalization, and international entrepreneurship are critically reviewed. Second, a model of industry structural and competitive influences on foreign direct investment by SMEs is developed and 12 propositions on the directional impact of these forces are formulated. The study concludes with a discussion of the theoretical and practical implications of the framework.

THEORETICAL PERSPECTIVES ON THE SMALL MULTINATIONAL

Research on small multinationals falls in the intersection of international business and international entrepreneurship research. International business theories explain the 'causes and consequences' (Caves, 1971) of the multinational enterprise, while research in international entrepreneurship focuses on the internationalization process of new and small companies, primarily international new ventures.

International Business Theories

International business scholars have traditionally related the emergence of multinational enterprises to industry structural and competitive forces. Multinational enterprises have been posited to emerge in oligopolistic market settings in order to economize on transaction costs (Buckley and Casson, 1976); exploit locational (Dunning, 1988), product pioneering (Vernon, 1966), or other proprietary advantages (Hymer, 1976), or react to the international expansion of competitors (Knickerbocker, 1973).

Developed in the context of large-scale manufacturing in the 1960s and 1970s, the constituent streams of international business research have formally linked multinationality to large firm size and oligopolistic market structure (Giddy and Young, 1982). The monopolistic advantage theory (Hymer, 1976), for example, argues that a firm needs certain proprietary advantages in order to compete globally. These advantages, however, such as scale economies (Caves, 1971), resource levels (Penrose, 1959), ability to absorb risks and uncertainty (Hirsch and Adar, 1974), or product innovations (Vernon, 1966), are all highly correlated to company size. Similarly, the oligopolistic reaction perspective (Knickerbocker, 1973) presents international expansion as a defensive strategy of rivals who seek to block the advantage of the first mover. In the lens of the oligopolistic reaction theory, multinationals also tend to be large in size and dominant market players. Overall, international business research has treated the small multinational as an 'unconventional form of multinational enterprise' (Giddy and Young, 1982) and has limits in providing an explanation for the drivers of foreign direct investment by SMEs (McDougall *et al.*, 1994; Dana *et al.*, 1999).

Theories of Internationalization

Theories of internationalization, such as the Uppsala model (Johanson and Vahlne, 1977), or the innovation model (Cavusgil, 1980) explore the drivers and evolution of internationalization of new and small companies, maintaining an internal perspective and focusing on firm-specific and managerial-related issues. Foreign involvement is conceptualized to proceed in a gradual and carefully controlled manner, so that extensive resource commitments are initiated only when significant experiential knowledge has been acquired (Camino and Cazorla, 1998; Oviatt and McDougall, 1997; Andersen, 1993). Internationalization process models have looked mainly at tacit managerial knowledge (Johanson and Vahlne, 1977) or experience (Cavusgil, 1980) as determinants of internationalization. With a few notable exceptions (McDougall, 1989; Boter and Holmquist, 1996), industry char-acteristics, though generally acknowledged, have been under-researched or blurred by prevailing cross-sectional sampling frames (Miesenbock, 1988). Theories of internationalization, therefore, while focusing on processes dis-tinguishing new and small companies, have limits in explaining industry drivers of foreign direct investment.

International Entrepreneurship

Recent work in international entrepreneurship has sought to include indus-try structural and competitive elements into the emerging theory of inter-national new ventures – companies international at inception (McDougall *et al.*, 1994). Summarizing case-based research, Oviatt and McDougall (1995) linked international business networks – an industry structural char-acteristic – to six managerial attributes, to analyse a pattern characteristic of successful global start-ups. Similarly, Knight and Cavusgil (1997) in their study of 'born global' firms, found that industry characteristics, such as globalization of markets, advances in technology, salience of global niche markets, or growing role of global networks, facilitated 'early, rapid, and substantial internationalization'. These authors also observed that 'born global' companies tend to be clustered in knowledge-intensive indus-tries, a finding supported by other researchers (Bloodgood *et al.*, 1996; Coviello, 1997; Zahra *et al.*, 2000).

Despite the apparent applicability of the international entrepreneurship lens to study small foreign investors, three issues need to be noted. First, international entrepreneurship considers internationalized companies from an 'age' perspective, looking at 'new', rather than 'small', international ven-tures. Second, international entrepreneurship is focused on 'born globals' and does not provide guidance on the internationalization of 'born domes-tic' ventures. Finally, international entrepreneurship maintains a broad view of internationalization (from exporting to foreign direct investment). It can be argued, however, that industry-level drivers of exporting differ from those of foreign direct investment. While the size limitation of the domestic market may be a key driver of exporting, it is also market disequilibrium, govern-ment-imposed distortions, market structure imperfections, or market failure imperfections that determine foreign direct investment (Calvet, 1981).

To summarize, theoretical perspectives from related disciplines do not fully explain industry influences on foreign direct investment by SMEs.

International business theories are concerned with large rather than small multinationals, traditional theories of internationalization discuss internal, rather than external, drivers of internationalization, whereas international entrepreneurship is interested in new rather than small international new ventures. To understand industry influences, it is, therefore, necessary to develop a theoretical framework which links constructs from several complementary theoretical disciplines and maintains an industry-level perspective. This is the purpose of the next section of the study.

INDUSTRY-LEVEL INFLUENCES ON FOREIGN DIRECT INVESTMENT BY SMES: A THEORETICAL FRAMEWORK

The relevance of the industry as a unit of analysis is predicated on the role of industries as 'the international arena[s] in which competitive advantage is gained or lost' and the pattern of international competition which 'differs markedly from industry to industry' (Porter, 1986, p. 17). The theoretical framework developed in this study is based on the industrial organization perspective (Bain–Mason's Structure–Conduct–Performance paradigm), which posits that industry structure shapes the pattern of competition, and determines the performance of industry players (Bain, 1956; Porter, 1980). Industry structure refers to certain stable attributes of the market that create the competitive context of the industry and influence the firm's conduct in the marketplace (Bain, 1972; Porter, 1980).

In the context of this study, it is proposed that these structural and competitive attributes (or structural and competitive forces) determine the foreign direct investment SMEs. The theoretical framework captures the impact of six supply-side structural forces: scale economies, R&D scale, advertising scale, capital scale, industry age and industry growth; two demand-side structural forces: market demand, and market size; and four competitive forces: oligopolistic rivalry, mimetic isomorphism, strategic networks, and community influences. Figure 4.1 presents the theoretical framework, followed by the development of 12 propositions on the directional impact of industry structural and competitive attributes on the foreign direct investment by SMEs.

Structural Forces: Supply Side

Multinational enterprises are posited to be 'logically incompatible' with a purely competitive organization of an industry (Hymer, 1976). Multinational enterprises tend to emerge in industries with concentrated sellers,

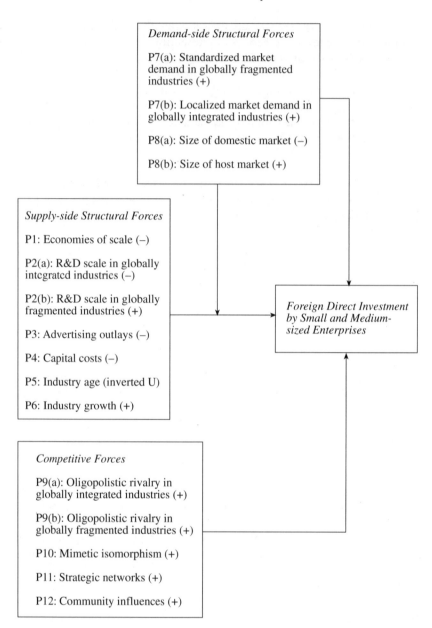

*Figure 4.1   Industry-level effects on foreign direct investment by small and
medium-sized enterprises: a theoretical framework*

i.e. oligopolistic industries '. . . because the influences giving rise to multi-national companies are identical with the bases of several barriers to entry into industries, and entry barriers cause sellers concentration' (Caves, 1971, p. 94). Hymer extended Bain's (1956) discussion of barriers to new competition to argue that the same advantages that deter the entry of new competitors into an industry can be used in the incumbents' international expansion in order to overcome the advantages of indigenous firms.

Scale economies in manufacturing

The potential for global integration is greatest when significant benefits are gained from worldwide volume because of the large optimal scale in relation to market size (Hout *et al.*, 1982). Industries characterized by substantial economies of scale tend also to be structurally globally integrated (Prahalad and Doz, 1987; Kobrin, 1991) and global in competitive scope (Porter, 1986). The list of global industries includes most manufacturing, chemicals, electronics, and automobiles (Kobrin, 1991). Scale economies present extremely high barriers to foreign direct investment by small companies, which operate on a small scale relative to the size of the market, because of the resource requirements (notably capital and management skills), investment scale, scale efficiencies, learning curve effects, concentration, and market power of industry incumbents (Buckley, 1989; Kohn, 1988).

SMEs, on the other hand, are most likely to undertake foreign direct investment in industries characterized by 'diseconomies of scale', e.g. industries fragmented into well-defined specialist segments, or market niches (Gomes-Casseres and Kohn, 1997; Knight and Cavusgil, 1997). These industries 'present a small firm in equilibrium with a small market' (Buckley, 1999, p. 70). In a market niche, a firm small in absolute scale, as defined by employment, assets, or sales, can be relatively large compared to the size of the market niche it occupies and a dominant player compared to its rivals (Buckley, 1989; Gomes-Casseres, 1997). Thus, small multinationals have been found to emerge in 'small-firm industries' (Buckley and Mirza, 1997, p. 3) – fragmented industries with low economies of scale and significant entry barriers for larger operations, where they are the technological leaders and dominate the niche segment within their narrow area of specialization. Examples include industries requiring a wide range of specialist intermediate inputs (Buckley, 1989).

In his study of small French multinationals – technology suppliers – Delapierre (1997) established that in seven of the nine cases the companies were world monopolies, commanding over 50 per cent of the world market share within their niche. Another case in point are the emerging hi-tech industries, which feature numerous well-defined global market niches. The

1997 OECD synthesis report estimated that SMEs in new niche industries, such as precision equipment, machine tools, and specialist software, are the most likely to undertake foreign direct investment (37 per cent of the small companies in the OECD countries). Two per cent of these small companies had multiple establishments and affiliates in many countries and in all major international regions.

Within the globally integrated industries themselves, innovation-led production and upgrading of consumer demand are reversing the trend towards world-scale plants and allow differentiation and segmentation with smaller cost penalties (Doz, 1987). As economic activity is becoming more interdependent, small businesses can be linked in the value chain of global manufacturing, because of their operational and organizational flexibility (Dunning, 1999). Similarly, Buckley (1997) posited that lean production and outsourcing meant greater opportunities for the globalization of smaller companies. Overall, then, our first proposition is:

P1: The lower the economies of scale achieved through worldwide production volume, the higher the likelihood that an SME will undertake foreign direct investment.

Technological intensity and speed of diffusion

Optimal economic scale is necessary to amortize research and development costs over a broader base (Kobrin, 1991). For example, the automakers' optimal scale of production to amortize R&D costs for new auto models is about two million units. This economic scale is, of course, a barrier to entry for small companies in traditional manufacturing industries characterized by high economies of scale.

On the other hand, small companies are found to be the innovators in innovative industries (Acs and Preston, 1997) and can successfully compete internationally if they focus on a narrow scope of technologies (Boter and Holmquist, 1996), becoming technological leaders in a specialized business (Kohn, 1988; Gomes-Casseres and Kohn, 1997). Fujita (1998) reported that up to 70 per cent of his cross-national sample of small multinationals were involved in an R&D activity, often with specialized research departments. Based on his case studies of six small companies emerging as multinationals, Prasad (1999, p. 4) noted that: 'the more technology-based the firm has been, the higher the probability that it would skip some or all of its pre-FDI stages'. The 'temporary monopoly' (Acs and Preston, 1997) afforded by technological leadership gives small multinationals a monopolistic advantage and allows them to behave as 'mini monopolies' in their respective market niche. Therefore interaction between industry scale and technological intensity can be expected, so that:

P2(a): The lower the technological intensity of a globally integrated industry, the higher the likelihood that an SME will undertake foreign direct investment.

P2(b): The higher the technological intensity of a globally fragmented industry, the higher the likelihood that an SME will undertake foreign direct investment.

Advertising outlays

Advertising outlays 'are associated with an entry barrier in certain types of industries where advertising dominates the information sought by buyers and its dissemination is subject to scale economies' (Caves, 1971, pp. 94–5). The importance of advertising as a barrier to foreign direct investment by SMEs is determined by its two linked effects: first, without the dominance of advertising as an information source, the new entrant (i.e. a small company) could use alternative marketing tactics for competitive positioning. Second, the scale economies in the dissemination of information put the new entrant at a 'pecuniary' disadvantage (Bain, 1956, p. 16), particularly serious in the case when the new entrant is also a resource-constrained small company with limited access to financing (Buckley, 1989). Therefore:

P3: The lower the advertising intensity of an industry, the higher the like-lihood that an SME will undertake foreign direct investment.

Capital cost barriers

Capital cost barriers arise where 'large outlays are required to enter an industry at an efficient scale of production', so that 'only an established firm with a large cash flow of internally generated funds can contemplate entry into such markets' (Caves, 1971, p. 95). Similar to the advertising-intensity mechanism, cost-of-entry has two linked effects discouraging foreign direct investment by SMEs. First, small companies cannot afford the amount of the capital outlay itself. Second, money market conditions impose higher cost of capital upon potential entrants than upon established firms, putting the small companies at an even more disadvantaged position compared to large established companies (Bain, 1956, p. 15). Therefore:

P4: The lower the capital cost intensity of an industry, the higher the likelihood that an SME will undertake foreign direct investment.

In addition to these stable structural characteristics, brought forward by the industrial organization paradigm, it is necessary to consider two dynamic structural attributes relevant to small ventures in competition: industry age and industry growth.

Industry age

This attribute is a key contextual variable in evolutionary theories. The entry of small ventures is posited to be concentrated in two phases of an industry's life cycle: the emergence/growth and decline stages of an industry (Carroll, 1994). Even though almost all populations of organizations show an inverted-U shaped growth pattern as the number of organizations rises and falls with population age, the number of organizations in declining populations increases with the entry of vigorous specialist organizations (Aldrich, 1999, p. 223; Carroll, 1994). It could be argued that the same industry structural conditions which favor the emergence of small organizations in general also foster their international expansion. Therefore, the impact of industry age on foreign direct investment by SMEs should be considered. All else being equal, the younger the global industry, the lower the barriers to entry. Interstices in new industries are still large enough to offer productive opportunities to small firms (Penrose, 1959), and firms in emerging industries do not have to be very large to be dominant players (Kohn, 1997). Buckley (1997, p. 72) further notes:

> The role of small companies varies with the life cycle of the industry. As the industry matures, economies of scale become prevalent and only a few survive. In the decline phase, established competitors face a threat from new entrepreneurial companies.

Therefore,

P5: The relationship between industry age and the likelihood of foreign direct investment by SMEs is curvilinear, where the likelihood of foreign direct investment by an SME is lowest at the maturity stage of the industry.

Industry growth

The other dynamic attribute is brought forward by the theory of the growth of the firm. This theory argues that small companies' growth is dependent on industry growth (Penrose, 1959). Since internationalization is one form of firm growth through geographic expansion (Penrose, 1959), it can be surmised that the emergence of small multinationals will also be contingent on the industry growth rate. Growing industries are a favorable milieu for small business internationalization. In fact, Penrose (1959, p. 222) suggested that small, resource-constrained firms should look for growth in growing economies and growing industries:

If, therefore, the opportunities for expansion in the economy increase at a faster rate than the large firms can take advantage of them and if the large firms cannot prevent the entry of small firms, there will be scope for the continued growth in size and number of favorably endowed small firms, some of whom will themselves enter the "large" category in time.

Moreover, environmental munificence, of which industry growth is a measure, is positively associated with the range of strategy options open to the small firm. When resources are not scarce, organizations can pursue goals other than survival and survival is possible under alternative goals and strategies. Therefore,

> *P6: The higher the growth rate of an industry, the higher the likelihood that an SME will undertake foreign direct investment.*

Structural Forces: Demand Side

Standardized market demand
As mentioned above, fragmented industries present a natural milieu for the development of small companies, because of the well-defined specialist niches and the equilibrium between the size of the firm and the size of the market. Industry fragmentation, however, does not preclude global homogenization of market demand within each specialist segment (Doz, 1987). The standardization of market demand across different markets, and the location of the majority of a company's customers outside of the domestic market, create global market niches in which small companies compete (Kohn, 1988, 1997; Oviatt and McDougall, 1997). Industries distinguished by well-defined global market segments include predominantly industrial markets, such as precision manufacturing, sophisticated medical equipment, industrial measuring and monitoring devices, and precision machine tools (Ozawa, 1997). The standardization of market demand within globally defined market niches increases returns to scale achieved through a worldwide production volume, reduces uncertainty, and lowers the information-seeking costs associated with extensive international resource commitments, thus promoting foreign direct investment by small and medium-sized enterprises.

Conversely, many globally integrated industries are experiencing increasing pressures for local customization (Prahalad and Doz, 1987). Under these conditions, attributes commensurate with smaller size, such as production expertise, adaptation to meet a particular market or use conditions, or expertise in production engineering (Giddy and Young, 1982), can promote foreign direct investment by SMEs. Based on the results of a 1993

UNCTAD survey of small and medium-sized transnational corporations, Buckley (1999, p. 153) concluded that 'where local skills are needed, small scale is a positive advantage, and information processing is required (speed-ily), then SMEs are likely to feel more confident of success'.
    Therefore,

P7(a): The higher the degree of standardization of market demand in a globally fragmented industry, the higher the likelihood that an SME will undertake foreign direct investment.

P7(b): The higher the degree of localization of market demand in a glo-bally integrated industry, the higher the likelihood that an SME will under-take foreign direct investment.

The size of the domestic market is another important demand-side struc-tural characteristic. The size of the domestic market is expected to affect the internationalization efforts of SMEs, especially if the domestic market is not large enough to support a sufficient level of sales (Reuber and Fischer, 1999, p. 87). Alternatively, the larger the focal host market, the more attractive it is as an investment opportunity. In fact, the United Nations cross-national survey of 98 small and medium-sized multinational enterprises revealed that the strongest motivation for foreign direct invest-ment was 'the expectation of growth in the focal market' (UNCTAD, 1993, p. 41). Therefore:

P8(a): The smaller the size of the domestic market relative to the global market, the higher the likelihood that an SME will undertake foreign direct investment.

P8(b): The larger the size of the host market relative to the domestic market, the higher the likelihood that an SME will undertake foreign direct investment.

Competitive Forces

Oligopolistic rivalry

It follows from the industrial organization paradigm that the structural attributes of the market determine the competitive context in the industry. An industry in which seller concentration is high, the products are close substitutes, and there is a substantial market interdependence of the players in the market is characterized as an 'oligopoly'. An oligopoly is both a definition of the market structure and of the behavior of the firms selling in the market (Knickerbocker, 1973, p. 4). Oligopolistic industries, in which seller concentration is high enough to create interdependence among the players, but not so high as to eliminate uncertainty and evoke collusion, are characterized by a distinctive pattern of foreign direct investment, clustered by time periods and markets. Knickerbocker (1973) argued that the herding pattern of foreign investment could be explained by the multinationals' fear of jeopardizing their market position after the first mover established a base in the foreign market. He proposed that oligopolists 'w[ould] try to nullify the anticipated consequence of their rivals' moves by countering with similar moves and with some kind of a blocking strategy' (Knickerbocker, 1973, p. 6). Therefore the emergence of multinationals could be the result of the defensive strategy, i.e. the oligopolistic reaction of market rivals.

Though the oligopolistic reaction theory refers to the defensive moves of peers to counter and block the first-mover advantage of their rival, the argument can be extended to provide an explanation for certain patterns of foreign direct investment by small and medium-sized enterprises. As large players in globally integrated industries engage in global multi-market competition, small companies are left free to fill in the 'interstices' of competitive space. Carroll (1994) proposed that competition among large generalist organizations in a population to occupy the center of the market frees peripheral resources that are most likely to be used by small specialist members of the population. In other words, the more similar a focal organization is to its competitors, the greater the intensity of competition it will experience. The less similar a focal organization to its competitors, the lower the intensity of competition. This argument explains why small companies effectively internationalize following specialist 'deep niche' strategies (Gomes-Casseres and Kohn, 1997) and why they are found 'at the edges' of oligopolistic industries, where they operate without disturbing the big players (Fujita, 1998).

In globally fragmented industries, on the other hand, small companies quickly fill in market niches and compete in their narrowly defined industry segments in a mini oligopolistic fashion resembling that of their larger-size counterparts. Since 'the ultimate leaders in global industries are often first movers' (Porter, 1986, p. 36), the speed of reaction to competitors' entry might be an important success factor for an internationalization strategy. Thus, small companies seek to match the international expansion of their rivals in much the same way as predicted by the oligopolistic reaction theory. In fact, the United Nations (1993, p. 41) cross-national survey revealed that the goal 'of strengthening competitive capacity' was the second strongest motivation for foreign direct investment, second only to the growth expectations in the host market. Overall:

*P9(a): The higher the degree of oligopolistic rivalry in a globally inte-
grated industry, the higher the likelihood that an SME will undertake
foreign direct investment.*

*P9(b): The higher the degree of oligopolistic rivalry in a globally frag-
mented industry, the higher the likelihood that an SME will undertake
foreign direct investment.*

Mimetic isomorphism

In industrial settings where large and small companies coexist, small players
mimic the behavior of similar and successful organizations or of market
leaders in a move which could be characterized as 'mimetic isomorphism'.
Mimetic isomorphism, a concept brought forward by the institutional literature, suggests that firms become similar to one another over time by the imitation of one another's structures and actions (DiMaggio and Powell, 1983).
Mimetic isomorphism is a response to uncertainty. In situations in which a
clear course of action is unavailable, organization leaders may decide that
the best response is to mimic a peer that they perceive to be successful
(Mizruchi and Fein, 1999, p. 657). Haunschild and Miner (1997) proposed
that organizations often imitate practices previously used by large numbers
of other organizations (frequency imitation); practices previously used by
large organizations (trait-based imitation); or practices that appear to have
had good outcomes for other organizations (outcome-based imitation).
Mimetic isomorphism in market entry, in particular, is documented in the
literature as a process of imitating large and profitable organizations rather
than imitating similarly sized organizations (Haveman, 1993). Therefore:

*P10: The higher the degree of mimetic isomorphism in an industry, the
higher the likelihood that an SME will undertake foreign direct investment.*

Strategic linkages and global networks

Brought forward by the network perspective of internationalization, this
attribute refers to the organization's set of network relationships rather
than a concrete firm-specific advantage (Johanson and Mattsson, 1988).
Large players in global industries rely increasingly on support groups of
suppliers and other horizontal alliances to adopt and diffuse innovations
(Nohria and Garcia-Pont, 1991; Knight and Cavusgil, 1997; Acs and
Preston, 1997). Dunning (1995) argued that large multinationals are divest-
ing themselves of non-core activities and are replacing them with keiretsu-
style relationships with small and medium-sized enterprises, reconfiguring
the boundaries of international business activity and entering an age of

alliance capitalism. Thus the international expansion of large multinationals in oligopolistic industries can have 'a drag effect' (Fujita, 1998) on the small companies gravitating in the dominant firms' global networks.

As large oligopolies move into the international arena and establish operations abroad, their suppliers and subcontractors follow suit for fear of losing major customers. This special status of SMEs as 'captives' to global players has accounted, for example, for the transformation of a great number of Japanese part and component manufacturers into small multinationals (Ozawa, 1997). Further, the OECD 1997 synthesis report revealed that small companies in mature global industries (automobiles, pharmaceuticals, chemicals, aerospace, and computers) are mainly subcontract suppliers, dependent on the large firms in the process of their internationalization, and operating 'at the edge' of their respective industries. Participation in alliances reduces the risks and transaction costs associated with international exchange, and is more flexible than hierarchical fiat through forward integration (Gomes-Casseres, 1997). Overall,

P11: The higher the degree of development of strategic linkages in a global industry, the higher the likelihood that an SME will undertake foreign direct investment.

Community effects

The organizational community perspective emphasizes the interaction between populations of related organizations (Martin *et al.*, 1998). Organizational theorists have increasingly emphasized processes through which individual organizations can be influenced by other organizations (Haunschild and Miner, 1997). Based on the organizational community, or collective (symbiotic) strategy perspective, Martin *et al.* (1998) argued that the international expansion of non-direct competitors would have a positive effect on the international expansion of a focal firm. The foreign market entry of a non-direct competitor increases the market visibility of the domestic industry, provides industry-wide information on the host market, and transplants the domestic supply base to a foreign market. Overall:

P12: The higher the community effects in a global industry, the higher the likelihood that an SME will undertake foreign direct investment.

The Relative Impact of Structural and Competitive Forces

The theoretical framework suggests that the influence of the structural and competitive forces is not equidirectional. Thus, competitive forces affect both large and small firms in the same manner. Increased oligopolistic competition, increased mimetic isomorphism, and increased degree of strategic links and community influences all foster foreign direct investment by small and medium-sized enterprises. Oligopolistic rivalry, in particular, tends to increase the likelihood that SMEs will undertake foreign direct investment in both globally integrated and globally fragmented industries.

The direction and effect of structural forces is attenuated by industrial context (globally integrated versus globally fragmented) as well as the type of market demand (standardized versus localized). Technological intensity promotes foreign investment in globally fragmented industries, but impedes foreign investment by SMEs in globally integrated industries. Standardized market demand in globally fragmented industries and localized market demand in globally integrated industries tend to promote foreign direct investment by SMEs. Industry growth generally favors international expansion; however, the emergence of multinationals is contingent on the stage in the industry life cycle. These comparisons allow the extension of traditional international business theories to provide an explanation for the phenomenon of foreign direct investment by SMEs.

IMPLICATIONS, LIMITATIONS AND DIRECTIONS FOR FUTURE RESEARCH

The theoretical framework developed in this chapter encompassed industry-level drivers of foreign direct investment by small and medium-sized enterprises. It sought to address a gap in the understanding of foreign direct investment by SMEs provided by international business research, internationalization theories, and work on international new ventures. The theoretical implications of the framework for each of these three perspectives, as well as the directions for future research, will be reviewed next, followed by public policy and managerial implications.

International Business Theories

The theoretical framework developed in the present study suggests that traditional international business theories cannot be used directly to explain industry influences on foreign direct investment by SMEs. This proposition supports Giddy and Young's argument (1982, p. 59) that the conventional theory of the multinational enterprise fails to explain the 'sources, size, and technological level' of some 'deviate multinationals'. Similarly, Lau (1992), in his study of the foreign operations of Hong Kong garment manufacturers, found that the traditional theory of the multinational enterprise did not apply to small, low-technology multinationals from developing countries.

The framework developed in the present study offers three avenues to extend traditional international business (IB) theories to the context of small companies. First, the framework suggests that traditional IB theories can be 'extended by negation', that is, used to explain the emergence of small multinationals in industries that do *not* favor large multinationals. The extension of traditional international business theories by negation has served as a theoretical platform for several studies of the pattern of foreign direct investment by SMEs (for example Kohn, 1988, 1997). Apparently more conceptual development is needed to reconcile the original theory of the multinational with the theory of the small multinational.

Second, the framework suggests that traditional international business theories can be 'extended by association', that is, explain the emergence of small multinationals in industries where small companies dominate their market niche in a manner similar to the large monopolies in globally integrated industries. This explanation has served as a theoretical perspective for several studies of foreign direct investment by SMEs, predominantly in specialized market segments and the high-technology industries (for example Buckley, 1997; Acs and Preston, 1997).

Finally, the traditional theory can be 'extended by evolution', that is, explain the emergence of small multinationals in industries that are evolving away from their traditional highly concentrated structure under the influence of technological breakthroughs or simply following the course of their life cycle. This theoretical background has been used to explain the patterns of foreign direct investment by non-dominant firms in industries characterized by a high level of organizational interdependence (for example Martin *et al.*, 1998).

The three avenues for extension brought froward by the framework imply that some of the theoretical perspectives developed in the context of research on large multinationals could be fruitfully used in the analysis of their small counterparts. Apparently, future conceptual development and empirical work would better determine which of the approaches holds the most promise and explanatory power in the context of small multinationals.

Theories of Internationalization

With regard to internationalization theories, the framework developed in the present study suggests that the industry-level influences on foreign direct investment by SMEs can be used to complement traditional internationalization process models. While research in the lineage of internationalization process has elucidated the specifics of managerial foreign investment decision making (Apfelthaler, 2000), as well as the increasing resource commitments to foreign market operations (Buckley, 1989), the understanding of industry-level factors can present a more complete picture of the foreign investment process. As Oviatt and McDougall (1999, p. 35) observed, 'Any theory that ignores . . . industry conditions is severely crippled in its ability to explain current processes of firm internationalization'.

On the other hand, a limitation of the present study is that it looked only at the direct effects of industry-level factors on the direct foreign investment by SMEs. Several structural and competitive factors, such as the size of the domestic market, are mediated by firm-level characteristics, for example international business competencies, innovative competencies, or product-specific competencies (Arora and Gambardella, 1997). Future research should develop models which consider these relationships.

International Entrepreneurship

The theoretical framework can fruitfully complement research in the area of international entrepreneurship. First of all, as most of the emerging international ventures are also small, the framework can be used to explain the direction of impact of structural and competitive industry-level forces on the emergence of international new ventures. Second, by focusing on the drivers of foreign direct investment of already established companies, the framework can be used to provide theoretical guidance on the 'early, rapid, and substantial internationalization' (Knight and Cavusgil, 1997) of 'born domestic' companies, a phenomenon of interest also to international entrepreneurship scholars. Finally, by focusing on the drivers of foreign direct investment, e.g. one type of international activity, the theoretical framework presented in the study offers a finer-grained approach to the conceptualization of internationalization, an issue noted by several students of international entrepreneurship (for example Oviatt and McDougall, 1997).

Managerial and Public Policy Implications

The theoretical framework suggests that not all industries are equally conducive to foreign direct investment by small and medium-sized enterprises. This proposition is of relevance to public policy makers seeking to promote the international activities of the small business sector. In fact, one important recommendation stemming from the present theoretical exploration is that public assistance directed at accelerated internationalization of small, resource-constrained enterprises in globally integrated industries may be misdirected, a contention supported by other researchers as well (for example Acs and Preston, 1997). Another public policy recommendation concerns government antitrust activities. The theoretical framework suggests that in industries characterized by a high level of symbiotic interdependence between large and small players, the international expansion of large multinationals promotes the growth of smaller, non-dominant firms. Therefore public policy makers would be well advised to consider carefully the actions likely to impede the expansion of large multinationals in industrial settings where the international growth of these large players also fosters the growth of small and medium-sized enterprises.

The theoretical framework developed in the study has important implications for managerial practice. Managers of SMEs should carefully consider the foreign direct investment options so as not to spread the limited resources of their companies too thinly. This recommendation is especially relevant in industries with high levels of uncertainty and strong pressures for mimetic isomorphism. Because of the differential impact of industry structural forces on small and large players, international expansion in settings characterized by high levels of success-based imitation can be especially risky. Small-business managers should be well advised of the expected direction of industry impact on the international expansion of their enterprises.

CONCLUSION

In conclusion, the theoretical framework developed in the present study linked concepts and relationships from a range of complementary perspectives to develop a theoretical framework explaining industry-level effects on foreign direct investment by small and medium-sized enterprises. The most important lesson from the preceding discussion is that global industries are not *terra incognita* for small companies. In their dynamic international expansion, increasing numbers of small companies establish affiliates abroad and thus emerge and compete as small multinationals. However, industry does matter. The proposed theoretical framework suggests that more conceptual development and empirical studies are necessary to understand the critical influence on industry structural and competitive factors on the emergence patterns of small multinationals in global industries. The critical importance of industry forces should be taken into consideration also by policy makers seeking to encourage the growth and internationalization of SMEs. Notably, the small-business owner would be wise to contemplate in what way industry factors are likely to affect the international expansion of the small venture.

REFERENCES

Acs, Z.J. and L. Preston (1997), 'Small and medium-sized enterprises, technology, and globalization: Introduction to a special issue on small and medium-sized enterprises in the global economy', *Small Business Economics*, 9: 1–6.

Aldrich, H.E. (1999), *Organizations Evolving*, London: Sage.

Andersen, O. (1993), 'On the internationalization process of the firm', *Journal of International Business Studies*, 24(2): 209–31.

Apfelthaler, G. (2000), 'Why small enterprises invest abroad: The case of four Austrian firms with US operations', *Journal of Small Business Management*, 38(3): 92–8.

Arora, A. and A. Gambardella (1997), 'Domestic markets and international competitiveness: Generic and product specific competencies in the engineering sector', *Strategic Management Journal*, 18 (Summer, Special Issue): 53–74.

Bain, J.S. (1956), *Barriers to New Competition*, Cambridge, MA: Harvard University Press.

Bain, J.S. (1972), *Essays on Price Theory and Industrial Organization*, Boston: Little Brown.

Bloodgood, J.M., H.J. Sapienza and J.G. Almeida (1996), 'The internationalization of new high potential U.S. ventures: Antecedents and outcomes', *Entrepreneurship Theory and Practice*, 20(4): 61–76.

Boter, H. and C. Holmquist (1996), 'Industry characteristics and internationalization process in small firms', *Journal of Business Venturing*, 11: 471–87.

Buckley, P.J. (1989), 'Foreign direct investment by small and medium-sized enterprises: The theoretical background', *Small Business Economics*, 1: 89–100.

Buckley, P.J. (1997), 'International technology transfer by small and medium-sized enterprises', *Small Business Economics*, 9: 67–78.

Buckley, P.J. (1999), 'International technology transfer by small and medium-sized enterprises', in Zoltan J. Acs and Bernard Yeung (eds), *Small and Medium-Sized Enterprises in the Global Economy*, Ann Arbor, MI: The University of Michigan Press, pp. 147–63.

Buckley, Peter J. and Mark Casson (1976), *The Future of the Multinational Enterprise*, London: Macmillan.

Buckley, Peter J. and Hafez Mirza (1997), 'Introduction', in P.J. Buckley, J. Campos, H. Mirza and E. White (eds), *International Technology Transfer by Small and Medium-Sized Enterprises: Country Studies*, New York: St Martin's Press, pp. 1–5.

Calvet, A.L. (1981), 'A synthesis of foreign direct investment theories and theories of the multinational firm', *Journal of International Business Studies*, 12(2): 43–59.

Camino, D. and L. Cazorla (1998), 'Foreign market entry decisions by small and medium-sized enterprises: An evolutionary approach', *International Journal of Management*, 15(1): 123–9.

Carroll, G.R. (1994), 'Organizations . . . The smaller they get', *California Management Review*, 37(1): 28–41.

Caves, Richard E. (1971), *Multinational Enterprises and Economic Analysis*, Cambridge, UK: Cambridge University Press.

Cavusgil, S.T. (1980), 'On the internationalization process of firms', *European Research*, 8(6): 273–81.

Coviello, N. (1997), 'Foreign market entry and internationalization: The case of

Datacom Software Research', *Entrepreneurship Theory and Practice*, 20(4): 95–109.

Dana, L.-P., H. Etemad and R.W. Wright (1999), 'The impact of globalization on SMEs', *Global Focus*, 11(4): 93–105.

Delapierre, M. (1997), 'Technology suppliers: The case of France', in Peter J. Buckley *et al.* (eds), *International Technology Transfer by Small and Medium-Sized Enterprises: Country Studies*, New York: St Martin's Press, pp. 113–38.

DiMaggio, P.J. and W.W. Powell (1983), 'The iron cage revisited: Institutional isomorphism and collective rationality in organizational fields', *American Sociological Review*, 48: 147–60.

Doz, Y. (1987), 'International industries: Fragmentation versus globalization', in B.K. Guile and H. Brooks (eds), *Technology and Global Industry*, Washington, DC: National Academy Press, pp. 96–118.

Dunning, J.H. (1988), 'The eclectic paradigm of international production: A restatement and some possible extensions', *Journal of International Business Studies*, 19: 1–31.

Dunning, J.H. (1995), 'Reappraising the eclectic paradigm in an age of alliance capitalism', *Journal of International Business Studies*, 26(3): 461–91.

Dunning, J.H. (1999), 'Reconfiguring the boundaries of international business activity', in Zoltan J. Acs and Bernard Yeung (eds), *Small and Medium-Sized Enterprises in the Global Economy*, Ann Arbor, MI: The University of Michigan Press, pp. 24–44.

Fujita, M. (1995a), 'Small and medium-sized transnational corporations: Trends and patterns of foreign direct investment', *Small Business Economics*, 7: 183–204.

Fujita, M. (1995b), 'Small and medium-sized transnational corporations: Salient features', *Small Business Economics*, 7: 251–71.

Fujita, M. (1998), *The Transnational Activities of Small and Medium-Sized Enterprises*, Boston, MA: Kluwer.

Giddy, I.H. and S. Young (1982), 'Conventional theory and unconventional multinationals: Do new forms of multinational enterprise require new theories?', in Alan M. Rugman (ed.), *New Theories of the Multinational Enterprise*, New York: St Martin's Press, pp. 55–78.

Gomes-Casseres, B. (1997), 'Alliance strategies of small firms', *Small Business Economics*, 9: 33–44.

Gomes-Casseres, B. and T.O. Kohn (1997), 'Technology suppliers: The case of the United States', in Peter J. Buckley *et al.* (eds), *International Technology Transfer by Small and Medium-Sized Enterprises: Country Studies*, New York: St Martin's Press, pp. 280–98.

Haunschild, P.R. and A.S. Miner (1997), 'Modes of interorganizational imitation: The effects of outcome salience and uncertainty', *Administrative Science Quarterly*, 42: 472–500.

Haveman, H.A. (1993), 'Follow the leader: Mimetic isomorphism and entry into new markets', *Administrative Science Quarterly*, 38: 593–627.

Hirsch, S. and Z. Adar (1974), 'Firm size and export performance', *World Development*, 2(7): 41–6.

Hout, T., M.E. Porter and E. Rudden (1982), 'How global companies win out', *Harvard Business Review*, 60(5): 98–108.

Hymer, S. (1976), *International Operations of National Firms: A Study of Direct Foreign Investment*, Cambridge, MA: MIT Press.

Johanson, J. and L.G. Mattsson (1988), 'Internationalisation in industrial systems

– A network approach', in Neil Hood and J.E. Vahlne (eds), *Strategies in Global Competition*, London: Croom Helm, pp. 287–314.

Johanson, J. and J.-E. Vahlne (1977), 'The internationalization process of the firm – A model of knowledge development and increasing foreign commitments', *Journal of International Business Studies*, 8(3): 23–32.

Knickerbocker, Frederik T. (1973), *Oligopolistic Reaction and Multinational Enterprise*, Boston, MA: Division of Research, Graduate School of Business, Harvard University.

Knight, G.A. and S.T. Cavusgil (1997), 'Early internationalization and the born-global firm: Emergent paradigm for international marketing', Working paper, Michigan State University, CIBER.

Kobrin, S.J. (1991), 'An empirical analysis of the determinants of global integration', *Strategic Management Journal*, 12 (Special Issue, Summer): 17–31.

Kohn, T.O. (1988), 'International Entrepreneurship: Foreign Direct Investment by Small U.S. Based Manufacturing Firms', unpublished doctoral dissertation, Harvard University.

Kohn, T.O. (1997), 'Small firms as international players', *Small Business Economics*, 9: 45–51.

Lau, H.-F. (1992), 'Internationalization, internalization, or a new theory for small, low-technology multinational enterprise?', *European Journal of Marketing*, 26(10): 17–31.

Martin, X., A. Swaminathan and W. Mitchell (1998), 'Organizational evolution in the interorganizational environment: Incentives and constraints on international expansion policy', *Administrative Science Quarterly*, 43: 566–601.

McDougall, P.P. (1989), 'International versus domestic entrepreneurship: New venture strategic behavior and industry structure', *Journal of Business Venturing*, 4: 387–400.

McDougall, P.P., S. Shane and B.M. Oviatt (1994), 'Explaining the formation of international new ventures: The limits of theories from international business research', *Journal of Business Venturing*, 9(6): 469–87.

Miesenbock, L.J. (1988), 'Small business and exporting: A literature review', *International Small Business Journal*, 6(2): 42–61.

Mizruchi, M.S. and L.C. Fein (1999), 'The social construction of organizational knowledge: A study of the uses of coercive, mimetic, and normative isomorphism', *Administrative Science Quarterly*, 44: 653–83.

Nohria, N. and C. Garcia-Pont (1991), 'Global strategic linkages and industry structure', *Strategic Management Journal*, 15 (Special Issue, Summer): 113–29.

Organization for Economic Co-operation and Development (1997), *Globalization and Small and Medium Enterprises (SMEs): Synthesis Report*, vol. 1, Paris: OECD.

Oviatt, B.M. and P.P. McDougall (1995), 'Global start-ups: Entrepreneurs on a worldwide stage', *Academy of Management Executive*, 9(2): 30–44.

Oviatt, B.M. and P.P. McDougall (1997), 'Challenges for internationalization process theory: The case of international new ventures', *Management International Review*, 37(2): 85–99.

Oviatt, B.M. and P.P. McDougall (1999), 'A framework for understanding accelerated international entrepreneurship', in Alan M. Rugman and Richard W. Wright (eds), *International Entrepreneurship: Globalization of Emerging Businesses*, Stamford, CA: JAI Press, Inc., pp. 23–42.

Ozawa, T. (1997), 'Technology suppliers: The case of Japan', in Peter J. Buckley *et al.* (eds), *International Technology Transfer by Small and Medium-Sized Enterprises: Country Studies*, New York, US: St Martin's Press, pp. 212–42.

Penrose, E.T. (1959), *The Theory of the Growth of the Firm*, New York: John Wiley.

Porter, M.E. (1980), *Competitive Strategy*, New York: The Free Press.

Porter, M.E. (1986), 'Competition in global industries: A conceptual framework', in Michael E. Porter (ed.), *Competition in Global Industries*, Boston, MA: Harvard Business School Press, pp. 15–61.

Prahalad, C.K.and Yves. L. Doz (1987), *Multinational Mission: Balancing Local Demand and Global Vision*, New York: The Free Press.

Prasad, S.B. (1999), 'Globalization of smaller firms: Field notes on processes', *Small Business Economics*, 13: 1–7.

Reuber, R. and E. Fischer (1999), 'Domestic market size, competencies, and the internationalization of small- and medium-sized enterprises', in Alan M. Rugman and Richard W. Wright (eds), *International Entrepreneurship: Globalization of Emerging Businesses*, Stamford, CA: JAI Press Inc., pp. 85–100.

Small Business Administration (SBA) (2000), *America's Small Business and International Trade: A Report*: http://www.sba.gov.

United Nations Conference on Trade and Development (1993), *Small and Medium-sized Transnational Corporations: Role, Impact, and Policy Implications*, New York: United Nations.

Vernon, R. (1966), 'International investment and international trade and the product cycle', *Quarterly Journal of Economics*, May: 190–207.

Zahra, S.A., R.D. Ireland and M.A. Hitt (2000), 'International expansion by new venture firms: International diversity, mode of market entry, technological learning and performance', *Academy of Management Journal*, 43(5): 925–50.

PART 2

Facilitating Small-firm Internationalization

5. Internationalization of Australian SMEs: challenges and opportunities

Quamrul Alam and John Pacher

INTRODUCTION

Globalization encompasses a wide range of issues and developments. It includes changes in business strategies in production, marketing, finance, and research and development (R&D). The increase in globalization has significantly influenced global trade and investment. Rapid technological changes in communications and transport, and an increasing trend toward deregulation of foreign exchange, foreign investment and financial markets have significantly affected the structure of industry and business competitiveness. Globalization has created greater incentives and opportunities for companies to access the various markets and knowledge sources needed to build lasting competitive advantages through continuous innovation (OECD, 2000). As well, it has brought about new competitors for SMEs in the industrialized world, especially in countries with high labour costs, such as Australia. SMEs need to search for competitive advantages across national borders in order to sustain their existence. They are faced with pressures to reduce production costs, increase productivity, and become more knowledge intensive. To achieve this end they have to internationalize their business activities. Consumers today want the best and the cheapest products, with little concern about where they are produced. Australian SMEs need to establish themselves as critical partners in the new internationalization process.

This chapter examines the challenges and the opportunities that face Australian SMEs which want to internationalize their operations. The aim is to demonstrate that as the economy becomes more integrated into globalized trade and business, there is an increased need for a supportive domestic environment to help SMEs become globally competitive, whether they actually venture abroad or not. The organizational capabilities of Australian SMEs are analysed regarding competencies, knowledge base, technology, and vision, all of which are essential to devise appropriate market-entry strategies. Such an analysis will help to explain whether SMEs have the right understanding of the global markets and the ability to manage cross-border transactions. It is also important to understand the relationships between upstream and downstream firms, which are critical to the transition of all firms as the market environment in advanced industrialized economies moves to a globally open, competitive, time-compressed, and digitalized economy (Porter, 1998a; Sahlman, 1999).

OPPORTUNITIES FOR AUSTRALIAN SMEs

The Australian economy has undergone significant structural changes during the last 15 years. Economic reform measures, such as lower tariffs, financial deregulation, labour market reform, and tax reform have been implemented. These reforms, together with the growing convergence of markets, are creating new demands and challenges for Australian businesses. Australia is an open and flexible economy integrated into the key global markets of Asia, America and Europe. It also has a high take-up rate of computers, Internet and information technology (*The Australian*, 6 July 2000). During 1998–99 foreign investment in Australia rose by $43.4 billion to $613.2 billion. Of this, direct investment rose by $16.3 billion to $172 billion; portfolio investment rose by $15.1 billion to $353.6 billion; and other investment rose by $12.0 billion to $87.5 billion (Australian Bureau of Statistics, 2000).

SMEs play a crucial role in the industrialized economies. Over 80 per cent of manufacturing exporters and 65 per cent service of exporters are SMEs. Many of them exist to service the demands of their larger counterparts, using alliances to enter foreign markets. In the absence of such alliances with large multinational corporations (MNCs), SMEs find it difficult to sustain their competitive advantage as they enter global markets as independent entities (Hine and Kelly, 1999).

SMEs play a particularly important role in the Australian economy. At the last count (the latest Australian Bureau of Statistics figures are from February 1997), there were 846,000 businesses with fewer than 20 employees: 6.5 per cent more than two years earlier. In Australia, SMEs in the manufacturing sector employ fewer than 100 people and SMEs in the service sector fewer than 20 (Australian Bureau of Statistics, 1997). The small-business sector makes up 96.6 per cent of all business operations in the private non-agriculture sector and accounts for more than 56 per cent of private sector employment (w.w.w.smallbusiness.info.au). Small businesses have adopted e-commerce eagerly. Nearly 500,000 businesses are operated from home and rely on an expanding range of telecommunications services to keep in touch with clients.

According to Allan Moss, Managing Director, Macquarie Bank, Australia is a good place from which to run an international investment fund. Australia has efficient professional groups and businesses now have access to high-quality professionals and a multicultural workforce, which enables it to use native speakers of every major language (Ries, cited in the *Australian Financial Review*, 2 May 2000).

Australian trade links with the Association of South East Asian Nations (ASEAN), North Asia, and Australia–New Zealand Closer Economic Relations (CER) provide an opportunity to deepen economic integration in the immediate region, thus expanding markets for Australian goods, services and investment.

CHALLENGES FOR AUSTRALIAN SMEs

For much of the twentieth century, governments have pursued a protective position in economic management, and competition was all but absent in many industries. The protectionist policies have stifled the incentives for enterprises to become proactive, to find new opportunities, and to expand their business horizons. Australia's economic development was largely determined by protective tariffs, which in turn contributed to the growth of an inward-looking, but relatively efficient economy in the 1970s and the 1980s. The government actively encouraged selected industries. There was, however, a great deal of confusion about the government-sponsored business programmes. SMEs, in particular, were baffled by the large number of uncoordinated assistance packages; the lack of any coherent policy framework; the perplexing array of and lack of linkages between agencies delivering programmes; and the lack of clarity about roles and accountability of outcomes (Mortimer, 1997). Business programmes supporting SMEs did not operate within a clear policy framework or strategy: there were no specific directions on how to adapt to changes and become more international.

One of the most important implications of globalization is that the comparative advantage of countries like Australia is shifting away from traditional factors of production, such as land, labour and capital, towards knowledge-based economic activities. The ability of SMEs to create, access, and commercialize knowledge on global markets will be a fundamental source of their new competitiveness. The introduction of national competition policy (NCP) in 1995 and the substantial tariff reductions since then have alerted Australian SMEs to the need to become more internationally competitive. Deregulation of financial and foreign exchange markets has further opened the economy to international market forces: a quantum change in Australia's long-standing interventionist and inward-looking industry policy.

Knowledge has become one of the tools of transition and a source of competitive advantage. To compete with lower costs in foreign locations, SMEs in high-cost countries like Australia need to develop strategic global options. Many will have to restructure their businesses, substitute capital and technology for labour, and shift production to lower-cost locations. Due to the lack of a proper strategic direction and the absence of supportive macroeconomic policies, Australian SMEs have lost much of their comparative advantage. The global demand for innovative products in knowledge-based industries is high and growing rapidly; but the move to introduce knowledge-based economic activity has been very slow in Australia.

SMEs need to respond to the important driving forces behind globalization to find their own competitive position. They also need to increase participation in, and integration of, world trade; understand changes in liberal trade and business policies; change business strategies; enter into global capital markets; understand the revolution in information technology; and increase their presence in foreign markets (Dodgson, 1999).

National competition policy, privatization policy, public sector reform, reforms in the local government systems, deregulation, introduction of the Goods and Services Tax (GST), and reforms in the Industrial Relations Act have created an environment in which SMEs are forced to find new ways to survive. The volume of imported goods, services, and components of many manufacturing firms in Australia has increased. Local SMEs have to go offshore and find partners to survive. Businesses need to change their strategies: either to become more export-oriented, to introduce technology for more value-adding activities, or to partner with other firms. There is a strong link between their survival and their ability to internationalize their business operations. The slow move to internationalize generates a high risk of SMEs going out of business. Global competition puts these firms under pressure to find ways to achieve a competitive edge at home and abroad. Australian SMEs will find this new policy regime both an opportunity to expand their businesses in different markets and a new challenge to survive.

INTERNATIONALIZING AUSTRALIAN SMEs

Policies

Since the early 1990s firms have become aware that competition, rather than protectionist policies, provides better incentives for businesses to improve their operations, acquire and develop new products and respond to the environment in which they operate (Sahlman, 1999). SMEs are trying relentlessly trying to increase efficiency, introduce intelligent business processes, find new overseas markets, and give customers more of what they want. Austrade is the Australian government trade office that provides services to SMEs to internationalize their operations, with an integrated network of 14 offices in Australia and more than 80 offices in 50 other countries. It has provided financial assistance to 3,300 SMEs under the Export Marketing Development Scheme. Seventy-one per cent of Austrade's clients are SMEs. An analysis of its client base shows that while Australian SMEs are internationalizing, a high proportion of them export less than 10 per cent of their turnover. Austrade provides the following services to SMEs to help them win businesses overseas and to bring investment to Australia:

- Information and advice about overseas markets and export opportunities.
- Practical assistance both in Australia and in the target markets, including identifying foreign investment partners.
- Grants and loans to assist businesses to market their products overseas.

Austrade also assists SMEs to internationalize their operations, in three ways:

- Exporting goods and services.
- Making outward investments, especially to establish final-stage manufacturing and marketing presence close to export customers.
- Attracting inbound investment to achieve joint venture with overseas companies in international marketing, and to access technology.

The IT outsourcing initiative taken by the Australian government has helped many SMEs to grow. A new definition over the past three financial years defines a medium enterprise as having an average aggregate annual revenue of less than $250 million, and a small enterprise as less than $20 million. Under this new system, SMEs have received more than $400 million in payments. The system offered SMEs 'the opportunity to partner with the larger IT companies giving them the exposure and expertise they require to develop their businesses. The advent of the Internet is promoting new forms of work that allows SMEs to export services in a range of sectors' (Australian Industry Group, 2001 and *The Australian*, 25 April 2000).

Strategies

Large enterprises use different strategies to cope with competitive pressure, such as outsourcing, downsizing, and subcontracting. These strategic choices can be major contributors to the growth of SMEs. On the other hand, they can also put pressure on SMEs to internationalize. To meet the demands of competition and to avoid diseconomies of scale, SMEs must find new markets and establish contractual relationships with large companies. Their lack of internationalization makes Australian SMEs dependent upon larger firms for their growth and survival. The recent trend toward mergers and acquisitions makes it especially urgent for SMEs to change their focus.

SMEs in the export sector are changing their attitudes, values, perception of risks, continuous learning, and managerial and marketing commitment and skills. They are acquiring the capability and resources to adopt structural changes, ensure availability and use of information, and continuously use the information superhighway to find new ways of doing business.

Thirty years ago, manufacturing contributed 25 per cent of Australia's gross domestic product; in 2000, the figure was 13 per cent. Manufacturers have had to weather two decades of tariff reductions, more open trading policies, deregulated markets and a floating currency. Because of the decline of manufacturing, SMEs are moving to higher-value service and technology industries (*BRW*, 12 May 2000).

Global competition has forced firms in the manufacturing sector – both large and small – to concentrate more on core activities and to outsource non-core functions. SMEs are now actively involved in providing services to large manufacturing firms. This has opened up opportunities to SMEs for internationalized operations. According to the Department of Foreign Affairs and Trade (DFAT, 1995), there are 4,500 SMEs actively involved in international operations. SMEs are developing linkages and networks both at home and abroad in order to become internationally competitive. According to the Bureau of Industry Economics (BIE, 1995), 40 per cent of SMEs were involved in co-operative arrangements, of which 40 per cent were with overseas firms. These relationships have enabled SMEs to gain better knowledge of markets.

Use of Information Technology

More recently, manufacturers have been exploring the potential of using the Internet for direct sales to consumers. By cutting intermediaries out of the supply chain they can reduce the cost of their products. Another trend is the 'virtualization' of manufacturing, which involves outsourcing the physical manufacturing to low-cost suppliers while retaining control over product design, brand marketing and business relationships. There are, however, risks in pursuing this approach. Manufacturers that choose to sell direct may risk their distribution networks. Another potential liability is that overseas manufacturers will use e-commerce to sell direct to consumers in the Australian market.

PROBLEMS IN INTERNATIONALIZING AUSTRALIAN SMEs

The processes of structural change and intensifying competition are seriously threatening the survival of SMEs. SMEs in Australia are extremely vulnerable to competitive pressures. The most important reasons for their vulnerability are: the ownership of small businesses is restricted to a small number of individuals who are often related by ties of friendship or family; and small businesses are often managed by owners, or part-owners, rather than by professional managers with little or no equity in the enterprise. As well, most small organizations have rudimentary management structures, with few specialized management functions; operate in one location only and sell to nearby customers; and have limited market power (Productivity Commission, 1999). SMEs tend to be less aware of environmental externalities and of legislation that affects their activities. As a result of all these handicaps, SMEs find it difficult to internationalize their businesses.

Owners of small businesses, especially farmers, are constantly busy and traditionally leave things until the last minute (*The Weekly Times*, 8 March 2000). According to a recent survey, 83 per cent of businesses in Australia are family-run operations, ranging from home-based operations to large, listed companies. Single families controlled slightly over 50 per cent of the businesses surveyed; most of the rest were owned by two families. These owners tend to emphasize financial and marketing skills more than others, such as the ability to compete globally, adopt new technology, and understand competitors' behaviour (*AFR*, 2 May 2000).

Lack of Strategic Direction

A study of 6,000 small businesses (*The Morgan and Banks Survey*, 1998, cited in *AFR*, 21 September 1998) suggests that 95 per cent of them have experienced changes since deregulation began. However, only 57 per cent of them had taken the initiative to restructure their organizations, and only

57 per cent had given managers some external training. Changes in the structure of 26 per cent of businesses came about because of mergers and acquisitions (*AFR*, 21 September 1998).

According to a Monash research report (1998, cited in *AFR*, 22 September 1998), 80 per cent of Australian family businesses do not have a proper succession plan, and 70 per cent lack a business plan. Three hundred thousand businesses have reached a crisis point. Although 43 per cent of the family businesses had discussed succession plans, only one third had had them approved (Ken Mores, cited in *AFR*, 22 September 1998). In May 2000 Frank Lowy, CEO of Westfield Ltd, expressed concern that Australian businesses do not have succession plans (*AFR*, 2 May 2000). Without such a plan, no business can adequately implement a strategic path for global operations. As a consequence, Australian business managers take an inordinately long time to understand and exploit new opportunities. The number of SMEs in services is increasing, but growth of the sector has been slower than in other advanced economies, which have shifted their trading base from primary and manufactured goods to services. Service industries now account for 38 per cent of all international trade but make up only 22 per cent of Australia's exports (*BRW*, 12 May 2000).

Foreign Direct Investment (FDI)

As a small economy Australia's business activities have always depended on trade and on foreign direct investment (FDI). While Australia long followed a protectionist policy with regard to its goods market, it has always favoured a very open policy towards FDI, becoming an active recipient of international investment far out of proportion to the size of its economy. Inbound FDI has played a significant role in increasing economic opportunities in Australia, as well as increasing competition, both domestically and from overseas. As a result, many Australian MNCs are moving to other countries and regions, with globally integrated production and marketing strategies. Australia's economy is increasingly integrated with the triad economies of North America, the EU, and Japan. As a result of this integration, foreign investment in Australia has grown fivefold, almost twice as fast as domestic investment; and outbound FDI from Australia has grown ninefold – more than three times the rate of domestic investment (Bryan and Rafferty, 1999). Foreign ownership has increased significantly, now comprising 100 per cent of the baby food industry, 80 per cent in abattoirs, 90 per cent in biscuits, 50 per cent in beer, 98 per cent in computers, 85 per cent in frozen vegetables, and 50 per cent in mining (Deveson, 1998, p. 199).

Emphasis on Export Strategy

Due to globalization of trade and investment there has been a significant shift in the sectoral balance of the Australian economy, especially in the shift from manufacturing to services. Most successful manufacturing companies are now producing at least some of their outputs outside of Australia. According to a survey report of the Australian Manufacturing Council (AMC, 1993), SMEs play an important role in the growth of high-value-added manufacturing exports. Mahmood (1997) suggests that SMEs also employ a variety of other modes of international operation such as licensing, franchising, distribution networks, co-operative networks and overseas production. Primary products still account for 58 per cent of merchandise exports, but manufactures have moved from 22 to 28 per cent over the past decade. Though exports to Asia Pacific fell, APEC (Asia-Pacific Economic Cooperation) still accounted for 70 per cent of merchandise exports in 1998 (DFAT, media release, 1999).

It is clear that Australian SMEs have used export strategy as their primary foreign-market entry mode. But unlike SMEs in the US and elsewhere, they have not used the knowledge they gained about different markets as a means of further expanding the range of their international operations. Australian SMEs have been selective in going to foreign markets and have used a very concentric diversification strategy. Their exposure to overseas markets is limited, and their understanding of the business culture of different markets is narrow. They have made limited use of modes of foreign-market entry other than exporting. Managers of Australian SMEs have been unable to see the opportunities available in different markets. In many cases they were critically dependent on Austrade's advice and support. Through the 1980s, exporting offered an effective means for Australian SMEs to achieve an international position. However, their lack of ability to skip stages in the export development process and to use other modes of internationalization have created a relative disadvantage for them.

Inadequate Managerial Expertise

Globalization has produced intense competition in which businesses need to have the ability to produce to customer needs at lowest costs and with short lead times. They should have the management capability to understand and react to continuous change in customer requirements. Customers must have confidence that their suppliers can respond to specific needs. A close customer–supplier relationship has to be established. In many industry sectors, there seems to be inadequate understanding of this crucial relationship between competing forces. As a result, businesses could not produce improved and differentiated products. Foreign competitors have in many instances replaced the non-innovative firms. Many SMEs failed to extend their operations to new markets as they relied on existing core competencies and did not have the capability to create new ones.

Australian managers have many good qualities, but they lack some of the critical ones, which are essential for businesses to compete internationally. They need international exposure to develop a global perspective. Table 5.1 illustrates some strengths and weaknesses of Australian managers.

Table 5.1   Strengths and weaknesses of Australian managers

Strengths	Weaknesses
Hard-working	Short-term view
Flexible, adaptable, resourceful around product and process	Lack of strategic perspective
Innovative/inventive	Lack of open-mindedness and rigidity towards learning
Technically sound	Complacent
Egalitarian	Poor at team work and empowerment
Independent thinking	Inability to cope with differences
Open, genuine, direct	Poor people skills
Honest and ethical	Lack of self-confidence

Source: AGPS (1995).

According to a recent survey, only 22 per cent of SME managers in Australia had completed an apprenticeship, technical or vocational, or had a tertiary qualification; the remaining 78 per cent had completed five to six years of secondary schooling (ABARE.gov.au website).

Inadequate Use of Information Technology

Approximately 15,000 Australian companies are on the Internet, but only 10 per cent of these are presently embarking on effective electronic commerce. The Internet can be used to deal directly with overseas buyers, enabling such enhanced value-added services as 24-hour delivery, better pick-up hours, tracking, and delivery confirmation, etc. Export-oriented firms can use electronic data interchange (EDI) to submit documents to buyers and customs officials. Customers and suppliers can be encouraged to initiate shipments, request services and track deliveries on their website. E-commerce is a medium of doing business better, faster, and differently, offering opportunities to expand business operations. SMEs in Australia, however, lag far behind their competitors. Many of these businesses are tackling e-commerce from the wrong direction. They are being caught up in the frenzy surrounding dot.com companies when they should be concentrating on finding effective business-to-business (B2B) solutions. Dot.com businesses have the tendency to put up a storefront on line instead of concentrating on B2B transactions. They should try to become efficient supply-management organizations (Terry Walsh, CEO, CISCO, cited in *The Australian*, 11 April 2000).

The growth rate of information and communications technology (ICT) is slow in Australia. A recent study states that ICT diffusion remains in its infancy. Only 21 per cent of all businesses have access to the Internet, and a mere 5 per cent have websites, the majority of which are in the finance, manufacturing and wholesale industries. The Internet presence is also strong in the service industry: 49 per cent of medium businesses and 19 per cent of small ones have access to the Internet; and 18 per cent of medium businesses and 3 per cent of small ones have websites. In contrast, 85 per cent of large businesses have access to the Internet and 50 per cent have websites (ABS, 1997).

The use of the Internet in Australian businesses is mainly concentrated on e-mail, information acquisition, data transfer and marketing. Slightly over 40 per cent of medium-sized businesses and less than 20 per cent of small businesses use the Internet to gather information. Only 18 per cent of medium businesses and less than 5 per cent of small businesses use the Internet for marketing. Its use for selling and purchasing is almost negligible (ABS, 1997).

E-commerce requires a complete and fundamental change in company culture, process, practice and technology. It is more than a homepage and an online technology (Archibugi and Michie, 1995). Businesses need to integrate and streamline their entire operation from store to the call centre in order to provide products and services faster and cheaper. By introducing this change they can gain a 360-degree view of their organization. They need to know the art of doing business online with their suppliers, facilitating supplier-managed inventory and trading through global electronic trading consumers.

In the area of the diffusion of technology internationally, European firms have been successful in developing technology in their home markets, then exporting it, which in turn leads to overseas production. This progression helped these firms to introduce simple R&D activities, amending products to fit local tastes and requirements. Some companies undertook R&D in different markets, resulting in a more globalized approach towards technology development and use (Vernon, 1979). In some sectors R&D has become an important strategic tool to sustain competitive advantage. European firms are more internationalized in their overseas R&D investments than either US or Japanese firms (Roberts, 1994). Businesses in Australia do not have a large domestic market, which prevents the SMEs from taking risky strategies that might help propel them internationally. There is no long-term Australian policy to achieve excellence in this area (Mortimer, 1997).

E-commerce is the third of four stages required to obtain value from the Net (the first two being e-mail, and the use of websites to convey information). Stage three is commercial interaction: using the Web to buy and sell products and to deliver customer service. The fourth stage involves using the Web to get work done. According to Oracle's regional marketing manager for Australia and New Zealand, Australian businesses are 12 to 18 months behind the rest of the cyber world (*The Australian*, 11 April 2000). SMEs often lack a clear objective before they start. The Internet is a great tool for researching the market and the product: it helps to find out who else is doing the same business and where are they doing it. One of the biggest problems for Australian SMEs is that they do not have long-term strategic plans and are not good at anticipating future trends (Brad Berman, Manager of Sydney Branch of Small and Medium Business Enterprise Centre, cited in *The Australian*, 13 July 2000).

Lack of Support for Innovation

In Australia the recognition of the importance of innovation is still in the formative stages (Smith, 1999). The processes and best practices used in other countries need to be disseminated in Australia. The capital gains tax and the lack of R&D support are clear evidence that the country has a long way to go. The business expenditure on R&D as a percentage of national GDP is very low. In Sweden it is about 2.7 per cent, in the US and the UK it is 1.8 per cent and 1.5 per cent respectively, but in Australia it hovers around 0.8 per cent (OECD, 1998).

In the area of innovation Australia has a long history of creative environment in which many technology-driven breakthroughs have occurred. But the link to market opportunities or to potential manufacturing routes or infrastructure too often appears weak (Smith, 1999). A European Commission study (cited in OECD, 2000) shows that 33 per cent of 4,000 internationalized SMEs were technology developers and 31 per cent were technology users. Australian SMEs lag behind in technology innovation. They are mainly users, and most are slow to reorient their strategic focus in order to find new market opportunities (Sheehan *et al.*, 1995).

Australian SMEs have near-term strategies with a local market vision. As they are mainly followers, they lack an innovation-driven culture. Managers have only recently begun to develop an export orientation. As they were late to introduce lean manufacturing (which could drive high-quality, low-cost capability), they are slow to move on to 'flexible manufacturing'. While SMEs in most other industrialized countries benefited from their early move to these newer management techniques, businesses in Australia have been less able to use the same equipment to produce small lots of different products at lowest cost, to cater to customer needs. Australia needs to strengthen its strategic development of technological targets and the links of these emerging technologies to new industrial capabilities.

Lack of Well-defined Industry Policy

Australia's processed food exporters are missing out on the boom in world demand for processed food because of poor industry strategy. Their market share is dropping steadily. Processed food exports had been growing at more than 5 per cent or approximately $10 million annually. Exporters from the US, Germany and France, however, began to outpace Australia in the late 1990s, causing its share of global markets to slump below 3 per cent (Gastin, 2000).

The majority of Australian processed food exports are concentrated at the lower end of the value chain: transforming grains, meats, horticultural and dairy products. Though the highly processed food sector is now finally growing, it is here that Australia's industry performance is the weakest (Gastin, 2000). Australian SMEs have failed to streamline operations, cut costs, and produce world competitive products because of lack of innovation in the industry ('Exporting Australian Processed Food: Are We Competitive?' cited by Carole Bate; Gastin, 2000). The lack of understanding of the demand of the international market and the changes in customer preferences have prevented Australian firms from reaching the important convenience-store market in Japan and in other industrialized countries.

Lack of an Export Culture

Australia's history of insularity is a severe hindrance to operating in the global economy. Most Australian businesses remain nationally focused and have not made strategic moves to globalize. Most of them derive the bulk of their revenue from the domestic market, and concentrate their efforts on controlling distribution and protecting market share by exerting oligopolistic power – essentially a defensive strategy. Some Australian companies have made attempts to internationalize, using a low-level multidomestic strategy. They have established small overseas operations to 'see how they go'. But they have little grasp of what is required to have a genuinely global strategy (*BRW*, 25 September 2000).

Australian producers lack an export culture, and are not prepared to put in necessary efforts to cultivate markets, especially in Asia. They have failed to respond effectively to changing customer trends in Asia, where buyers are looking for quality and specific product advantages rather than low prices. Australian SMEs do not have a wide understanding of consumer behaviour and demographic changes taking place in the emerging economies of the Asia–Pacific.

It is important for Australian SMEs to be exposed to foreign exchange transactions, the understanding of which is a vital business tool. Given the recent volatility in the currencies of Australian trading partners in Asia, it is crucial for SMEs that trade internationally to formulate risk management strategies. Many SMEs in Australia have limited understanding of foreign exchange exposure or hedging. Some SMEs choose not to hedge as they believe it does not make a marked difference to their performance (Scott, 1999).

Low Labour Productivity

The cost of raw materials is high in Australia and labour productivity lags behind that of other nations. The Australian food industry has a 'reputation for unreliable supply of products and inconsistent quality' (Gastin, 2000). A key to competitiveness is differentiation through quality and safety, and launching innovative products in niche markets. Australian SMEs lack both commitment and scale. The marginal cost of transmitting information across geographic space has been drastically reduced due to the telecommunications revolution. However, the marginal cost of transmitting knowledge actually rises with distance. Internationalization through entry modes other than export can be a useful tool to transmit knowledge. The industry's R&D efforts, however, have fallen by 38 per cent since the 1970s (Gastin, 2000).

Protectionism in the Industrialized Countries

Protectionism among developed countries has risen sharply over the past two years. This policy shift is wiping out the gains achieved since the Uruguay Round of world trade talks. The US is pushing hard to get a new round of farm trade negotiation under way. The industrialized countries increased their agricultural assistance from 32 per cent to 37 per cent of production value by 1998. But commodity prices remain weak and farm-level incomes have fallen (Gerald Viatte, The Food and Agriculture Director, OECD, 2000). Australian companies have been hard hit by the assistance policies of many of its trade partners: Australia offers only 6 per cent assistance, compared to 70 per cent in South Korea, Japan, Switzerland and Norway (*The Weekly Times*, 8 March 2000). Policy changes in the US to aid farmers with $17 billion of extra money will put Australia's agricultural SMEs further into the doldrums. In the context of this uncertainty SMEs are reluctant to make further moves to internationalize their operations.

Inadequate Relationships with Overseas Companies

Businesses in Australia find it difficult to form relationships with overseas companies. Very few Australian companies make successful overseas acquisitions because they try to manage them from Sydney and Melbourne. It is especially challenging for SMEs, located in regional cities, to find overseas partners. Australian multinationals believe that the push for the removal of national barriers to trade and investment is good for them. As Australia is a small domestic market, they believe they will find opportunities overseas. But their investments in high-growth areas may actually limit the business opportunities remaining for SMEs. Globalization may be good for consumers, but it has been a double-edged sword for SMEs concentrating on the domestic market. If the head offices of large businesses continue to migrate to the Northern Hemisphere, the pool of opportunity for local management and service providers and related SMEs in Australia will shrink 'like a billabong in a drought' (*AFR*, 2 May 2000).

To become global, SMEs need to obtain comprehensive knowledge about their targeted international markets. They need access to relevant, reliable, timely information. The most effective form of collecting information is export networks, which can be established with businesses in a wide range of industries. To achieve ISO standards, it is important that the SMEs have strategic links with customers and suppliers. In Australia, SMEs lack well-developed links with international customers and suppliers, although a substantial amount of export promotion development funds has been spent in the last few years to improve the competitiveness of individual businesses.

IMPLICATIONS AND RECOMMENDATIONS

Effective Use of Best Practice Principles

Throughout the 1980s the main focus in the US was on business improvement. Total quality management (TQM), time to market, variability reduction, re-engineering, and cost reduction helped businesses to achieve efficiency. In many companies R&D was decentralized and outsourcing evolved as a strategic tool. The focus on business improvement helped companies to understand the strategic importance of investment in technology. A new business culture evolved with the implementation of acquisitions, mergers, strategic alliances and joint ventures. This culture is aligned with rapid growth through new products. Organizations with these strategies have moved rapidly into global markets. The emphasis on improved value-chain activities has helped the emergence of new businesses (Smith, 1999). SMEs in Australia should take well-planned, strategic moves to catch up.

Partnership with Large Firms

SMEs can enter global markets either independently or in partnership with larger firms. To maximize their opportunities they need to obtain knowledge on foreign market culture, utilize networks and strategic alliances and develop long-term, mutually beneficial relationships with enterprises operating in the target markets. SMEs need to develop overseas markets and establish wider links through various entry modes (Ruthven, in *BRW*, 12 May 2000).

Australian SMEs consider exporting to be the most preferred option for competing in the international market, with a few also using FDI, licensing, franchising and distribution networks. Those with product quality, product differentiation, and competitive prices are well positioned to compete. There is, however, a need to invest more in R&D so that they can enter into co-operative arrangements with other firms. Australia now ranks below Iceland, Denmark, Canada, and Austria in its gross expenditure on R&D as a proportion of GDP (*The Australian*, 28 August 2000).[1] It is also important that management attitudes be changed: managers should have a global orientation, create a management culture, and cultivate organizational capability and proactive decisions to take advantage of the new opportunities created in the era of globalization.

To secure a competitive edge, SMEs must change their traditional business models to establish alliances with large businesses. With the accelerating rate of technology change, small businesses have to establish both equity and non-equity alliances earlier to keep ahead. They also need access to the distribution channels of big business, to piggyback on their networks to ensure that their products and services get to market earlier.

---

[1] R&D expenditure during 1996–97 and 1998–99 shows that Australia's gross expenditure as a percentage of GDP fell from 1.65 per cent to 1.49 per cent, a fall of 9.7 per cent (Australian Bureau of Statistics cited in *The Australian*, 28 August 2000).

Change in Strategic Direction

One of the most important sources of competitive advantages for SMEs is the ability to work as agents of change to generate new ideas and innovative activities. Germany's SMEs, commonly referred to as the *Mittelstand*, employed a niche strategy. Companies such as Krones, Korber-Hauni, Weinig, Webasto, and Terta Wereke are not well known to the public, but their global market shares exceed those of the giant companies of Germany. The *Mittelstand* firms have between 70 and 90 per cent of the global market shares in their fields and account for the bulk of Germany's international trade surplus (OCED, 2000, p. 13). The main strategic instruments they used were product specialization with geographic diversification. They focused on a particular market niche, using their technical expertise and company resources to maintain market leadership in that niche. Because of their small size these firms were at a disadvantage in terms of economies of scale. To address this issue, SMEs sought to have a global presence and to follow a product market specialization strategy. They also gained leverage across broad geographic markets so that the globalization of marketing and sales created sufficient scale to recover R&D expenses and to maintain costs at a reasonable level (OECD, 2000, p. 13). Key success factors behind the success of the German SMEs were:

- strong commitment to global expansion
- investment in plant, technology, equipment, and people
- strategy to ensure high standard in the host market
- servicing their products through the creation of strong and reliable service networks.

Big businesses are under pressure to cut costs and increase profitability, and they are keen to make alliances with small companies to develop innovative products and services to plug holes in their strategies and expand into new markets. SMEs in Australia have taken a positive approach. Seventy-eight per cent of the fastest-growing private companies were establishing alliances, often with big businesses (*BRW*, Annual Survey, 1999).

Australian SMEs can focus on the interface of technology and customer needs and take special measures for customer training. As the complexity of products increases, customers require more instruction in operating and maintaining products. *Mittelstand* firms provided this by expanding their businesses in the region or differentiating products and/or services for various customer groups.

Industry Clusters

Australian SMEs have failed to use business clusters effectively. Only near Sydney is there a cluster of information-processing firms. Alone, SMEs cannot easily create industry-specific knowledge and develop the supplier and buyer networks they need. Clusters can become repositories for industry-specific skills and capabilities that can help innovation. Other OECD countries have used clusters to help develop industry-specific knowledge (OECD, 2000a). Learning the ropes of internationalization requires cultivating skills and know-how. To internationalize, SMEs need to establish a base of operations from which they can begin to test the waters of export activity and develop the tacit knowledge necessary for export success (Wolf and Pett, 2000). They can use different strategies because of their different resource endowments.

Australian SMEs are good at new product development and have access to superior technology, but internationalization also requires significant sophistication in the marketing function. Customizing products for international markets requires significant organizational effort on a sustained basis. It also demands well-developed distribution systems, innovation in marketing effort, and new organizational resources to tailor products to clients' needs. Due to the absence of different modes of market entry, the low degree of interaction with overseas business enterprises, and the lack of strategic, long-term vision, Australian SMEs are unable to benefit from improved international communication, complementary resources and information networks.

Development of industry clusters in different geographical regions can help SMEs to work together to create new pools of resources, use existing location specific skills, and create factor conditions to gain avail opportunities in globalized markets.

CONCLUSION

Australian businesses need to move on from a 'Crocodile Dundee' existence to a new emphasis on entrepreneurship. Australian businesses need a modern economy image. The country did not have the scale or the incentive to lead the manufacturing age. However, the new economy offers opportunity for Australian businesses, because they do possess abundant skills and intellectual capital. And Australia has a 'free-wheeling and creative culture that suits the internet economy' (Ira Magaziner, *AFR*, 27 May 2000). Peter Coroneos, head of Australia's Internet Industry Association, suggests that 'we are not selling ourselves well. We are not being seen as a happening new economy' (*AFR*, 27 May 2000).

Australian businesses, especially the SMEs, need to address the following issues to reposition themselves.

- Globally competitive, fast and efficient processes must be developed to take full advantage of Australian innovation.
- New business leaders must be trained with the skills to identify the best ideas and to manage an efficient down-selection process through business incubation, to commercial development, and then on to formation of independent, commercially successful business.
- Value creation from commercialized technologies has to be achieved in terms of the formation of globally competitive companies with export-oriented new businesses, offering knowledge-based jobs and growth through value-chain integration.

It is important that SMEs in Australia form alliances with big companies to have access to new markets. They need to learn to form alliances with competitors and to develop integral links with large foreign and domestic firms. As the economy has developed and as costs have risen, SMEs need to move on to another lower-cost base, or to move upmarket to higher-quality, higher-technology subcontracting. International subcontracting is going through a structural shift worldwide. Government policy support is essential to help subcontracting SMEs adjust and remain competitive. To become internationalized, they must maintain acceptable quality control standards and be able to demonstrate their capability. Subcontracting arrangements can be a major source of technology and skill transfer. SMEs need to devise strategies to facilitate this and find ways to reduce transaction costs.

SMEs in Australia should try to use innovation strategy to appropriate return from their knowledge base and to employ information technology strategy. These organizations can exploit quality-based niche strategies to become global players in a narrow product or service line. Due to their resource constraints and lack of experience in diversified markets, niche strategies may be particularly appropriate for SMEs. By using network strategy, SMEs should seek to collaborate with international firms to access information and widen their knowledge about markets. A well-thought-out cluster strategy can be used to locate businesses in close proximity with competitors to take advantage of knowledge spill-overs and to exploit firm-specific ownership or partnership advantages (Vickery, 1999; Porter, 1998b). Globalization is not likely to recede. To survive, both Australia's public policies and its SMEs will need to develop new skills and awareness suited to operating in the new, global business environment.

REFERENCES

ABARE website: www.ABARE.gov.au

Archibugi, D. and J. Michie (1995), 'The Globalisation of Technology: A New Taxonomy', *Cambridge Journal of Economics*, 19: 121–40.

Australian Bureau of Statistics (ABS) (2000), *International Trade in Goods and Services*, Canberra: AGPS.

ABS (1997) Catalogue No. 8141.0.

AGPS (1995), *Industry Task Force Report*, Canberra.

Australian Industry Group (AIG) (2001), *Industry in the Regions 2001*, Australian Industry Group and the Commonwealth Bank of Australia, Sydney.

The Australian Financial Review (AFR), 21 and 22 September, 1998; 2 and 27 May, 2000.

Australian Manufacturing Council (AMC) (1993), *Emerging Exporters: Australia's High Value-Added Manufacturing Exporters*, Melbourne.

The Australian, 11 and 25 April, 6 and 13 July, and 28 August 2000.

Bryan, D. and M. Rafferty (1999), *The Global Economy in Australia*, St Leonards, NSW: Allen and Unwin.

Bureau of Industry Economics (BIE) (1995), *SMEs in an Open Economy: The Australian Experience*, Canberra: AGPS.

Business Review Weekly (BRW) (1999), Annual Survey.

BRW, 'Globalisation: The end of trade', 25 September 2000.

BRW, 12 May 2000.

Department of Foreign Affairs and Trade (DFAT) (1995), *Exports of Primary and Manufactured Product Australia*, Canberra: AGPS.

DFAT (1999), media release, Canberra.

Deveson, I. (1998), *Evolution of Australian Management Style*, Singapore: John Wiley and Sons.

Dodgson, M. (1999), ' Globalisation', National Innovation Summit, Melbourne, October.

Gastin, G. (2000), ABARE's Annual Conference, March, Canberra, Australia.

Hine, D. and S. Kelly (1999), 'Standing Alone and the Global Market', *Small Enterprise Research*, 7 (2): 66–83.

Mahmood, M. (1997). 'Internationalisation of Manufacturing SMEs in Australia', *The Journal of Small Enterprise Association of Australia and New Zealand*, 5 (2): 20–28.

Monash research report (cited in *AFR*, 22 September 1998).

The Morgan and Banks Survey (1999).

Mortimer, D. (1997), *Going For Growth*, Canberra: AGPS.

OECD (1998), *Main Science and Technology Indicators* (MSTI database), November, Paris: OECD.

OECD (2000), 'Enhancing the Competitiveness of SMEs Through Innovation', *Workshop 1*, Bologna, Italy, June.

OECD (2000a), 'Enhancing the Competitiveness of SMEs in the Global Economy: Strategies and Policies', *Workshop 2*, Bologna, Italy, June.

Porter, M. (1998a), 'Competing Across Locations: Enhancing Competitive Strategy Through a Global Strategy', in M. Porter (1998), *On Competition*, Cambridge, MA: Harvard Business School Publishing.

Porter, M. (1998b), 'Clusters and Competition: New Agendas for Companies,

Governments, and Institutions', in M. Porter (1998), *On Competition*, Cambridge, MA: Harvard Business School Publishing.

Productivity Commission (1999), *Impact of Competition Policy Reforms on Rural and Regional Australia*, Draft Report, Canberra: AGPS.

Ries, I. (2000), 'Why our best companies are leaving Australia', *Australian Financial Review* (AFR), 2 May.

Roberts, E. (1994), *Benchmarking the Strategic Technology*, Cambridge, MA: MIT Sloan.

Sahlman, W. (1999), 'The New Economy is Stronger Than You Think', *Harvard Business Review*, November/December: 99–106.

Scott, M. (1999), 'Foreign Exchange Transaction Exposure Management Practices of Australian SMEs: An Exploratory Analysis', *Small Business Research*, 7 (2): 29–42.

Sheehan, P., N. Pappas, G. Tikhomirova and P. Sinclair (1995), *Australia and the Knowledge Economy*, Melbourne: Centre for Strategic Economic Studies.

Smith, G. (1999), 'Australia's Innovative Environment Compared with USA Experience', paper presented at AATSE Seminar, Melbourne.

Vernon, R. (1979), 'The Product Cycle Hypothesis in a New International Environment', *Oxford Bulletin of Economics and Statistics*, 41 (4): 255–67.

Viatle, Gerald (2000), Director, Food and Agriculture, OECD, interview, ABC Lateline, July.

Vickery, G. (1999), 'Business and Industry Policies for Knowledge-based Economies', *The O.E.C.D. Observer*, No. 215: 15–18.

The Weekly Times, 8 March 2000.

Wolf, J.A and T.L Pett (2000), 'Internationalisation of Small Firms: An Examination of Export Competitive Patterns, Firm Size, and Export Performance', *Journal of Small Business Management*, 32 (2): 34–47.

www.smallbusiness.info.au.

6. Cluster development programmes: panacea or placebo for promoting SME growth and internationalization?

Peter Brown and Rod McNaughton

INTRODUCTION

Regional cluster development is the latest panacea in government initiatives to encourage home-based competitive advantage for small firms trying to operate in an international market. Where governments once focused on general network strategies to address issues of growth, competitiveness and internationalization (McNaughton and Bell, 1999), they now embrace the concept of localized networks. These clusters of similar firms, found in distinct geographical regions, apparently derive support and competitive advantage through highly localized inter-firm relationships, place-specific history, economic factors, values and culture. Drawing on a range of research – including that related to industrial districts (Marshall, 1910), economic geography (Weber, 1929; Krugman, 1991), localized competitive advantage (Porter, 1990, 1998), local milieu (Aydalot and Keeble, 1988; Camagni, 1991), location-specific knowledge and innovation (Maskell and Malmberg, 1999; Feldman, 1994) – the concept of dynamic SME development through inter-firm relationships and spatial proximity has achieved international currency. Underlining the intrinsic developmental advantages of location is the frequently cited evidence that clusters result in dynamic regional economic development. Areas like Northern Italy (Putnam, 1993), Baden-Wurttemberg (Staber, 1998), Silicon Valley and Boston's Route 128 (Saxenian, 1990, 1994) have been held up as proof that economic and competitive advantages accrue where similar firms cluster together.

There should be little surprise that government agencies in at least 35 different instances (Porter, 1998) have focused on policy implementation designed to stimulate and encourage the development of dynamic clusters of industrial activity within specific regional economies. This championing of clusters as vehicles for dynamic economic development is based on correlation rather than causation. The result has been a variety of publicly funded programmes that are not based on an explicit model of when and how cluster dynamics lead to improved economic performance. It is this gap between policy and reality that the following research seeks to explore.

This chapter contributes to the discussion of public promotion of clusters by reviewing and synthesizing the diverse literature on geographical co-location, and then by following the programme of cluster development initiated in New Zealand informed by data gathered from firms in an electronics cluster located in Christchurch. By matching the theory and reality of New Zealand's cluster development programme, the chapter identifies strengths and weaknesses of its implementation and addresses implications for public policy and firms.

LITERATURE REVIEW

The linking of clusters, comparative advantage and competitiveness dates back to before Marshall (1910), the acknowledged father of the cluster concept. Adam Smith (1979 [1776]) first posited the concept of division of labour and increasing specialization of productive units. These discrete units were able to inter-link with other production units clustered together in one location, creating a vertically disintegrated system of organization that led to individual regions specializing in particular types of products. But it was Ricardo (1817, reprinted 1971) who most clearly articulated the competitiveness of location with the concept of comparative advantage. The underlying premise on which this is based is that different countries, cities and regions have distinctive kinds of resource or factor endowments, which manifest themselves in efficient forms of local specialization and trade. It was this principle that '... determines that wine shall be made in France and Portugal, that corn shall be grown in America and Poland, and that hardware and other goods shall be manufactured in England' (Ricardo, 1971, p. 152).

Marshall (1910) developed this argument further in examining the industrial districts found in Europe in the late 1800s. He cited the chief causes of industry localization as physical conditions – such as the character of the climate and the soil, the existence of mines and quarries in the neighbourhood, or within easy access by land or water. These industrial districts resulted in benefits or externalities for the firms within them such as technological spill-over, access to a skilled labour pool, access to intermediate inputs–outputs and marketing advantages. It was these externalities that provided competitive advantage for the region both domestically and internationally.

Subsequent researchers have challenged the idea that the competitive

advantage of firms within a cluster is solely dependent on resource endowments or pre-conditions. Economic geographers have tried to explain the
existence of clusters on the basis of cost minimization (e.g. Weber, 1929;
Hoover, 1948; Williamson, 1985), or maximization of profit and maximization of space utility (Lösch, 1954; Isard, 1956). Because of economies of
scale, producers concentrate production in a limited number of locations.
Because of transaction costs, the preferred locations for each individual
producer are those where demand is large or supply of inputs is particularly
convenient – which is often where other producers choose to locate.
Location within these clusters of manufacturing results in competitive
advantage over manufacturers located in more dispersed regions.

Perhaps the single most important contribution to this discussion comes
from Porter, who argues that competitiveness is dependent on productivity
but also depends on more than the comparative advantage Ricardo posited.
Porter states that national, or regional, competitiveness must move beyond
comparative advantage and existing endowments. He points to the economic
and competitive success of nations such as Germany, Japan and Italy as evidence that natural resources are not the answer (Porter, 1998). Similarly,
cheap labour, government intervention and differing management practices
cannot explain why some countries or regions are more competitive and economically productive than others. Porter argues that it is competition that
underpins competitiveness and he links dynamic and evolving competition
to firms that are located in clusters. The competition that exists between firms
located together drives productivity, innovation and new firm development
(Porter, 1998). This environment of competition creates new and different
resource endowments such as skilled staff and technological knowledge.

Porter also acknowledges that 'social glue' (Porter, 1998, p. 225) contributes to the value creation process of clusters. This refers to the social structure, inter-firm relationships and embeddedness of the cluster. The notion
of embeddedness comes from Granovetter (1985) and has been used to
develop concepts such as social capital to describe the positive benefits of
networks within business communities (Coleman, 1990; Putnam, 1993).
The concept of new growth theory identifies human capital as the engine
of growth, and postulates that economic actors influence the productivity
of each other (Lucas, 1988; Martin, 1999). The manner in which people
interact determines the extent to which externalities and spill-overs will
advantage firms in proximity to each other. Lucas (1988) stresses that the
economic mechanism at the heart of growth requires social interactions
and external effects, which are mostly local in nature.

It is possible to link this aspect of new growth theory with the social
capital theorists by thinking of the two as twin elements in explaining mon-

etarily uncompensated information exchanged between firms. The social capital concept provides the social structures that determine *who* is going to interact, while the human capital concept determines *how* they interact. Along with new growth theory, Granovetter's influence and that of social capital theorists such as Coleman, Putnam, and Bourdieu (1986) has been significant in cluster literature, particularly that related to industrial districts.

Neither Porter's eloquent and persuasive case for the importance of clusters to competitive advantage, nor the efforts to explain cluster dynamism by embeddedness and social interaction, actually provides a definitive explanation for why clusters form at all and why some regions are more competitive than others. Porter's competitiveness can be seen as a result of clustered activity, not a cause, and embeddedness is a contingent concept dependent on the existence of appropriate resources that can be accessed, but not created, by local networking within a cluster.

In fact, the concepts of competitive advantage and social embeddedness appear to pre-suppose an existing cluster of firms – indeed require it – to be of relevance in this discussion. On their own, Porter's theory and the embeddedness concepts that can be placed under industrial district theory do not explain why the first firm set up shop in a particular location. The economic theories of Weber and others, grafted on to Marshallian resource endowments, intuitively provide a more complete understanding of a cluster's inception. This is especially so if the concept of serendipity or historical accident is considered.

The basic competitive model of economic equilibrium implies inevitability in location decisions due to resource and factor endowments, and transportation costs. But uncertainty exists in industrial location and agglomeration, which means several alternative equilibria are possible (Martin, 1999). Which particular spatial pattern emerges will depend on history. The initial catalyst for a cluster may be an accident of history but, once it is established, it may become locked in through processes of cumulative causation based on increasing returns. 'Thus "irrational" economic decisions can generate suboptimal but equilibrium distribution' (Martin, 1999, p. 70). Therefore, it can be argued that the establishment of early firms at a particular location is as much a matter of historical accident as anything else. The subsequent attraction of other firms depends on the existence of increasing returns, in the form of economies of scale and positive externalities (which is where the importance of embeddedness becomes apparent).

The world's most examined cluster, Silicon Valley, was started by a mix of serendipitous events and watershed changes. Frederick Terman's desire to settle in California because of its climate meant he pursued an applied electrical engineering research and business start-up programme as

Stanford's vice-president rather than at a university on the East Coast. Military demands from the Korean War provided a stimulus to the nascent electronics industry (Saxenian, 1990). Similarly, the United States call-centre hub based in Omaha, Nebraska is a direct result of the US armed forces locating their strategic command centre there. This required the installation of a huge communications infrastructure and capacity, which provided the opportunity for firms to establish national call centres.

Clusters of firms can also originate from a single successful start-up or parent firm. Thirty-one semiconductor firms were started in Silicon Valley during the 1960s and a majority could trace their origins back to one company (Saxenian, 1994). The concept of lead firms as the focal point in cluster and network development is common within the literature (Arthur, 1990; Axelsson and Easton, 1992; Humphrey and Schmitz, 1996; Porter, 1998; Scott, 1998). Once the initial location is determined (through historical conditions or accident, resource endowment or unique market demand) there are compelling reasons for firms to continue to locate near similar firms. As the first firms become successful, suppliers, workers and investors become available. This lowers the cost of entry for subsequent firms, making the area relatively more attractive than other areas (Pouder and St John, 1996). If the net benefit of externalities increases with the number of firms in the region, positive feedback to other firms will see a predominant share of an industry cluster in a single region or location. (This holds up to a point where congestion and other negative externalities begin to impact adversely on firms.) Far from there being any intrinsic locational advantage, it is the attraction of subsequent firms that consolidates the location as an industry cluster (Storper, 1997).

Arthur (1990) argues that the first firms to enter an industry choose their location either by chance or to maximize individual benefits (in line with economic theory discussed above). If benefits increase by locating near other similar firms, then, over time, the industry becomes locked in to that location. New entrants then choose their location based on the positive feedback created by existing firms and they reinforce the geographic concentration of that particular industry. Even though researchers acknowledge that each cluster has a unique development path based on different historical pre-conditions (Piore and Sabel, 1984; Saxenian, 1990; Putnam, 1993; Porter, 1998; Scott, 1998), most have failed to acknowledge the impact of this on subsequent development of the cluster.

CLUSTER DEVELOPMENT POLICY IN NEW ZEALAND

The development of a cluster formation and development strategy in New Zealand began in 1996, when the New Zealand Trade Development Board's (TradeNZ) Strategic Development Unit introduced the concept of clusters to local economic development agencies via a series of regional presentations. This initiative built on previous TradeNZ work to develop New Zealand's export base through the concept of *Co-operating to Compete*. The first building block in this initiative was the establishment of Joint Action Groups (JAGs) that were export-focused national associations of firms within specific industry sectors. The second building block was the development of a Hard Business Network (HBN) programme, which attempted to stimulate alliances between small and medium-sized exporters. (See Perry (1995) for a discussion of JAGs, and McNaughton and Bell (1999) for a discussion of HBNs.) This progression from JAGs to HBNs to clusters does not appear to be based on empirical analysis of the benefits of any of the programmes. There has been no formal evaluation of the HBN programme (McNaughton and Bell, 1999). TradeNZ has, in effect, mimicked government agency activity in a number of other countries that sought to imprint the cluster model on their own particular environment. TradeNZ accepted the correlation between clustered industrial activity and strong economic performance at face value without exploring the existence of any causal link.

In the cluster development initiative begun in New Zealand during May 1996, participants heard about established clusters in the US and Italy. They were able to study the definition and key elements of successful dynamic clusters based largely on the 1995 work of Stuart Rosenfeld, Regional Technology Strategies, Inc. (Rosenfeld, 1995). These regional presentations always included a discussion of local industrial activity and an attempt to identify potential or existing clusters of activity (Ffowcs-Williams, 1997).

In July 1996, a workshop was held in Auckland to explore the cluster concept further and to establish some parameters for identifying regional needs and developing local government policy to meet those needs. Key representatives from local development agencies, business development boards, research institutions and business support organizations attended this workshop. Out of this workshop, TradeNZ's Strategic Development Unit produced a four-pronged cluster development process that was to form the basis of future training and development initiatives (see Figure 6.1).

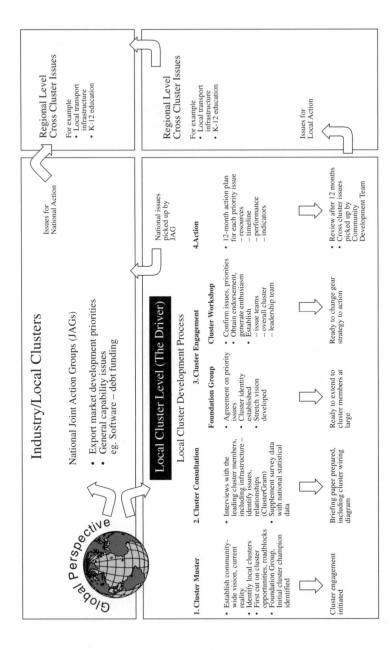

Source: TradeNZ workshop materials. (Reproduced with permission of Ifor Ffowcs-Williams.)

Figure 6.1   TradeNZ's cluster development process

Perhaps the key element of the cluster development programme developed by TradeNZ was the role of central government in initiation and then withdrawal. It was anticipated that once central government had provided the impetus for cluster development through cluster musters, local regional government and local industry would take over the process and drive future growth.

In March 1997 a cluster training course was held in Rotorua. Regional economic development personnel from throughout New Zealand, and from Australia, South Africa and Canada, spent two days exploring the cluster concept as it existed in Italy and elsewhere. This training course sought to disseminate the key components of clusters – core, specialist supporting firms, supporting social and physical infrastructure (Ffowcs-Williams, 1997) – and relate them to specific regional environments.

A series of Cluster Musters was then organized by local regions with the support of TradeNZ. These one-day workshops typically consisted of 100–200 senior representatives of the local economy – mayors, civic leaders, chief executives of exporting/manufacturing businesses, support organizations, banks and tertiary institutions. In most cases, these Cluster Musters were the first time many of these participants had met together to discuss the economic future of their community. Through a series of workshops, an outline of the participants' vision for their community was developed and compared to reality. Clusters within the region were identified and opportunities and threats for each cluster discussed. At the end of each Cluster Muster a senior member of each cluster was to have 'volunteered' to act as the initial champion and as a foundation member for each cluster established. The Cluster Musters were held in six cities, with the first occurring in Christchurch on 7 August 1997 in association with the Canterbury Development Corporation.

In reporting on the outcome of this Cluster Muster, Chris Pickrill, Chief Executive of the CDC, said that the exercise had created an awareness of the key areas where a co-ordinated focus would be required to build on the realities and perceptions of Canterbury in 1997. The overwhelming majority of people attending signified their willingness to be further involved in identifying and developing a range of such initiatives (Pickrill, 1997). The clusters identified are electronics, telecommunications and software, engineering (food, agriculture and high-tech), wool, apparel, outdoor equipment, education, tourism, agribusiness and biotechnology. Key executives in each of these sectors were identified and charged with the role of co-ordinating an industry group designed to progress cluster activity within that particular industry sector. The research outlined in this chapter focuses on the implications of this development programme for the electronics cluster.

RESEARCH APPROACH

Clusters are by definition spatially bounded systems, so the basic unit of analysis in this case is the cluster followed by the firms within it. Because each cluster is unique, research must involve an intense examination of relationships between firms and support organizations including government agencies.

Much of the cluster research undertaken in the past has focused on economic or survey data that have been statistically analysed for the existence of patterns and location factors between regions (e.g. Porter, 1990; Krugman, 1991; Saxenian, 1994; Swann and Prevezer, 1996). This analysis has been useful for comparing cluster regions, levels of growth and development patterns. But the result is descriptive and does not provide insight into why firms within a particular cluster act the way they do.

More recent research, focusing on the relationships between cluster members, has taken a different approach. Larson (1992), Lazerson (1995), Romo and Schwartz (1995), and Uzzi (1997) among others have utilized qualitative techniques such as in-depth interviews and observation to explore and understand the relationships and inter-firm activity within individual clusters.

Because this research seeks to understand a contemporary phenomenon and explain its development, the method employed followed this latter approach. It involved an industry analysis within the Christchurch electronics cluster. Extensive, multiple sources of information were used to provide a detailed in-depth picture of the cluster, including interviews with cluster members and support organizations as well as secondary source material. Cluster firms were asked to discuss the development of the electronics cluster in Christchurch. Interviews explored the key elements of location decisions, and the cluster development path. Particular emphasis was placed on the role of support organizations and government policy in influencing that developmental path.

The sample of 27 firms was drawn partly from a directory of electronics and software businesses, which lists firms actively engaged in the Christchurch electronics cluster, and further information from the University of Canterbury and several firms within the cluster itself. The 27 firms represented the entire population of the Christchurch electronics cluster at the time the research was undertaken. In-depth interviews were conducted with the founders or managing directors of 23 of the 27 firms over a ten-day period. (Interviews were unable to be conducted with four company representatives because of their unavailability due to business travel.) Founders or managing directors (often one and the same) were selected for interview because they were in the best position to provide information on the topic of interest. A profile of the firms within the cluster is presented in Table 6.1.

FINDINGS

Research from the Christchurch electronics cluster indicated that a firm's location decision within that cluster was overwhelmingly based on the family origins of a firm's principal. This was certainly true for firms that were more than ten years old. However, there was also evidence that suggested younger firms were locating within the cluster because of other factors such as the existence of externalities. This suggests that pre-existing initial factors may be key to the foundation of a geographical cluster of like firms. However, the externalities that derive from the cluster then draw in other firms to drive cluster growth forward. The Christchurch cluster is relatively young compared to most international counterparts and it may yet exhibit the type of growth driven by firms locating in Christchurch because of apparent externalities. It appears that a firm's location decision can be separated into two distinct stages, depending on the cluster's level of development. This finding is relevant to development of policy or programmes for the growth or attraction of firms to a cluster, which is discussed further in the Conclusions section of this chapter.

The Canterbury Development Corporation has been one of New Zealand's leading local government agencies in initiating a cluster development programme. Since jointly sponsoring a Cluster Muster with TradeNZ in August 1997, the CDC has also sponsored background research and data collection on the Christchurch electronics and software clusters (Canterbury Development Corporation, 1997; BERL, 1998) and has been working on draft cluster development proposals since 1997. It recently launched a regional science, technology and innovation strategy called ICAN (Innovation Canterbury) that outlines its priorities and initiatives to achieve long-term competitive advantage for the Canterbury regional economy grounded on its science and technology base. Key components of the ICAN strategy are fostering a technological infrastructure and entrepreneurial network that encourages the creation of high-technology firms and supports their survival.

In view of this apparent effort, it was expected that firms within the

Table 6.1 Cluster profile

Firm	Year Est.	Ownership	Size	Staff (FTE)	Product	Sales	% Export
A	1995	Private NZ	Small	3	Design/Manu.	$250,000	40
B	1978	Private NZ	Medium	32	Design/Manu.	$10m	90
C	1991	Private NZ	Small	8	Encryption	$2m (est)	100
D	1948	Private NZ	Medium	30	Moldings	$5m	70
E	1984	Private NZ	Medium	35	Hard. peripherals	$35 m	2
F	1974	Foreign	Large	300	Motor Controls	$50m (est)	99
G	1989	Private NZ	Medium	30	Contract manu.	$6m	5
H	1939	Private NZ	Medium	100	Metal fab.	$16m	50
I	1974	Private NZ	Medium	80	Cables	$20m (est)	50
J	1990	Private NZ	Small	14	Design	$1.5m	5
K	1974	Private NZ	Medium	32	Ind. Measurement	$5m	20
L	1992	Private NZ	Small	5	Automotive	$650,000	33
M	1993	Private NZ	Small	5	Telecomm.	$1.5m	100
N	1996	Private NZ	Small	1	Marketing	$500,000	10
O	1984	Private NZ	Small	4	Design	$500,000	0
P	1988	Private NZ	Medium	55	Medical	$18m	95
Q	1985	Private NZ	Medium	14	Design	$2m	5
R	1996	Private US	Small	7	Design	$500,000	50
S	1964	Private NZ	Medium	35	PLC Controls	$3m	66
T	1985	Foreign	Large	400	Power DC	$90m	95
U	1968	Private NZ	Large	1000	Telecomm	$100m	90
V	1997	Private NZ	Small	2	Measuring	>$50,000 (Start-up)	0
W	1991	Foreign	Large	180	GPS Systems	$80m (est)	99
Total: 23				2372		$447m	

Source: Author's research.

116

electronics cluster would positively identify the contribution of TradeNZ and the CDC in cluster development initiatives. Surprisingly, this was not the case. Many firms could not recall the specifics of the 1997 Cluster Muster and several claimed nothing had happened since. Most firms were able to recall the establishment of an industry foundation group but said it had not functioned effectively, or at all, after the first few meetings. No initiatives had come from the foundation group and most firms felt the Cluster Muster had been a '. . . waste of time and no use . . .' to firms within the cluster (respondent from Firm M).

Other firm respondents remarked on the long delay between cluster development initiatives sponsored by TradeNZ or the CDC. The launch of the ICAN strategy was viewed positively but there were fears that it too would be a one-shot wonder that looked good but did not receive the on-going support from local government that it required.

There was criticism from firms of the *ad hoc* nature of TradeNZ policy towards clusters, with a feeling that they had presented a new export initia-tive and then abandoned it after only a short time. The General Manager of Firm N (a firm engaged in network activity with other firms) felt that the support agencies, particularly the CDC and TradeNZ, did not understand what the network was established for or what its true potential was. There was a feeling that TradeNZ in particular had moved away from its Hard Business Network and cluster development initiatives because tangible benefits had not been evident quickly enough. This respondent said, 'polit-ically, if it doesn't give immediate benefits, they lose interest. There is too much short-term thinking and not enough long-term planning. Everyone wants something now and it doesn't work that way.'

Several firms echoed these sentiments and observed that the support agencies did not really understand the organic nature of clusters, the elec-tronics sector or what it specifically needed. The respondent from Firm J claimed it was as though '. . . they think all you have to do is point us in the right direction and leave us to it. But we've all got businesses to run and we haven't got time to muck about with something new'. This high-lighted the gap between government's expectation that their involvement in cluster development could be brief and the expectation or need of firms within the cluster. The Chief Executive of the Chamber of Commerce pointed out: '. . . firms within Italian clusters are all run by family members so they already have that interfirm relationship going. It's not quite like that here.'

While there were generally negative perceptions of the Cluster Muster and subsequent development programme, many firms expressed support for informal cluster initiatives. TradeNZ initiated business sector breakfasts, which targeted particular industry groups and encouraged networking between firms on an informal basis. (These have subsequently been discontinued.)

The interview respondent from Firm G claimed the TradeNZ breakfasts were good for exchanging information. They provided an opportunity to discuss '. . . where you're at with different projects, design work, industry things and funding like TBG [Technology for Business Growth grants] . . .' in an informal setting. (Interestingly, Firm G is heavily involved in network activity.) Several other respondents also expressed support for the business breakfasts held monthly by TradeNZ and bemoaned the fact that these had been discontinued, as they were one of the few opportunities for firms within the same industry sector to meet and discuss issues that affected them all.

While most firms acknowledged the existence of soft network relationships between firms, there were only three specific groups of firms that had formed cluster networks and begun working together. All three cluster networks acknowledged the importance of soft networking in their initial development, with one group crediting the TradeNZ Hard Business Network programme as the catalyst for coming together. This highlights a significant difference between the perception of much of the cluster literature and reality. Clusters are generally perceived to be about networks between firms, with the dynamism of a cluster dependent on inter-firm relationships. This was clearly not the case within the Christchurch electronics cluster where few firms had leveraged their informal relationships into hard networks.

Similarly, strong relationships between firms and tertiary research institutions appeared to be expected by policy developers. This research found that many firms had experienced significant barriers to accessing information, research or facilities from these institutions. While several larger, or leading-edge, firms experienced a close relationship with the local university, many smaller firms considered it to be anachronistic and irrelevant to their activities. This suggests that government policy needs to place greater emphasis on the issue of relationships both between firms and between firms and support organizations.

When respondents were asked what they needed in terms of support programmes, there was no overall consistency in responses received. One surprising finding was the desire expressed by several firms, and the Chief Executive of the Chamber of Commerce, for more competition within the cluster. Competition within a cluster is credited with stimulating innovation and growth in the literature, especially in Italian industrial districts (Porter, 1998; Pyke *et al.*, 1990). The Managing Director of Firm H, one of the larger firms engaged in contract manufacturing, admitted that competition would drive the cluster forward. He acknowledged that competition might impact on his firm but he felt confident it would grow the cluster, not destroy it. Several firms stated that one of the roles of government policy should be to attract inward investment to the cluster to create competition. It should be noted that enthusiasm for competition was strongest amongst smaller firms and those that did not possess leading-edge technology or had not heavily invested in their own research and design activity. Support for competition from contract manufacturing firms might have been because it would increase the number of firms to manufacture for, rather than any innovation potential for the cluster.

Some respondents (from Firms D and G) felt there needed to be more networks established locally so that there was less competition. Other respondents (from Firms D, M and V) wanted assistance (grants or information) with marketing aspects – finding opportunities and help with developing them. Still others (from Firms I, R and W) claimed there was no role for local government or other support organizations beyond informal networking and lobbying – that firms within the cluster should develop on their own. Respondents from two of the larger firms (Firms F and T) expressed dismay at central government policies and believed they were stifling local business development by making the macro-environment too competitive. Some firms did not know what they needed.

DISCUSSION AND CONCLUSIONS

Porter (1998) emphasizes the importance of government policy in facilitating cluster development. It would appear that New Zealand government policy on cluster development has been based on an international trend and correlation rather than hard evidence of a causal link between clusters and economic development. There has been little or no consideration given to the location-specific factors influencing cluster development in New Zealand, and TradeNZ's original cluster development programme grew out of an assumption that firms simply needed to be introduced to the concept to adopt it and drive it themselves. This research indicates that this is not the case. Firms acknowledged the original efforts of TradeNZ and the CDC but felt there was little support or understanding of what was required for real development of the cluster. Firms believed they needed programmes tailored to New Zealand and based on local research rather than programmes taken from international observation.

Firms also felt that TradeNZ's efforts were *ad hoc* and inconsistent. This was generally acknowledged to be the result of central government pressure to achieve immediate results for political advantage. This failed to recognize the organic nature of clusters and the delay between policy implementation and effect.

The key element that must be grasped by both government and support agencies is that most clusters, including the Christchurch electronics cluster, form and develop not through the actions of any government but by a random combination of locational factors or advantages. Governments must accept this reality if they are to understand the dynamics of how clusters work. Only then can policy and support be directed at upgrading and reinforcing existing clusters, rather than merely attempting to create new ones.

The current stage of cluster development in Christchurch was frequently described as organic. Little credit was given by firms, or claimed by support agencies, for development stimulation. Combined with evidence on the location decision of firms, this suggests that it is important for a cluster to have at least some of the pre-conditions necessary to develop at all. It follows that an effort to stimulate cluster activity in an area where there is not at least some form of nascent cluster activity is unlikely to succeed. This is particularly important for government policy as it would appear that regional development must be founded on an existing, identified strength that can be nurtured rather than transplanted.

If clusters occur organically and firms locate in a particular location because of certain initial pre-conditions, then cluster development programmes may need to address how locational advantages, and a few originating firms, can be leveraged into a dynamic economic force. The fact that dynamic clusters grow out of the degree and strength of inter-firm relationships rather than just economic considerations suggests that government stimulation measures must focus on more than technological innovation through research and development funding. There may need to be a focus on management development so that firms can take advantage of cluster network opportunities. There may also need to be a focus on market development for the cluster members.

Firms within the Christchurch cluster made a clear call for real services from government agencies that included access to applied research, promotional activities, market development, and dissemination of market information. Some Christchurch firms suggested network brokers who could draw together groups of firms would be useful, especially if they had credibility within the industry. These brokers could help leverage the informal ties that many firms had into harder networks that would create a more dynamic edge to the cluster. In addition, cluster firms called for government agencies to re-institute the soft networking opportunities that had previously occurred within the cluster through trade functions and meetings.

From the preceding research analysis and discussion, several recommendations for cluster development policy or programmes can be suggested:

1. Government agencies need to accept the organic nature of cluster development and acknowledge that cluster development programmes can only be successful where there is an appropriate foundation to build on. Moreover, positive benefits from policy support may not be apparent in the short term.
2. Government agencies need to clearly identify clusters, the firms and institutions within them and the capabilities and gaps that exist. This then needs to be combined with gathering market intelligence about the industry sector, international competition and opportunities that will guide the type and direction of support programmes necessary.
3. Governments and support agencies need to actually help build the link between firms and research organizations rather than just paying lip service to it. This relationship needs to be accelerated to enhance cluster growth.
4. Governments should consider attracting new, leading-edge firms to the cluster. This would stimulate competition that could drive externality growth, provide more opportunities for existing subcontractors and possibly lead to small firm spin-offs.
5. Support policy must also focus on network management education to enable managers to maximize the benefits cluster externalities provide. Much of the New Zealand focus on cluster development has revolved around the need for management up-skilling in vital areas such as financial, operations and marketing management. However, the concept of management skill has been restricted to aspects of individual firm management. With the importance of inter-firm relationships being underlined by this research, policy makers might consider training programmes for firm management within a cluster that focused on networking and communication skills within the cluster, and the benefits of co-operation in marketing and collaborative new product development.
6. Government policy requires a shift in focus away from production-oriented support towards demand-side support in the form of network development and market opportunity research. Firms need highly developed international networks to develop export activity. Strengthening the role of TradeNZ so that it can develop international networks and opportunities on an industry sector basis could be a crucial part of this focus. Demand-side support may *lead* firms to

innovate for export rather than current policies that attempt to *drive* firm production for export.

7. A specific recommendation is for TradeNZ or the Canterbury Development Corporation to provide a network broker service, experienced in the electronics industry, to lever soft, informal network ties into stronger marketing networks, and to investigate market opportunities for the cluster. The electronics sector in Christchurch is big enough to warrant this support and government agencies already have positive experience of network brokers through the Hard Business Network programme.

REFERENCES

Arthur, W.B. (1990), 'Silicon Valley locational clusters: Do increasing returns imply monopoly?', *Mathematical Social Sciences*, 19: 235–51.

Axelsson, Bjorn and Geoffrey Easton (1992), *Industrial Networks – a New View of Reality*, London: Routledge.

Aydalot, P. and D. Keeble (eds) (1988), *High Technology Industries and Innovative Environments: The European Experience*, London: Routledge.

BERL (Business and Economic Research Ltd) (1998), *Canterbury's Electronic and Information Technologies Cluster 1996*, Wellington, New Zealand.

Bourdieu, Pierre (1986), 'The Forms of Capital', in John Richardson (ed.), *Handbook of Theory and Research for the Sociology of Education*, New York: Greenwood Press, pp. 241–58.

Camagni, R. (ed.) (1991), *Innovation Networks: Spatial Perspectives*, London: Belhaven Press.

Canterbury Development Corporation (1997), *CDC Electronics and Software Directory of Business*, Christchurch, NZ.

Coleman, James (1990), *Foundations of Social Theory*, Cambridge, MA: The Belknap Press.

Feldman, Maryann P. (1994), *The Geography of Innovation*, Dordrecht: Kluwer Academic Publishers.

Ffowcs-Williams, Ifor (1997), 'Local clusters and local export growth', *New Zealand Strategic Management*, Summer: 24–9.

Granovetter, Mark (1985), 'Economic action and social structure: the problem of embeddedness', *American Journal of Sociology*, 91(3): 481–510.

Hoover, E.M. (1948), *The Location of Economic Activity*, New York: McGraw-Hill.

Humphrey, J. and H. Schmitz (1996), 'The triple C approach to local industrial policy', *World Development*, 24(12): 1859–77.

Isard, W. (1956), *Location and Space Economy*, New York: Wiley and Sons.

Krugman, Paul (1991), *Geography and Trade*, Boston, MA: MIT Press.

Krugman, Paul (1991a), 'Increasing returns and economic geography', *Journal of Political Economy*, 99(3): 483–99.

Larson, Andrea (1992), 'Network dyads in entrepreneurial settings: a study of the governance of exchange processes', *Administrative Science Quarterly*, 37: 76–104.

Lazerson, Mark (1995), 'A new phoenix: modern putting-out in the Modena knitwear industry', *Administrative Science Quarterly*, 40: 34–59.

Lösch, A. (1954), *The Economics of Location*, New Haven: Yale University Press.

Lucas, R.E. (1988), 'On the mechanics of economic development', *Journal of Monetary Economics*, 22: 3–42.

McNaughton, Rod B. and James D. Bell (1999), 'Brokering networks of small firms to generate social capital for growth and internationalization', *Research in Global Strategic Management*, 7: 63–82.

Marshall, Alfred (1910), *Principles of Economics* (6th edn), London: Macmillan.

Martin, Ron (1999), 'The new "geographical turn" in economics: some critical reflections', *Cambridge Journal of Economics*, 23: 65–91.

Maskell, P. and A. Malmberg (1999), 'Localised learning and industrial competitiveness', *Cambridge Journal of Economics*, 23(2): 167–85.

Pickrill, C. (1997), *Leading edge – Quarterly Newsletter of the Canterbury Development Corporation*, September–November.

Piore, M. and C. Sabel (1984), *The Second Industrial Divide: Possibilities for Prosperity*, New York: Basic Books.

Porter, Michael E. (1990), *The Competitive Advantage of Nations*, London: Macmillan.

Porter, Michael E. (1998), *On Competition*, Boston, MA: Harvard Business School Press.

Pouder, Richard and Caron H. St John (1996), 'Hot spots and blind spots: geographical clusters of firms and innovation', *Academy of Management Review*, 21(4): 1192–225.

Putnam, Robert D. (1993), *Making Democracy Work – Civic Traditions in Modern Italy*, Princeton, NJ: Princeton University Press.

Pyke, F.G. Becattini and W. Sengenberger (eds) (1990), *Industrial Districts and Inter-firm Co-operation in Italy*, Geneva: International Institute for Labour Studies.

Ricardo, D. (1971), *Principles of Political Economy and Taxation*, Harmondsworth: Penguin Books.

Romo, Frank P. and Michael Schwartz (1995), 'Structural embeddedness of business decisions: a sociological assessment of the migration behaviour of plants in New York State between 1960 and 1985', *American Sociological Review*, 60: 874–907.

Rosenfeld, Stuart A. (1995), *Overachievers – Business Clusters that Work: Prospects for Regional Development*, Carrboro, NC: Regional Technology Strategies Inc.

Saxenian, AnnaLee (1990), 'Regional networks and the resurgence of Silicon Valley', *California Management Review*, Fall: 89–112.

Saxenian, AnnaLee (1994), *Regional Advantage: Culture and Competition in Silicon Valley and Route 128*, Cambridge, MA: Harvard University Press.

Scott, Allen J. (1998), *Regions and the world economy: the coming shape of global production, competition and political order*, Oxford: Oxford University Press.

Smith, Adam (1979), *The Wealth of Nations*, Baltimore: Penguin.

Staber, Udo (1998), 'Inter-firm co-operation and competition in industrial districts', *Organization Studies*, 19(4): 701–24.

Storper, Michael (1997), *The Regional World*, New York: The Guilford Press.

Swann, Peter, and Martha Prevezer (1996), 'A comparison of the dynamics of industrial clustering in computing and biotechnology', *Research Policy*, 25: 1139–57.

Uzzi, Brian (1997), 'Social structure and competition in interfirm networks: the paradox of embeddedness', *Administrative Science Quarterly*, 42: 35–67.

Weber, Alfred (1929), *Theory of Location of Industry*, Chicago: The University of Chicago Press.

Williamson, Oliver (1985), *The Economic Institutions of Capitalism*, New York: Free Press.

7. Social capital, networks and ethnic minority entrepreneurs: transnational entrepreneurship and bootstrap capitalism

Teresa V. Menzies, Gabrielle A. Brenner and Louis Jacques Filion*

INTRODUCTION

> Comprehensive explanations of entrepreneurship must include the social context of behavior, especially the social relationships through which people obtain information, resources and social support. (Aldrich and Zimmer; 1986, p. 11)

Ethnic networks have long been recognized as a vital component of success for the ethnic entrepreneur (for example, Aldrich and Zimmer, 1986; Bonacich *et al.*, 1977; Boubakri, 1999; Deakins *et al.*, 1997; Dhaliwal, 1998; Dyer and Ross, 2000; Iyer and Shapiro, 1999; Light, 1984; Peterson and Roquebert, 1993; Ram, 1994; Teixeira, 1998; Waldinger, 1988; Waldinger *et al.*, 1990). Acting as an informal business incubator, ethnic networks nurture new businesses and assist in their growth by providing varying amounts of physical and intellectual resources (Greene and Butler, 1996; Greene, 1997). From the fledgling entrepreneur in a South Asian ethnic enclave in England to a venture-capital-funded, high-technology, transnational entrepreneurial team in Silicon Valley, each acquires a strong competitive advantage through the use of ethnic networks (Greene, 1997). Saxenian (1999) has studied the highly educated, transnational community of Chinese and East Indian immigrants who have started new technology businesses in Silicon Valley and found networks that help

* This research was made possible thanks to a SSHRC Research Grant No. 412–98–0025. We gratefully acknowledge the assistance of Linda Lowry, Brock University, Charles Perreault and Charles Ramangalahy, HEC. An earlier version of this paper was presented at the Second Biennial McGill Conference on International Entrepreneurship: Researching New Frontiers McGill University, Montreal, Canada.

create organizations specifically to further their technical, professional and entrepreneurial interests. Some businesses have a synergistic relationship between California and Taiwan whereby products, capital, skills, and information flow freely without the usual hindrance due to national borders. At least a quarter of the new high-technology ventures created in Silicon Valley in the last 20 years were started by the Chinese (17 per cent) or East Indian (7 per cent) (Saxenian, 1999). What Saxenian calls the 'trans-local' (homeland and new country) networks provide 'entry points' for entrepreneurs, 'duties and sanctions', but also an increase in trade for both countries due to industry integration. Meanwhile, the 'bootstrap capitalism' of South Asians in England (Werbner, 1999) conforms to more traditional perceptions of ethnic networks: support is provided by family and friends, or religious and other organizations as well as business people. Rath and Kloosterman (2000) say that today's economic sociologists call these social networks 'social capital', and they consider this an essential component of an ethnic entrepreneur's success.

Aldrich and Waldinger (1990) define *ethnicity* as 'self-identification with a particular ethnic group, or a label applied by outsiders' (p. 131) and ethnic *social structures* as 'networks of kinship and friendship around which ethnic communities are arranged, and the interlacing of these networks with positions in the economy (jobs), in space (housing), and in society (institutions)' (p. 127). They affirm that 'within complex networks of relationships, entrepreneurship is facilitated or constrained by linkages between aspiring entrepreneurs, resources, and opportunities [along with] chance, necessity, and purpose' (p. 9). Their three-part person-to-person transaction approach includes communication, exchange, and normative considerations (expectations of the parties concerned). A hierarchy of social networks starts with the *role-set* (people you know), *action-set* (purposeful alliances), and *network* ('the totality of all persons connected by a certain type of relationship' (Aldrich and Zimmer, 1986, p. 12)). Networks are distinguished by their *density* or connectedness, *reachability* (direct or indirect path), *centrality* of the individual in the network, and the group's 'internal organizing capacity' (p. 14). Bates (1994a) explains the relationship between social capital and networks as follows: 'The entrepreneur is seen as a member of supportive kinship, peer and community subgroups. These networks, in turn, assist in the creation and successful operation of firms by providing such social capital as sources of customers, loyal employees and financing' (p. 674, from Aldrich *et al.*, 1990).

Although interest in social capital and ethnic groups and businesses has a long history, theory building in the business literature is surprisingly underdeveloped (Rath and Kloosterman, 2000; Werbner, 1999). Knowledge about the process of venture creation, business success and problems, and growth characteristics may act as a guide to framing government policies and programs for potential and new immigrants, and also for 'under-represented as entrepreneurs' ethnic groups (Brenner *et al.*, 1992; Camarota, 2000; De Lourdes Villar, 1994). Immigrants or ethnic community entrepreneurs with strong links to their homeland may have formal and informal networks, which can be of use for both the entrepreneurs themselves and for companies intending to do business overseas (for example, Chamard, 1995; Kotkin, 1988; Razin and Langlois, 1996; Saxenian, 1999; Tseng, 1995; Wong, 1997; Wong and Ng, 1998).

FOCUS, METHOD AND ORGANIZATION OF THE REVIEW

Our objective in this review is to develop propositions concerning ethnic social capital and networks. We have searched the ethnic minority literature from 1988 to 1999 (Aldrich and Waldinger (1990) reviewed the literature to the late 1980s) for the purposes of a larger review. However, in this chapter we have drawn from the larger study to pursue the questions relating to ethnic social capital and networks. Table 7.1 shows the breakdown by topic of the 80 studies in our larger review, which focused on ethnic minority entrepreneurship in general. Many articles included information on social capital and networks, even if this was not the key focus of the specific article.

Table 7.1   Main topic(s) identified in each paper across review of 80 empirical studies in ethnic minority entrepreneurship

Main Topic(s)	No. of Studies
Social capital, networking	28
Motives for entrepreneurship, success factors	16
Ethnic enclaves	14
Characteristics and profiles of entrepreneurs	11
Factors leading to self-employment, incidence	10
Immigration and refugee issues	6
Problems of ethnic entrepreneurs	3
Gender (female) specific	3
Financing issues (not related to social resources)	3
Intra-ethnic differences	1
Total (some studies have multiple topics)	95

We define ethnic minority entrepreneurs (EMEs) as business owners or self-employed individuals who self-identify, or can be identified, with a particular ethnic (geographically or religiously based) minority group.

Our search strategy for garnering relevant papers was multidisciplinary. We include empirical studies published in refereed journals; business, economics, urban and regional geographical studies; politics and policy studies; and sociology literatures. Our review is a first step in theory building and as such makes no claim to include all studies in the area (for example, we have excluded papers from conference proceedings). Also, we did not conduct our review by selecting the principal journals in each field; rather, we adopted a keyword strategy and searched databases for relevant articles. Sociological Abstracts for the period 1988–99 was searched using the terms 'entrepreneurship' or 'small business' or 'self-employment' and 'ethnic groups' or 'ethnic minorities' or 'immigrants' or 'refugees'. ABI/INFORM Global database, Econlit, Canadian Business and Current Affairs and Social Sciences Index were also searched using similar terms, for the same period. Both English and French-language publications are included in our review. This chapter begins with a brief outline of some major theories and important reviews in the field. Findings on social capital and networks follow, and in our conclusion we summarize these findings as tentative propositions suitable for further discussion and research.

BACKGROUND LITERATURE

Early researchers into ethnicity and entrepreneurship include Simmel in the late 1800s (see Wolf, 1950), Weber (1930) and Schumpeter (1934). According to Butler and Greene (1997), these early writers developed ideas based on the stranger as trader, the social structure of society, the value systems produced and religious tenets. These fundamental issues led to the emergence of a theoretical framework for ethnic entrepreneurship. Historically, 'Enclave Theory', 'Middleman Theory' and 'Theories of Immigration' are the basis for much of the research. However, current studies suggest that these existing theories need to be augmented (Marger and Hoffman, 1992). Enclave Theory is concerned with immigrants, entrepreneurship and labor market issues (Nee and Nee, 1986). Ethnic enclaves, as well as being economically and culturally linked, have historically been geographically based (Wang, 1999). Middleman Theory relates to the type of business that immigrant or ethnic entrepreneurs engage in. They often act as traders or negotiators (Zenner, 1991). Theories of immigration are mostly concerned with migration patterns, networks and economic benefits (Muller, 1993). Research on ethnic entrepreneurs is found in the business, sociology, economics, labor market, urban studies, criminology, and gender literatures and includes qualitative, ethnographic, anthropological, quantitative, survey, and census-based methodologies (Weinfeld, 1998).

Aldrich and Waldinger's (1990) three-part framework included access to opportunities (markets, ownership, state policies); the characteristics of the group (predisposing factors like settlement characteristics, selective migration, culture and aspiration levels and resource mobilization); and finally the ethnic strategies ensuing from the two previous factors. They affirm 'The strategies adopted by the various ethnic groups in capitalistic societies around the world are remarkably similar' (p. 131). Butler and Greene's (1997) review of ethnic entrepreneurship, with a US focus, highlighted the following hypotheses with regard to social capital and networks: First, 'the importance of a community dimension inherent in the business creation process' and second, 'significant contributions of community resources to the entrepreneurial activities of group members' (p. 281). However, they cautioned that the stereotypes (for example, the previously mentioned affirmation of similar ethnic strategies worldwide) are open to re-examination.

Robichaud (1999) focused his literature review on the elements and models of the business creation process for immigrant entrepreneurs. He synthesized the literature into three general approaches: first, structural theory (social and economic structures, politics of the local community, 'middlemen minorities'), second 'cultural theory' (general culture and values of the ethnic), and finally, 'situational theory' (the 'social disadvantage' of the immigrant). Overlying the various theoretical approaches is the social and institutional structure of the wider community, and the strategic actions of the entrepreneur. Robichaud (1999) confirms the existence of ethnic enclaves and highlights the lack of studies in ethnic entrepreneurship. Deakins's (1999) four-part framework to summarize the literature on ethnic minority entrepreneurship consists of, first, accessing resources; second, accessing markets; third, motivation (for example, discrimination, push, pull factors); and finally, successful entrepreneurial strategies which include social capital factors within the framework of the first three categories. Deakins (1999) concluded that networking was vital to minority business success, that the diversity of ethnic minority enterprises has been overlooked and that:

> Ethnic enterprise development has succeeded largely outside mainstream support and largely without access to special support. . . . *Enterprise Forums* have been established by individual Asian community leaders, who have recognized the need to widen the contacts of the Asian (and other) business communities and to develop them with mainstream businesses and agencies. (Deakins, 1999, p. 91)

A highly critical review of current research into ethnic entrepreneurship (Rath and Kloosterman, 2000) stated that most research in this area was driven by government funding and mainly concerned policy directives, lacking an interactive model that included structural changes in economies and a specific focus on different markets, and thus had little theoretical value. They recommended that future studies focus on social capital and ethnic networks, with international comparisons of ethnic groups. These reviews of the literature from Canada (Robichaud, 1999), the Netherlands (Rath and Kloosterman, 2000), the UK (Deakins, 1999), and the USA (Aldrich and Waldinger, 1990) all point to the limitations of current knowledge, the lack of currently viable theoretical models and the necessity for future theoretically grounded research.

Iyer and Shapiro (1999), however, have proposed an evolutionary business model for successful ethnic business, which provides an interesting framework that we can adapt when considering social capital, networks and the relationship to international business. They posit that an immigrant begins by supplying co-ethnic labor in an enclave, then moves to self-employment in the enclave, then expands horizontally to the wider non-ethnic markets, next starts to make international investments in businesses back in their homeland, then initiates international expansion of their business to their homeland, and finally, develops lateral connections between their multiple business interests in their homeland and new country.

REVIEW FINDINGS

Our review includes a broad range of ethnic minority groups and studies conducted in Europe, North America and Asia. There was a range of methodologies used, which is to be expected. Almost half were quantitative (40) and included analysis of census data (20), mail surveys (14), and closed questionnaires administered at interviews (20). Eleven studies used hypotheses. These did not always use quantitative research methodologies. Only 31 papers used statistical analysis and a further 16 reported only frequencies. Just over half (49) were qualitative studies which used case studies (9), open (39) and semi-structured (3) interviews, along with a few which used personal observation, document analysis and focus groups. Nine of the studies used a mix of methodologies (quantitative and qualitative). Overall, 25 of the studies used a random sampling procedure and 55 did not. For our review purposes the authors found it difficult to compare findings when minority ethnic groups are defined in very broad terms (for example, 'Asians').

SOCIAL CAPITAL

If we see entrepreneurship as 'embedded in networks of continuing social relations' (Aldrich and Zimmer, 1986, p. 8), then social capital and networks are central themes. Social capital (sometimes called cultural capital) refers to the potential benefits derived from belonging to a specific group. In the entrepreneurship literature, social capital is illustrated by the use of co-ethnic employees, markets, suppliers, community sources of capital, advice and information, as well as belonging to ethnic and/or community organizations. Ethnic-based networks are an integral part of ethnic social capital. We will first present the findings relating to social capital and then discuss networks.

Co-ethnic Employees

Employing workers from the same ethnic group has obvious advantages in that they speak the same language, are part of the same culture and, if the customers are mainly drawn from the same ethnic group, can relate well to customers. Across the studies regardless of ethnic group, country, industry type, immigrant or non-immigrant entrepreneur or stage of business, the use of co-ethnic employees was very common (for example, Pessar, 1995; Phizacklea and Ram, 1996; Portes and Jensen, 1989; Ram, 1994; Shin and Han, 1990; Waldinger, 1995; Walton-Roberts and Hiebert, 1997; Yoon, 1995) but not universal: in a study of 59 Chinese immigrants in Canada, Wong and Ng (1998) found that 81 per cent used co-ethnic employees in addition to a major reliance on family members. Wong (1997) had earlier found that 89 per cent out of a group of 284 Chinese immigrant entrepreneurs had co-ethnic employees and 59 per cent employed *only* Chinese. But Light *et al.*, (1994), studying Iranians in the US, found that only 4.6 per cent of employees worked for a co-ethnic employer, which could point to either a low level of co-ethnic employment or a small number of Iranian-owned businesses. Marger (1990), studying East Indians in Canada, and Rafiq (1992) Muslims in the UK, found that there was a mix of employees, with some co-ethnic. For Cubans in the US, Cobas and DeOllos (1989) found that there was a greater chance of self-employment if there was a ready supply of co-ethnic labor. Self-employed Soviet Jews and Vietnamese refugees in the US were found to hire co-ethnic labor (Gold, 1992).

There is a flip side noted to the use of co-ethnic labor. Sometimes entrepreneurs feel they are training would-be competitors (Lee, 1999) and resent the lack of privacy in business matters. De Lourdes Villar (1994) found that the use of illegal co-ethnic labor, seen as an unfair business advantage by competitors, caused considerable conflict with other ethnic business owners. Bates, discussing African Americans and Korean immigrants in the US (1994b) and Asians in the US (1994a), indicated that co-ethnic labor was not a decisive factor in business success; in fact with Vietnamese owner-managers, a reliance on co-ethnic labor and markets increased the likelihood of failure.

Family Labor

An integral part of co-ethnic labor is the use of family members, some paid but mainly unpaid. Many studies in our review indicated a heavy reliance on family members as part or all of the business workforce (Dallalfar, 1994; Iyer and Shapiro, 1999; Juteau and Paré, 1996; Phizacklea and Ram, 1996; Portes and Jensen, 1989; Rafiq, 1992; Ram et al., 2000; Ram, 1994; Shin and Han, 1990; Simard, 1994; Walton-Roberts and Hiebert, 1997; Wong and Ng, 1998; Wong, 1997). Shin and Han (1990), studying Koreans in the US, found an employment pattern related to business growth and success, whereby ethnic businesses start out by using family labor, then with growth hire co-ethnic employees and subsequently non-ethnic employees. One of the stereotypes of ethnic business is the exploitation of female family members by using them as an unpaid or low-paid labor source in family businesses (Butler and Greene, 1997), and several studies indicated the presence of exploitation of female family members (for example, Juteau and Paré, 1996; Wong and Ng, 1998). Several studies mentioned a related form of exploitation by the existence of 'hidden women', women whose contribution to the business in the form of capital, family connections, management, and long hours of work is great but whose contributions are largely unacknowledged (Phizacklea and Ram, 1996; Rafiq, 1992; Ram, 1994). Iyer and Shapiro (1999) consider the strong dependency on family and co-ethnic labor to be one of the main distinguishing factors between ethnic minorities and small business owners in general.

Co-ethnic Markets

As with co-ethnic employees, a majority of studies mentioned the use of co-ethnic markets. A protected co-ethnic market is considered to be a positive attribute of ethnic social capital (Portes and Jensen, 1989) and is a common feature of small businesses that cater to ethnic minorities (Gold, 1992; Juteau and Paré, 1997; Pessar, 1995; Peterson and Roquebert, 1993; Tseng, 1995; Waldinger, 1995; Walton-Roberts and Hiebert, 1997). But certain drawbacks to reliance on these markets exist: excessive clustering may cause market saturation (Lee, 1999). Fierce competition among minority entrepreneurs chasing the same market is found in several studies (Iyer and

Shapiro, 1999; Lee, 1999; Marger, 1990; Ram *et al.*, 2000; Razin and Light, 1998), even to the extent that illegal immigrant employees will be hired and government regulations broken to gain a competitive advantage (Kloosterman *et al.*, 1999). Businesses that catered only to the ethnic market were found to be smaller and less successful than those that served the wider market or both the ethnic and the wider markets (Bates, 1994a,b; Phizacklea and Ram, 1996; Shin and Han, 1990; Torres, 1988; Walton-Roberts and Hiebert, 1997). Exclusive reliance on the ethnic market is often due to 'blocked mobility' because of either discrimination or poor language skills of the entrepreneur, or lack of capital to operate in non-ethnic minority areas (Wong and Ng, 1998).

Some ethnic minority entrepreneurs have been successful in serving both the co-ethnic and wider markets. For instance, a group of Chinese entrepreneurs in Canada, mostly involved in import/export, non-food retail and manufacturing, sold 40 per cent of their products in the co-ethnic market and 60 per cent in the non-ethnic (Wong and Ng, 1998). Also, in addition to the obvious benefits and drawbacks of a co-ethnic market, some studies have found that the larger the co-ethnic market, the greater the likelihood of self-employment for members of the minority group (Cobas and DeOllos, 1989; Evans, 1989), although this finding has been contradicted by Razin and Langlois (1996).

Co-ethnic Suppliers

The existence of co-ethnic suppliers is regarded as part of the social capital of a group when there is considerable vertical integration. This was found to be prevalent by Lee (1999) in the US for the Jewish and Korean communities (but not for the African Americans), by Juteau and Paré (1996, 1997) across four immigrant groups (Asian, Jewish, Sri Lankan, Vietnamese) in Canada, and by Peterson and Roquebert (1993) among the Cubans, and the Taiwanese (Tseng, 1995; Saxenian, 1999) in the US.

Co-ethnic Sources of Finance

As in previous research (Butler and Greene, 1997), it was found that personal and family members were the primary sources of financing for most entrepreneurs (for example, Bates, 1997; Deakins *et al.*, 1995; Feldman *et al.*, 1991; Huck *et al.*, 1999; Juteau and Paré, 1996; Pessar, 1995; Peterson, 1995; Shin and Han, 1990, Simard, 1994; Tseng, 1995, Walton-Roberts and Hiebert, 1997). There are, however, formal and informal mechanisms created and used by ethnic minority groups to provide sources of financing (Basu, 1998; Bates, 1997; Boubakri, 1999; Gold, 1992; Lee, 1999; Peterson and Roquebert, 1993; Phizacklea and Ram, 1996; Shin and Han, 1990; Saxenian, 1999; Yoon, 1995). Informal sources of finance are used by entrepreneurs largely due to the difficulties of obtaining formal financing (Basu, 1998; Deakins *et al.*, 1997; Iyer and Shapiro, 1999) Deakins *et al.*, (1995) found that ethnic minority entrepreneurs often provided inadequate information to banks that prevented them from obtaining financing. According to Bates (1997), these weaker start-ups rely on informal sources of financing, like Revolving Credit Associations (RCAs), which are used by the Haitian community in the US (Laguerre, 1998). Contributions to RCAs are made by each member, and each is entitled to share in the accumulated fund, according to pre-arranged guidelines. Boubakri (1999) found that Tunisians in Europe have access to another informal form of credit, ethnically based commerce funds, administered by a 'Godfather'. Tseng (1995) found that Taiwanese in the US, in finance, insurance and real estate, borrow money from ethnic banks. But not all immigrant groups have informal lending associations (for example, none was found by Marger (1989) among the East Indian entrepreneurs in Canada). And, regardless of whether they are informal or formal, these are mechanisms whereby ethnic minority entrepreneurs have access to capital that is not available to non-members of the ethnic minority. We can thus regard them as another attribute of social capital.

ETHNIC-BASED SOCIAL NETWORKS

We will use the *role-set*, *action-set*, and *network* framework of Aldrich *et al.* (1989) to discuss social networks. The *role-set* will depend on factors like the existence of an ethnic enclave, the language fluency of the entrepreneur, the personality of the individual or the culture of the group, and whether he is part of a chain migration, highly connected to his homeland and other immigrants. The *action-set* can be analyzed by looking at the formal and informal organizations and alliances of ethnic minority entrepreneurs. The *network* (for our purposes) will include everyone known to the entrepreneur who can in any way further his business interests. Table 7.2 gives specific information regarding the network by ethnic minority group, country in which the study was conducted and author(s). Included within the network details is information on the format of the network and its relationship to business success. There are two broad categories within Table 7.2. First is the grouping of all the studies that found dense networks (large role-set and action-sets); the second category includes studies which found low-density networks (smaller role-set and action-sets) among their entrepreneurs.

Table 7.2 Incidence, usage and importance of co-ethnic networks

Group	Country	Network details	Author(s) of study
		HIGH-DENSITY NETWORKS – Considered essential for business success (unless otherwise stated)	
African	UK	Network of contacts, key to new markets, best if not just co-ethnic. Network essential to success.	Deakins et al., 1997
Tunisian	France	Formal Godfather, free association, commerce funds, sponsored association. Strong community solidarity.	Boubakri, 1999[F]
Asian	Canada	Strong network. Mostly co-ethnic labor, clients and suppliers. Network part of success.[1]	Juteau and Paré, 1996[F]
	UK	Informal network.	Dhaliwal, 1998
		Network of contacts, key to new markets, best if not just co-ethnic.	Deakins et al., 1997
		Network includes family and community, central role in business operations.	Ram, 1994; Ram et al., 2000
		Ethnic enclaves are embedded networks by industry, vital for bootstrap capitalism = cultural capital.	Werbner, 1999
	US	Informal network overcomes low education barrier to self-employment.[1]	Boyd, 1990
Bangladeshi	UK	Informal sources of capital and advice. Network part of success.	Basu, 1998
Chinese	Canada	Network at pre-start-up stage includes family, friends, associates, professionals, govt agencies. Start-up stage uses, in addition, partners, staff, buyers/suppliers.[1+] Ethnic enclave. Sub-economy includes institutions, contacts, support, co-ethnic labor.[1]	Chu, 1996 — Marger and Hoffman, 1992

Table 7.2 (continued)

Group	Country	Network details	Author(s) of study
Hong Kong		Ethnic enclaves. Community moving to institutional completeness, cultural division of labor theory.	Wang, 1999
		Capitalist transmigration, trans-Pacific networks, astroraut syndrome. 'Family/personal, ethnic, business transnational fields.'[1]	Wong, 1997
		Strong family and friends network. Informal: 42% had family in Canada, 88% had friends network, 67% used it. 50% transnational and used Asia to help Canadian business. Network essential to success.[1]	Wong and Ng, 1998
	Hong Kong	Network at pre-start-up stage includes family, friends, associates. Start-up stage uses, in addition, partners, staff, buyers/suppliers. Maturity stage uses professionals, govt agencies.	Chu, 1996
	UK	Network of contacts, key to new markets, best if not just co-ethnic.	Deakins *et al.*, 1997
	US	Solidarity among ethnic group, informal yet strong network for credit, info. etc., strong competition. Extensive use of family and co-ethnic labor. Network part of success.	Iyer and Shapiro, 1999
		Ethnic business clustering. Co-ethnic advantages (access capital + lower wholesale costs), vertical integration, fierce competition.	Lee, 1999
		Formal and informal, extensive, trans-local, transnational (Taiwanese mostly) prof. and tech. organizations, ethnic linked subcultures. Networks provide entry-points but also duties and sanctions.[1+]	Saxenian, 1999
Indian	Canada	Informal, strong use of networks at every stage in business but differential use. Use female family labor, also source of capital, also co-ethnic labor. Network is used for getting first job, training on job, raising capital, acquiring labor, and clients.	Walton-Roberts and Hiebert, 1997

Group	Country	Description	Reference
		Small, dense co-ethnic and family. Business contacts: 28% no one, 24% one person. Wider community friends also.[1]	Birley and Ghaie, 1992
	UK	Network provides informal source of capital and advice. Network part of success.	Basu, 1998
		Network includes family and community, central role in business operations.	Ram et al., 2000
	US	Formal and informal, extensive, trans-local, transnational (Taiwanese mostly) prof. and tech. organizations, ethnic linked subcultures. Networks provide entry-points but also duties and sanctions.[1+]	Saxenian, 1999
Iranian	US	Informal network. Family–business overlap.	Dallalfar, 1994
		Clustered businesses, co-ethnic labor. Network part of success.	Light et al., 1994
Korean	Canada	Large ethnic community.[1+]	Razin and Langlois, 1996
	US	Solidarity among ethnic group, informal yet strong network for credit, info. etc., strong competition. Extensive use of family and co-ethnic labor. Network part of success.	Iyer and Shapiro, 1999
		Extensive, strong network. Supplies finance, labor, management. Determines success at start and early stages, less long term. Uses family at start, then co-ethnic labor, then non-ethnic. Authority stays with ethnic.	Shin and Han, 1990
		Informal, strong embedded networks, insulated. Access to information, finance, markets, labor. Network essential to success.	Waldinger, 1995
		Enclaves + wider. Extensive family and non-kin networks (church, school etc.). Source of finance and advice. Business clustering. Intra-ethnic business Succession, vertical integration.[1]	Yoon, 1995
Pakistani	UK	Informal sources of capital and advice. Network part of success.	Basu, 1998
		Network includes family and community, central role in business operations.	Ram et al., 2000
	US	Quasi-formal, like formal incubators, based on religion and community.	Greene and Butler, 1996
		Quasi-formal. Bounded solidarity, enforceable trust, no temporal constraints = strong competitive advantage. Network essential to success.	Greene, 1997

Table 7.2 (continued)

Group	Country	Network details	Author(s) of study
Sri Lankan	Canada	Strong network. Mostly co-ethnic labor, clients and suppliers. Network part of success.[1]	Juteau and Paré, 1996[F]
Taiwanese	US	Multi-nuclear economy, not enclave. Reliance on co-ethnic customers and suppliers varies by industry. Extensive and strong network. Linkages to homeland for capital + other resources. Dependency on local network depends on industry type.	Tseng, 1995
Vietnamese	Canada	Strong network. Mostly co-ethnic labor, clients and suppliers. Network part of success[1]	Juteau and Paré, 1996[F]
S. Asian	US	Solidarity among ethnic group, informal yet strong network for credit, info. etc., strong competition. Extensive use of family and co-ethnic labor. Network part of success.	Iyer and Shapiro, 1999
European	Canada	Formal, informal ethnic networks. Also, local networks. Network part of success.[1]	Simard, 1994[F]
Italian	Canada	All belonged to business and ethnic associations. All belonged to ethnic and non-ethnic associations. No strong transnational network to Italy.[1+]	Dana, 1993 Triulzi *et al.*, 1999
Jewish	Canada	Solidarity among ethnic group, informal yet strong network for credit, info. etc., strong competition. Extensive use of family and co-ethnic labor. Network part of success.[1] Large ethnic community.[1]	Juteau and Paré, 1996[F] Razin and Langlois, 1996
	US	Solidarity among ethnic group, strong network for credit, info. etc., strong competition.	Iyer and Shapiro, 1999
	US	Ethnic business clustering. Co-ethnic advantages (access capital + lower wholesale costs), vertical integration, fierce competition.	Lee, 1999

Group	Country	Description	Reference
Cuban	US	Ethnic enclave. Supportive Latin networks, operates like a quasi-formal incubator. Use of co-ethnic labor, markets, suppliers, finance.[1]	Peterson and Roquebert, 1993
	US	No ethnic enclave. Family vital to business success.[1]	Portes and Jensen, 1989
		No ethnic enclave. Family vital to business success.[1]	Portes and Zhou, 1992
Dominican	US	Social capital vital. Strong networks with bounded solidarity, enforceable trust.[1]	Portes and Zhou, 1992
Haitian	US	Extensive use of rotating credit associations, used for start-up, growth, personal financing needs. Risks attached to non-repayment.	Laguerre, 1998
Portuguese	Canada	Multi-nuclear enclaves. Rely on community resources for start-up (family, friends, community organizations, markets and info.) and growth. Extensive and strong network. Social embeddedness, chain migration.	Teixeira, 1998
Across Groups[1]	Canada	Network includes strong links to homeland. Don't transfer all wealth. Network part of success.[1]	Chamard, 1995
Census		Use some co-ethnic suppliers. Playing the 'ethnic card'. Language used to increase affiliation and integration. Network part of success.	Juteau and Paré, 1997[F]

LOW-DENSITY NETWORKS

Group	Country	Description	Reference
African Americans	US	Lack of informal support networks.[1] Lack of co-ethnic advantage. Intra-ethnic diversity leads to low network density and use.	Boyd, 1990; Lee, 1999; Waldinger, 1995

Table 7.2 (continued)

Group	Country	Network details	Author(s) of study
Asian	Canada	Scarcity co-ethnics, low usage networks. Family network mainly.	Bherer and Robichaud, 1997
East Indian	Canada	No enclave, little networking, family and co-ethnic labor but little social capital. Trades in ethnic and general market.[I+/I+]	Marger, 1990, 1989
Vietnamese[R]	US	Informal, small. Capital, labor, markets, info. From own community. Generally refugees have smaller networks.[R/R]	Gold, 1992, 1988
Haitian	Canada	No real use of ethnic network.	Brenner *et al.*, 1992[F]
	Canada	Little financial or legal assistance, small network.	Dana, 1993
Jews (Soviet[R])	US	Informal, small network. Capital, labor, markets, info. From own community. Generally refugees have smaller networks.[R/R]	Gold, 1992, 1988
Latino	US	No enclave. Distrust, social distance, individualistic, family, friends network only.	Pessar, 1995

Note: F = study written in French; R = Refugees; I = Immigrants; I+ = Immigrants and non-immigrants in same ethnic group.

The Role-set

Ethnic enclave
An ethnic enclave where ethnic minority residences and businesses are geographically clustered is a finding of several studies: it was found among the Cubans in Florida (Peterson, 1995, Peterson and Roquebert, 1993), Portuguese in Toronto (Teixeira, 1998) and South Asians in the UK (Aldrich *et al.*, 1989). But there were also multi-nuclear ethnic enclaves, where pockets of ethnic groups were found throughout a metropolitan area (Taiwanese in the US, Tseng, 1995; Chinese in Canada, Wang, 1999). The Koreans in the US have businesses both within the ethnic enclave and outside (Yoon, 1995). Werbner (1999) found that the enclaves were not so much geographical but rather clustered according to particular industry. Some ethnic minority entrepreneurs, like the Iranians (Light *et al.*, 1994), Latinos in the US (Marger, 1990) and East Indians in Canada (Marger, 1990), were not part of an ethnic enclave. Also, educational and financial resources may lead to entrepreneurs distancing themselves from the traditional ethnic enclave.

Language and culture
Our review found some instances where language was a barrier to the entrepreneur trading in the wider market (Boyd, 1990; Iyer and Shapiro, 1999; Min, 1990; Yoon, 1995). As would be expected, refugees did encounter more language problems (Lerner and Hendeles, 1996), which would limit the role-set to those speaking the same language. Regarding culture, some studies found that an individualistic culture, like the East Indians in Canada (Marger, 1990; Walton-Roberts and Hiebert, 1997) and Latinos in the US (Pessar, 1995), limits the role-set and network size.

Chain migration and ethnic solidarity
Some studies indicated there was a strong sense of bounded solidarity and enforceable trust due to shared experiences, culture including language, problems like discrimination and alienation, and shared history (Greene, 1997; Portes and Zhou, 1992; Saxenian, 1999). Chain migration was also found to lead to dense networks both in the new country and in the homeland (Teixeira, 1998).

The Action-set

Formal and informal organizations
Formal and informal ethnically based organizations can be included as part of the alliances of people which form an action-set. Organizations that

assist with financing are at the center of facilitating entrepreneurship (Butler and Greene, 1997), but are not alone. Saxenian (1999), in a qualitative study of entrepreneur and non-entrepreneur Chinese and East Indians in California, provided a rich source of information about organizations. The Silicon Valley Indian Professionals Association, founded in 1991, has 1,000 members and encourages co-operation between professionals in the US and India. The Indus Entrepreneur, founded in 1992, has 560 members and fosters entrepreneurship by mentorship and providing resources. Similar organizations exist for the Chinese. Some of these organizations very much resemble a business incubator whereby nascent entrepreneurs are nurtured by mentoring, seminars on business plan preparation, and introductions to angels and venture capitalists. The thrust of these organizations is to assist members to develop a dense transnational network between the Pacific Rim and the United States. These ethnic organizations can be deeply embedded within the social structures of the group. Kloosterman *et al.* (1999) found that ethnically based trade associations have more influence in stopping illegal practices than government regulations. However, not all ethnic minority entrepreneurs join an ethnic business organization. Birley and Ghaie (1992) found that only 6 per cent of the entrepreneurs in their study belonged to an ethnic-based organization, and in a study by the Centre de la PME de l'UQAH (Small Business Centre of University of Quebec–Hull) (1993), the respondents did not join any associations. In two studies of Italian business people in Canada (Dana, 1993; Triulzi *et al.*, 1999), membership in ethnic and non-ethnic associations was common. But there is little information in the studies we reviewed about the types of ethnic organizations and details about purpose and usage.

Informal advice, mentoring and role models

Our review of studies shows that ethnic entrepreneurs look to members of their ethnic group as a source of informal advice and support, for mentoring and contact with role models (for example, Basu, 1998; Dana, 1993; Yoon, 1995; Dadzie and Cho, 1989; Marger and Hoffman, 1992; Peterson, 1995; Saxenian, 1999).

The Network

A dense, and often transnational, ethnic-based network was present and used by nearly all the entrepreneurs. Still, there were instances where the entrepreneurs were found to have low-density networks consisting mostly of family. Also, the presence of dense ethnic networks was found to positively influence the propensity for self-employment for members of the group (Camarota, 2000).

Network patterns across ethnic groups

Some groups are disadvantaged in terms of ethnic social capital and networks, like the African Americans (Boyd, 1990; Lee, 1999; Waldinger, 1995) and Latinos (Pessar, 1995) in the US, and Haitians in Canada (Brenner *et al.*, 1992; Dana, 1993). Three studies found that East Indians (Marger, 1990, 1989) and Asians (Bherer and Robichaud, 1997) use only small and informal networks, but ten studies from Canada and other countries show evidence of dense networks (Table 7.2). As a group, refugees have smaller networks than immigrants in general (Gold, 1992, 1988). Reynolds and White (1997), studying nascent entrepreneurs (American Indians, Asians, Blacks, Hispanics) across the US, found an absence of dense ethnic networks, leading to the question: when does the accumulation of role-sets and action-sets reach a dense network? In our review we have omitted studies on nascent entrepreneurs. However, network development during the process of pre-start-up and start-up is required (see Chu (1996) in our review). Any other pattern, across different ethnic groups, or by country, is not obvious and further research is required in this area.

SOCIAL CAPITAL AND NETWORKS AS FACTORS IN BUSINESS SUCCESS

As shown in Table 7.2, in 33 instances studies of entrepreneurs from a particular ethnic group showed dense network to be an essential factor in business success. The use of dense networks was considered at least a part of business success in a further 14 studies (Table 7.2). Within the low-density network studies, there is a range of views on the use and value of ethnic networks, from low-density family networks to no real use of an ethnic network. Our review found strong support for the Social Capital Theory and Ethnic Network Advantage as being important factors of business success. Class resources, which include education and financial capital, however, are sometimes considered more important predictors of success (Basu, 1998; Bates, 1994a,b; De Lourdes Villar, 1994; Evans and Jovanovic, 1989; Marger, 1989; Rafiq, 1992; Torres, 1988; Tseng, 1995). For Koreans in the US, Pessar (1995) found that class resources precluded the use of ethnic resources, while Bates and Dunham (1993) found that business success is inversely correlated with the use of social resources among Asian immigrant subgroups in the US. It can be argued, of course, that class resources include other forms of social capital and networks. Selective use of ethnic social capital and dense ethnic networks along with class resources is perhaps a win–win situation (Saxenian, 1999).

SUMMARY AND CONCLUSIONS

We have reviewed some of the multidisciplinary literature on ethnic minority entrepreneurship, social capital and networks. Many studies in our review found strong use of ethnic social capital, including co-ethnic labor, co-ethnic markets and co-ethnic sources of finance. We also found overwhelming evidence of the existence and use of dense co-ethnic networks, in many instances considered to be essential to business success. Often the networks were transnational and integral to international business. We also found that a few ethnic groups did not make use of ethnic resources and lacked dense networks, and mostly used informal family networks. We conclude this chapter by framing our findings as tentative propositions that can act as a guide for further discussion, as research questions for empirical studies and first steps in theory-building.

Social Capital

- Ethnic minority entrepreneurs (EMEs) employ a high percentage of co-ethnic employees, but there are differences linked to ethnicity, industry, market served, language fluency and tenure in a country.
- Co-ethnic labor is a form of social capital but is not always a positive attribute of EME businesses.
- At start-up and during the early stages of a venture, EMEs use family members, particularly women, as a source of low-cost or free labor. Moreover 'hidden women' are often found.
- Co-ethnic family labor is a form of social capital.
- EMEs in the retail and service industries serve mostly co-ethnic markets.
- Excessive clustering of EME businesses in the same co-ethnic market leads to fierce competition and may trigger the use of illegal practices.
- Growth of an ethnic business depends on reaching beyond the co-ethnic market.
- Co-ethnic markets are a form of social capital.
- Co-ethnic suppliers are a form of social capital.
- EMEs utilize personal and family sources of financing as their primary source of start-up and operational funding.
- EMEs, especially the weaker start-ups, experience problems in obtaining early-stage financing.
- Beside personal and family sources of funding, EMEs will utilize ethnic-community-based funding sources, both formal and informal, for start-up and operations.
- Community-based sources of financing are a form of social capital.

Ethnic-based Social Networks

- EMEs' role-set will vary according to whether they are members of an ethnic enclave.
- The class resources of an EME will influence their role-set.
- EMEs host-country language fluency will influence the size of the role-set.
- The size of the role-set will vary according to ethnic group and status of the entrepreneur (immigrant or refugee).
- EMEs belong to ethnic-based social and business organizations with variances in types among groups and entrepreneurs' class resources.
- Well-organized ethnic communities develop means of helping nascent entrepreneurs through use of formal and informal organizations, and act as informal business incubators.
- Dense, often transnational, ethnic-based networks are utilized by EMEs.
- The existence of dense, ethnic-based networks increases the likelihood of self-employment for members of that ethnic group, with repercussions on groups which lack dense co-ethnic networks.
- Ethnic social capital and dense ethnic-based networks are essential components of business success.
- With increased class resources (for example, education and resources), EMEs will place less reliance on the ethnic network.

Theory-building in relation to social capital and ethnic-based social networks can provide valuable information about the process of venture creation, business success and problems, and growth characteristics of ethnic minority business owners. There is considerable scope for future research as relatively few studies focus mainly on social capital and/or networks. There are only a few studies that use a standardized research methodology with different ethnic groups, and more research is required, especially with larger sample sizes. Future studies should also adopt both quantitative and qualitative methodologies to provide a more complete picture of ethnic social capital and networks. A study of the process by which ethnic businesses are established, span the wider market, and eventually become transnational, allows considerable scope for building theory in future studies.[1]

[1] The authors of this chapter are engaged in a collaborative cross-Canada study of immigrant and ethnic entrepreneurs, funded by SSHRC. Over a four-year period, two ethnic groups will be investigated each year for a total of eight groups. Interviews are conducted with 150 entrepreneurs and 150 non-entrepreneurs from each of these ethnic groups (60 of whom are professionals and 90 non-professionals), and are conducted in Montreal, Toronto and Vancouver. The groups studied to date include Chinese, Italian, Jewish and Sikh. Preliminary findings from our research have been presented at learned conferences and included in Working Papers. A partial listing is included in the Appendix.

Research in the area of ethnic minorities and immigrants is often driven by a desire to inform government policy. Our conclusion and tentative propositions are particularly relevant in this respect as this review is firmly rooted in a strong theoretical base generated by scholars from a variety of disciplines. We hope our findings will generate greater interest and research with implications for theory, practice and policy.

REFERENCES

Aldrich, H.E. and R. Waldinger (1990), 'Ethnicity and entrepreneurship', *Annual Review of Sociology*, 16: 111–35.

Aldrich, H.E., R. Waldinger and R. Ward (1990), *Ethnic Entrepreneurs*, London: Sage.

Aldrich, H.E. and C. Zimmer (1986), 'Entrepreneurship through social networks', in D.L. Sexton and R.W. Smilor (eds), *The Art and Science of Entrepreneurship*, Chicago: Upstart, pp. 3–20.

Aldrich, H.E., C. Zimmer and D. McEvoy (1989), 'Continuities in the study of ecological succession: Asian business in three English cities', *Social Forces*, 67(4): 920–44.

Basu, A. (1998), 'An exploration of entrepreneurial activity among Asian small businesses in Britain', *Small Business Economics*, 10(4): 313–26.

Bates, T. (1994a), 'Social resources generated by group support networks may not be beneficial to Asian immigrant-owned small businesses', *Social Forces*, 72(3): 671–89.

Bates, T. (1994b), 'An analysis of Korean-immigrant-owned small-business start-ups with comparisons to African-American and non minority-owned firms', *Urban Affairs Quarterly*, 30(2): 227–48.

Bates, T. (1997), 'Financing small business creation: the case of Chinese and Korean immigrant entrepreneurs', *Journal of Business Venturing*, 12(2): 109–24.

Bates, T. and C. Dunham (1993). 'Asian-American success in self-employment', *Economic Development Quarterly*, 7(2): 199–215.

Bherer, H. and D. Robichaud (1997), *Immigration et entreprenariat dans la région de Québec – Étude sur l'attraction et la rétention d'entrepreneurs immigrants en région*, Québec: Université Laval, mai, 125pp.

Birley, S. and S. Ghaie (1992), 'Networking by the Indian community in Northern Ireland', London, UK: Imperial College, Working Paper.

Bonacich, E., I. Light and C. Wong (1977), 'Koreans in business', *Society*, 14: 54–9.

Boubakri, H. (1999), *Les entrepreneurs migrants d'Europe*, Paris: Culture & Conflits, Sociologie Politique de l'International, Printemps–Été.

Boyd, R.L. (1990), 'Black and Asian self-employment in large metropolitan areas: a comparative analysis', *Social Problems*, 37(2): 258–74.

Brenner, G., G. Célas and J. Toulouse (1992), *New Immigrants and New Businesses: the Chinese and the Haitians in Montreal*, Montréal: Chaire d'Entrepreneurship Maclean Hunter, École des HEC de Montréal, Cahier de recherche #92-03-01.

Butler, J.S. and P.G. Greene (1997), 'Ethnic entrepreneurship: the continuous rebirth of American enterprise', in D.L. Sexton and R.W. Smilor (eds), *Entrepreneurship 2000*, Chicago: Upstart, pp. 267–89.

Camarota, S.A. (2000), *Reconsidering Immigrant Entrepreneurship: an Examination of Self-employment among Natives and the Foreign-born*, Washington, DC: Center for Immigration Studies.

Centre de la PME de l'UQAH (1993), *Profil des gens d'affaires néo–québécois en Outaouais*, Hull: Ministère des communautés culturelles et de l'immigration, Conseil régional de développement de l'Outaouais.

Chamard, R. (1995), *L'entrepreneurship ethnique et les gens d'affaires immigrants*, Montréal: Conseil des communautés culturelles et de l'immigration, février.

Chu, P. (1996), 'Social network models of overseas Chinese entrepreneurship: the experience in Hong Kong and Canada', *Canadian Journal of Administrative Sciences*, 13(4): 358–65.

Cobas, J.A. and I. DeOllos (1989), 'Family ties, co-ethnic bonds and ethnic entrepreneurship', *Sociological Perspectives*, 32(3): 403–11.

Dadzie, K.Q. and Y. Cho (1989), 'Determinants of minority business formation and survival: an empirical assessment', *Journal of Small Business Management*, 27(3): 56–61.

Dallalfar, A. (1994), 'Iranian women as immigrant entrepreneurs', *Gender & Society*, 8(4): 541–61.

Dana, L. (1993), 'An inquiry into culture and entrepreneurship: case studies of business creation among immigrants in Montreal', *Journal of Small Business & Entrepreneurship*, 10(4): 16–31.

De Lourdes Villar, M. (1994), 'Hindrances to the development of an ethnic economy among Mexican migrants', *Human Organization*, 53(3): 263–68.

Deakins, D. (1999), 'Ethnic minority entrepreneurship', in A. Lindsay (ed.), *Entrepreneurship and Small Firms* (2nd ed), Toronto: McGraw-Hill Publishing Company, pp. 80–100.

Deakins, D., D. Hussain and M. Ram (1995). 'Ethnic entrepreneurs and commercial banks: untapped potential', *Regional Studies*, 29(1): 95–100.

Deakins, D., M. Majmudar and A. Paddison (1997), 'Developing success strategies for ethnic minorities in business: evidence from Scotland', *New Community*, 23(3): 325–42.

Dhaliwal, S. (1998), 'Silent contributors: Asian female entrepreneurs and women in business', *Women's Studies International Forum*, 21(5): 463–74.

Dyer, L.M. and C.A. Ross (2000), 'Ethnic enterprises and their clientele', *Journal of Small Business Management*, 39 (2): 48–66.

Evans, D.S. and B. Jovanovic (1989), 'An estimated model of entrepreneurial choice under liquidity constraints', *Journal of Political Economy*, 97(4): 808–27.

Evans, M.D.R. (1989), 'Immigrant entrepreneurship: effects of ethnic market size and isolated labor pool', *American Sociological Review*, 54(6): 950–62.

Feldman, H.D., C.S. Koberg and T.J. Dean (1991), 'Minority small business owners and their paths to ownership', *Journal of Small Business Management*, 29(4): 12–27.

Gold, S.J. (1988), 'Refugees and small business: the case of Soviet Jews and Vietnamese', *Ethnic and Racial Studies*, 11(4): 411–38.

Gold, S.J. (1992), 'The employment potential of refugee entrepreneurship: Soviet Jews and Vietnamese in California', *Policy Studies Review*, 11(2): 176–85.

Greene, P.G. (1997), 'A resource-based approach to ethnic business sponsorship: a consideration of Ismaili–Pakistani immigrants', *Journal of Small Business Management*, 34(4): 58–71.

Greene, P.G. and J.S. Butler (1996), 'The minority community as a natural business incubator', *Journal of Business Research*, 36(1): 51–8.

Huck, P., S.L. Rhine, P. Bond and R.Townsend (1999), 'Small business finance in two Chicago minority neighborhoods', *Economic Perspectives*, 23(2): 46–63.

Iyer, G.R. and J.M. Shapiro (1999), 'Ethnic entrepreneurial and marketing systems: implications for the global economy', *Journal of International Marketing*, 7(4): 83–110.

Juteau, D. and S. Paré (1996), 'L'entrepreneurship ethnique', *Interfaces*, 17(1): 18–28.

Juteau, D. and S. Paré (1997), *Usages linguistiques des entrepreneurs ethniques: portrait des groupes immigrants et natifs de la deuxième ou troisième génération*, Montréal: Immigration et Métropoles, Université de Montréal, juin 1999.

Kloosterman, R., J. Van der Leun and J. Rath (1999), 'Mixed embeddedness: (in)formal economic activities and immigrant businesses in the Netherlands', *International Journal of Urban and Regional Research*, 23(2): 253–67.

Kotkin, J. (1988). *The Third Century*, New York: Crown.

Laguerre, M.S. (1998), 'Rotating credit associations and the diasporic economy', *Journal of Developmental Entrepreneurship*, 3(1): 23–34.

Lee, J. (1999), 'Retail niche domination among African-American, Jewish and Korean entrepreneurs', *American Behavioral Scientist*, 42(9): 1398–417.

Lerner, M. and Y. Hendeles (1996), 'New entrepreneurs and entrepreneurial aspirations among immigrants from the former USSR in Israel', *Journal of Business Research*, 36: 59–65.

Light, I. (1984), 'Immigrants and ethnic enterprise in North America', *Ethnic and Racial Studies*, 7: 195–216.

Light, I, G. Sabagh, M. Bozorgmehr and C. Der-Martirosian (1994), 'Beyond the ethnic enclave economy', *Social Problems*, 41(1): 65–80.

Marger, M.N. (1989), 'Business strategies among East Indian entrepreneurs', *Ethnic and Racial Studies*, 12(4): 539–63.

Marger, M.N. (1990), 'East Indians in small business: middleman minority or ethnic enclave', *New Community*, 16(4): 551–9.

Marger, M.N. and C.A. Hoffman (1992), 'Ethnic enterprise in Ontario: immigrant participation in the small business sector', *International Migration Review*, 26(3): 968–81.

Min, P.G. (1990), 'Problems of Korean immigrant entrepreneurs', *International Migration Review*, 24(3): 436–55.

Muller, T. (1993), *Immigrants and the American City*, New York: New York University Press.

Nee, V. and B. Nee (1986), *Longtime Californ': A Study of American China Town*, Stanford, CA: Stanford University Press.

Pessar, P.R. (1995), 'The elusive enclave: ethnicity, class and nationality among Latino entrepreneurs in Greater Washington, D.C.', *Human Organization*, 54(4): 383–92.

Peterson, M.F. (1995), 'Leading Cuban-American entrepreneurs: the process of developing motives, abilities and resources', *Human Relations*, 48(10): 1193–215.

Peterson, M.F. and J. Roquebert (1993), 'Success patterns of Cuban-American enterprises: implications for entrepreneurial communities', *Human Relations*, 46(8): 921–37.

Phizacklea, A. and M. Ram (1996), 'Being your own boss: ethnic minority entrepreneurs in comparative perspective', *Work, Employment & Society*, 10(2): 319–39.

Portes, A. and L. Jensen (1989), 'The enclave and the entrants', *American Sociological Review*, 54(6): 929–49.

Portes, A. and M. Zhou (1992), 'Gaining the upper hand', *Ethnic and Racial Studies*, 15(4): 491–522.

Rafiq, M. (1992), 'Ethnicity and enterprise: a comparison of Muslim and non-Muslim owned Asian businesses in Britain', *New Community*, 19(1): 43–60.

Ram. M. (1994), 'Unraveling social networks in ethnic minority firms', *International Small Business Journal*, 12(3): 42–53.

Ram, M., T. Abbas, B. Sanghera and G. Hillin (2000), '"Currying favour with the locals": Balti owners and business enclaves', *International Journal of Entrepreneurial Behaviour & Research*, 6(1): 41–55.

Rath, J. and R. Kloosterman (2000), 'Outsider's business: a critical review of research on immigrant entrepreneurship', *International Migration Review*, 34(30): 657–81.

Razin, E. and A. Langlois (1996), 'Metropolitan characteristics and entrepreneurship among immigrants and ethnic groups in Canada', *International Migration Review*, 30(3): 703–27.

Razin, E. and I. Light (1998), 'Ethnic entrepreneurs in America's largest metropolitan areas', *Urban Affairs Review*, 33(3): 332–60.

Reynolds, P.D. and S.B. White (1997), *The Entrepreneurial Process*, London: Quorum.

Robichaud, D. (1999), *L'entrepreneuriat immigrant: revue de la littérature*, Montréal: Chaire d'Entrepreneurship Maclean Hunter, École des HEC, Cahier de recherche #99-05, avril.

Saxenian, A. (1999), *Silicon Valley's New Immigrant Entrepreneurs*, San Francisco: Public Policy Institute of California.

Schumpeter, J.A. (1934), *The Theory of Economic Development: An Inquiry into Profits, Capital, Credit, Interest, and the Business Cycle*. New York: McGraw-Hill.

Shin, E. and S. Han (1990), 'Korean immigrant small businesses in Chicago: an analysis of the resource mobilization process', *Amerasia Journal*, 16(1): 39–60.

Simard, M. (1994), *Les entrepreneurs agricoles immigrants européens: insertion dans la société rurale québécoise*. Montréal: Ministère des Affaires internationales, de l'immigration et des Communautés culturelles, Décembre.

Teixeira, C. (1998), 'Cultural resources and ethnic entrepreneurship: a case study of the Portuguese real estate industry in Toronto', *The Canadian Geographer*, 42(3): 267–81.

Torres, D.L. (1988), 'Success and the Mexican-American businessperson', *Research in the Sociology of Organizations*, 6: 313–34.

Triulzi, U., R. Peterson and R. Blatt (1999), *Italian Canadian Business in the Toronto area: their characteristics and their links to Italy*, Paper presented at the ICSB Annual Meeting, Naples, Italy.

Tseng, Y. (1995), 'Beyond Little Taipei: the development of Taiwanese immigrant businesses in Los Angeles', *International Migration Review*, 29(1): 33–58.

Waldinger, R. (1988), 'The ethnic division of labour transformed: native minorities and new immigrants in post-industrial New York', *New Community*, 14 (4): 318–32.

Waldinger, R. (1995), 'The other side of embeddedness', *Ethnic and Racial Studies*, 18(3): 554–80.

Waldinger, R., H. Aldrich, R. Ward and Associates (eds) (1990), *Ethnic Entrepreneurs*, London: Sage.

Walton-Roberts, M. and D. Hiebert (1997), 'Immigration, entrepreneurship and the family: Indo-Canadian enterprise in the construction industry of greater Vancouver', *Canadian Journal of Regional Science*, 20(1–2): 119–40.

Wang, S. (1999), 'Chinese commercial activity in the Toronto CMA: new development patterns and impacts', *Canadian Geographer*, 43(1): 19–35.

Weber, M. (1930), *The Protestant Ethic and the Spirit of Capitalism*, New York: Charles Scribner and Sons.

Weinfeld, M. (1998), *A Preliminary Stock-taking on Immigration Research in Canada*, prepared for the Metropolis Project and Strategic Policy, Planning & Research Citizenship and Immigration Canada.

Werbner, P. (1999), 'What colour "success"? Distorting value in studies of ethnic entrepreneurship', *The Sociological Review*, 47(3): 548–79.

Wolf, K. (1950), *The Sociology of Georg Simmel*, Glencoe, IL: Free Press.

Wong, L.L. (1997), 'Globalization and transnational migration: a study of recent Chinese capitalist migration from the Asian Pacific to Canada', *International Sociology*, 12(3): 329–51.

Wong, L.L and M. Ng (1998), 'Chinese immigrant entrepreneurs in Vancouver: a case study of ethnic business development', *Canadian Ethnic Studies*, 30(1): 64–85.

Yoon, I. (1995), 'The growth of Korean immigrant entrepreneurship in Chicago', *Ethnic and Racial Studies*, 18(2): 315–35.

Zenner, W. (1991), *Minorities in the Middle: A Cross Cultural Analysis*, Albany: State University of New York Press.

APPENDIX

A sample of conference and working papers reporting our empirical studies is included below. For a copy contact: Professor L.J. Filion, Maclean Hunter Chair of Entrepreneurship, HEC, 3000, chemin de la Cote-Sainte-Catherine, Montreal, Quebec, Canada, H3T 2A7 (e-mail: louisjacques.filion@hec.ca)

- Ethnic entrepreneurship in Canada: Comparison of the Chinese communities in three Canadian cities: Montreal, Toronto and Vancouver (Brenner *et al.*, #2000–08)
- Problems encountered by ethnic Chinese entrepreneurs: A comparative analysis in three major Canadian cities (Brenner *et al.*, #2000–10)
- Ethnic entrepreneurship. Data from a survey of Chinese communities in the Canadian cities of Montreal, Toronto and Vancouver (Brenner *et al.*, #2000–12)
- Ethnic entrepreneurship: Data from a survey of Italian communities in the Canadian cities of Montreal, Toronto and Vancouver (Menzies *et al.*, #2001–02)
- Characteristics and features of Chinese and Italian ethnic entrepreneurship in Canada: Implications for business, research and government policy (Filion *et al.*, #2001–05)

- Chinese, Italian and Sikh Ethnic entrepreneuers in Canada: Implications for the research agenda, education programs and public policy (Filion *et al.*, #2001–08)
- Ethnic entrepreneurship: Data from a survey of Sikh communities in the Canadian cities of Montreal, Toronto and Vancouver (Ramangalahy *et al.*, # 2001–10)

8. Small business in the Czech Republic and Japan: successes and challenges for women entrepreneurs

Terri R. Lituchy, Philip Bryer and Martha A. Reavley*

INTRODUCTION

Throughout the world, women are starting and operating their own business at a much greater rate than are men (*Economist*, 1996; Chandler and Murphy, 1994; Capowski, 1992). Many of these entrepreneurs are involved in international business (Knight, 2000). From 1980 to 1994, the number of female entrepreneurs has tripled in the US to almost eight million. One-third of all US businesses are owned by women (Esters, 1997). On an international basis, the growth rate of women-owned businesses is similar to that of the United States (OECD, 1986; Silvestri and Lukasiewicz, 1987). In the Czech Republic, for the first time in over 50 years, women as well as men have the opportunity to start their own businesses and to earn a profit. In several Asian countries, such as Japan, the economic crisis has reduced the opportunities for women in large firms. The crisis has forced many Japanese women to work outside the home to supplement their husbands' incomes. These conditions have provided entrepreneurial Japanese women with a reason to start their own small businesses.

The purpose of this chapter is to understand women small-business owners in other cultures, specifically the Czech Republic and Japan. Interviews with women entrepreneurs in both countries were used as the basis for this qualitative case-study research.

Many researchers have examined the differences between male and female entrepreneurs in the United States. They have found differences in

* Earlier versions of this paper were presented at ASAC and Applied Business Research conferences. Partial funding for this research was provided by CIDA (through CCMS), FCAR (Quebec) and Concordia University to the first author while on faculty at Concordia University. The authors would like to thank S. Yadav and K. Hattori for their assistance with data collection.

demographics, personality characteristics and traits (Hisrich and Brush, 1983; Schwartz, 1979), education and experience (Birley *et al.*, 1987; Buttner and Rosen, 1988; Hisrich and Brush, 1983), and in obtaining finances (Brush, 1992). Schein and her colleagues have found differences in the perceived characteristics of successful men and women in different cultures (Schein *et al.*, 1996). One objective of this chapter is to examine the traits and characteristics of women small-business owners in the Czech Republic and Japan.

The democratization of Central and Eastern Europe marked the beginning of a transition to a free-market economy and privatization. The transition also liberated a new economic force: the female entrepreneur. In the wake of the Velvet Revolution of November 1989 in the Czech Republic, many small businesses were created, and women have started, own or manage a significant number of them. Many of these businesses were 'born global', which means that they were linked to international networks of suppliers and customers from the earliest stages. The global connection brings with it additional difficulties, of course, such as dealing with people from other cultures.

In Japan, the corporate world is perceived as a man's domain. Women are seldom part of corporate management, nor do they typically receive the benefits of lifetime employment. A woman is expected to quit her job after marriage or pregnancy to take care of children and run the household. Perhaps because of these inequities and expectations, women entrepreneurs in Japan remain relatively rare, although their numbers are increasing. According to Nakada (2000), the Teikoku Databank shows that the proportion of women-owned or women-run companies in Japan is 5.4 per cent. Over 2.5 million Japanese women run their own small business, usually with less than five employees (Steinhoff and Tanaka, 1998).

Hofstede's well-known study of national cultures is relevant here. It provides a means of understanding why women forge ahead on their own as entrepreneurs despite their previous experiences of glass ceilings and other forms of work-related discrimination and regardless of the widespread idea that women should stay at home to care for their families. For example, in Hofstede's 'masculinity index' Japan ranks number one among the 50 countries and three regions in the study. A 'masculine' society is one in which 'social gender roles are clearly distinct (i.e., men are supposed to be assertive, tough, and focused on material success whereas women are supposed to be more modest, tender, and concerned with the quality of life)'. On the other hand, a 'feminine' society is one 'in which social gender roles overlap (i.e., both men and women are supposed to be modest, tender, and concerned with the quality of life)'. The only Eastern European nation included in his study – Russia – shares with El Salvador the 40th position (which Hofstede labels 'strongly to moderately feminine') in the bottom third of the countries and regions (Hofstede, 1991, pp. 82–3, 84; 1993, Table 1). One might suppose from the differences related to the masculinity/femininity dimension that women in feminine societies would be more inclined to enter the business world or to start their own businesses because, according to Hofstede, boys and girls in a feminine society receive similar educations and because both share a concern for warm human relationships. This supposition, however, is incorrect:

> Ambitious women are more frequently found in masculine rather than feminine societies. In feminine societies the forces of resistance against women entering higher jobs are weaker; on the other hand the candidates are less ambitious. These two influences seem to neutralize each other so that women in feminine societies do not enter higher jobs in much larger numbers than in masculine societies. (Hofstede, 1991, p. 96)

In short, the masculine dimension of Japanese society is precisely what fosters ambition in Japanese women and helps them overcome many obstacles on the road to becoming successful entrepreneurs.

The successful woman entrepreneur in the Czech Republic and Japan can be an important mentor, role model and advisor to other women considering starting businesses throughout the former Communist Bloc or newly industrialized economies (NIEs) in Asia, respectively. Understanding the keys to their success and the challenges these women face may suggest public policy and foreign aid initiatives to support women entrepreneurs in general in other countries. Therefore, a second objective of this research is to explore the challenges and keys to success faced by women entrepreneurs in these countries in transition. A third objective is to determine whether any of three different models of entrepreneurship in North America (environmental, traits, and behavioral) apply to women small-business owners in Japan and the Czech Republic. As the field of international entrepreneurship expands, it is important to examine whether the theories and models of entrepreneurship developed in the West apply to other cultures. Three common models of entrepreneurship are described below and serve as the basis for this study.

Women Entrepreneurs

While American male and female entrepreneurs have much in common, the experience of women entrepreneurs has distinct differences as well. According to US literature, women entrepreneurs may choose to start businesses for reasons different from those of men and often face barriers that make it more challenging for them to establish, operate and grow their businesses (Brush, 1992). Many women decide to create their own businesses as a consequence of discriminatory treatment at work (Capowski, 1992). Like their Japanese counterparts, American women may perceive that a 'glass ceiling' has obstructed their career progress by preventing them from reaching the top positions in organizations. Therefore, starting a business serves as a means of accomplishing levels of personal success otherwise unattainable to them as employees.

Business ownership, however, is not necessarily a haven from gender discrimination. Even in the early stages of starting a business, women entrepreneurs often experience greater difficulty than men. Historically, for instance, the lending policies of many financial institutions in the United States have disadvantaged women in obtaining capital for their enterprises (Brush, 1992). All too often, therefore, female entrepreneurs have been forced to rely on personal and family financial resources. Consequently, female-owned businesses may be undercapitalized from start-up, a frequent cause of business failure.

Although American women entrepreneurs tend to be well educated, they frequently lack specific business education and training (Brush, 1992) as well as experience in management, accounting, marketing and finance (Buttner and Rosen, 1988; Hisrich and Brush, 1987). Training in skills such as writing a business plan, accounting, marketing and human resources management can contribute to the survival and success of new ventures. Where business-training programs are unavailable, however, women may be unable to acquire the necessary business knowledge, thus further reducing their chances of success.

The social and cultural roles played by women may place an additional burden on them (Stoner *et al.*, 1990; Capowski, 1992). In Japan and many other countries, women are still expected to take care of the children and the home (Hofstede, 1991, p. 81). In the Czech Republic, on the other hand, it is generally acceptable for women to hold jobs outside the home. Regardless of the cultural expectations or norms, however, women who work outside the home must juggle many roles as wife, mother, daughter and businesswoman. They are usually expected to take on most of the household duties while simultaneously working as employees, managers or business owners. The skill with which women perform the balancing act and the degree of support they receive from friends and relatives are key determinants of the success or failure of their enterprises.

Studies by Schein and her colleagues in the 1970s found that respondents tended to define a successful manager in terms of masculine characteristics, such as assertiveness, aggressiveness and competitiveness. Women were perceived as having more tender characteristics. This gender-based distinction had largely disappeared by the 1990s. By that time, respondents in the US were just as likely to attribute the characteristics of a successful manager to women as to men. In other countries, such as Thailand and Japan, however, women continued to be seen as less likely to be successful managers and to have more tender and caring characteristics than men (Schein *et al.*, 1996).

For self-employed women, success can be defined as length of time in business (Waddell, 1982). Since most small businesses that fail do so in the first three years, women in business longer than three years can be seen as successful. Several Western authors have stated that women entrepreneurs are less concerned with profits and more concerned with community than male small-business owners (for example, Godfrey, 1995). These differences in attitude are reflected in women's definitions of success, which often involve an emphasis on individual achievement and recognition from others. Another study found that women are more concerned than men about the quality of their relationships with clients and suppliers (as opposed to the number of such relationships) and about the welfare and happiness of their employees (Esters, 1997). Yet other studies show that many female small-business owners feel that they are not taken seriously. (See Godfrey, 1995.)

Based on the above discussion, the following research questions for women entrepreneurs are explored:

1. What is their definition of success?
2. What types of business and personal problems have they encountered and to what extent has being female played a role in those problems?
3. How do they describe their decision-making and leadership styles?
4. What, if any, business training or education did they receive and how would they assess the impact of such training?
5. How well do these women fit the North American models of entrepreneurship?

North American Models of Entrepreneurship

The entrepreneurial process includes the environmental, traits and behavioral models (Ibrahim, 1990, 1994). Each model provides an approach or way of understanding the most important motivational influences, character traits and necessary managerial skills of successful entrepreneurs. These three models will be used in this study. The environmental approach to entrepreneurship states that the entrepreneur may have either a role model (parent or spouse) or a rejection model. The rejection model applies to those entrepreneurs who start their own businesses because they have been rejected by the family, work, or society (Ibrahim, 1994). The rejection or 'push factor' may take the form of frustration about limited advancement, job dissatisfaction or an unreasonable boss (Buttner, 1997; Hisrich and Brush, 1987). Many North American women decide to create their own businesses as a consequence of discriminatory treatment in work organizations (Buttner, 1997; Capowski, 1992). They may feel that their career progress has been halted by a 'glass ceiling' that prevents them from reaching the top positions in organizations. Starting a business may thus serve as a means of accomplishing levels of personal success otherwise unattainable to them as paid employees.

A second model, the traits approach to entrepreneurship (Ibrahim, 1994; McClelland, 1987), shows that most entrepreneurs in North America display similar traits, such as a high need for achievement, risk-taking, tolerance of ambiguity, creativity, intuition, flexibility, high need for autonomy, self-confidence, internal locus of control, adaptability, dominance, low need for conformity, commitment, pro-activity and sense of observation. Studies in the US have found that women and men may have similar personality traits (Hisrich and Brush, 1985; Schwartz, 1979). One important characteristic that is not included in the Traits Approach, however, is humor. Graham and Duncan (1995) state, 'Good humor helps tremendously when you have just taken the giant step of opening your own law firm.' In this chapter, therefore, humor will be considered along with the other chief characteristics.

The third approach is behavioral (Ibrahim and Goodwin, 1986). It describes what managerial skills and competencies entrepreneurs should have and use in their small businesses. These include strategic niche or distinctive competencies, cash flow management, strategic planning, accounting and record keeping, marketing, networking and delegating. Previous research in the United States has found that women have more difficulties obtaining capital than do men (Schwartz, 1979). Women also lack experience in management, marketing and advertising, accounting and finance (Buttner, 1997; Brush, 1992; Hisrich and Brush, 1987).

Based on the above research and studies, questions were developed for the interviews with the Czech and Japanese entrepreneurs in order to find out about their small businesses, including such issues as start-up, globalization, successes and failures. The interview protocol, along with a description of the women interviewed, is described in the method section below. Qualitative results of these questions as well as of the three models of entrepreneurship follow.

METHOD

Participants

Six Czech and six Japanese women entrepreneurs participated in this study. In the Czech Republic, the Czech Business and Professional Women's Association (APM) was first contacted for help in locating entrepreneurial women. Women were chosen from the APM catalogue to participate based on two criteria: (1) their availability in either Prague or in the nearby sur-rounding region, and (2) their ability to meet with the researchers at a mutually convenient time.

In Japan, the Director of the Small and Medium Size Enterprise Asso-ciation was first contacted for help in locating entrepreneurial women. The Director made the arrangements for the meeting between the research-ers and the women based on two criteria: (1) their availability in either Tokyo or Nagoya, and (2) their ability to meet with the researchers at a mutually convenient time. All of the women contacted agreed to be inter-viewed.

Procedure

The researchers first contacted the women entrepreneurs by phone and explained the purpose of the study to them. The time and place of the inter-view were confirmed. Like research in this area conducted in other coun-tries (McCarthy *et al.*, 1997; Pellegrino and Reece, 1982), the case-study method was employed for the purpose of data collection. A bilingual research assistant conducted structured interviews in Czech or Japanese, and tape-recorded them with the permission of the interviewees.

Questionnaire

Structured, open-ended questions were used as the primary data-gathering instrument. In the first part of the interview, each participant was asked to provide demographic information, including name, educational back-ground, work experience, marital status and number of children. In the second part of the interview, each participant was asked (1) to give a brief history of her business and to explain why she decided to start it; (2) what problems she faced at the start-up stage; and (3) what she most enjoys about being in business.

In the third part of the interview, each participant provided further back-ground information on her business, including type, year registered, own-ership, products/services, customers, competition, size, growth in sales and number of employees. In part four of the interview, each participant was asked open-ended questions about the successes and challenges she faced. Specifically, she was asked to describe any problems she had encountered in several business management areas, including finance, marketing, technology, production, managing people and government regulations. Each woman was also asked to identify the decision-making style she used and to summarize what it means to her to be a woman in business. Finally, each entrepreneur was asked to discuss her plans for the future.

Analyses

The interview tapes were transcribed and translated into English by bilingual research assistants. The researchers coded the transcripts following the methods described by Yin (1984) and Miles and Huberman (1984). Transcripts were then analyzed and coded by two of the researchers, individually, for each dimension of the three models of entrepreneurship. Next, the researchers compared results. Inter-rater reliability ranged from 85 to 98 per cent for each of the women in the study. The researchers then reviewed any differences and came to an agreement on each of these items.

RESULTS

Demographics

Demographic information about the entrepreneurs interviewed is presented below and summarized in Table 8.1. The Czech entrepreneurs were all very well educated and most of them held master's degrees. Of the Japanese women interviewed only two attended universities, one in economics and one in business. Most of the women were currently married and had children or had been married. Like their counterparts in the USA, most of the Japanese entrepreneurs had to balance the role of wife and mother with that of businesswoman. The older, unmarried Japanese women had more business experience than the younger ones. On the other hand, because the Czech Republic is a newly industrialized economy, most of the Czech women did not have any previous business experience.

The names of the women who participated in this study have been changed to protect their anonymity. Fictitious names are used here in alphabetical order for the reader's convenience.

Czech entrepreneur Ana worked as a translator and interpreter immediately following the revolution. In 1993, she decided to open her own travel agency in Prague. She participated in the business skills training program

Table 8.1 Demographics

Name	Type of business	Year established	Location	Previous experience	Business education or training	Global?
Czech						
Ana	Travel agency	1993	Prague	Translator/ Interpreter	USAID training	Start-up
Beata	Import/Market research	1993	Prague	No	USAID training	Start-up
Catarina	Travel agency	1993	Prague	No	No	Start-up
Dana	Advertising agency	1996	Prague	No	No	Yes
Eva	Personnel-consulting firm	1996	Pilzen	No	USAID training	Yes
Frieda	Personnel-consulting firm	1992	Pilzen	No	USAID training	Start-up
Japanese						
Ando	Computer company	1993	Tokyo	Over 45 years	No	Yes
Ban	Sundries imports and sales	1993	Yokohama	No	No	Yes
Chiba	Newspaper publishing	1898	Tokyo	No	Studied economics	Yes
Doi	Marketing of handicrafts	1970	Yokohama	Over 30 years	Studied management	Yes
Egami	Sundries–apparel importing and sales	1990	Tokyo	Over 10 years	No	Start-up
Fuma	Medical supply company	1972	Nagoya	No	No	Yes

in the United States in the summer of 1996. Entrepreneur Beata opened an import company in Prague in 1990 and built it into a highly respected market research firm. She also attended the same training program as Ana in 1996. Entrepreneur Catarina started a travel agency in Prague. She has been in business for five years. She did not attend the training program. Entrepreneur Dana started an advertising agency in Prague in April 1996. She did not participate in the training program. Entrepreneur Eva is from Pilzen. After she participated in the training program in the United States (summer 1995), she decided to start her own personnel-consulting firm (January 1996). Entrepreneur Frieda is also from Pilzen. She has owned a personnel-consulting firm since 1992 and attended the training program in 1996.

Japan entrepreneur Ando has owned several of her own businesses since she graduated from high school over 45 years ago. She currently has a computer company. Entrepreneur Ban has been in business for six years. She sells sundries and trades with firms outside Japan. Entrepreneur Chiba started her own company in 1989 after she graduated from university where she studied economics. She publishes newspapers for women and mothers. Entrepreneur Doi founded her company when she was 26 years old after studying management at a university. She has been in business for well over 30 years and both markets handicrafts made by Japanese women and helps them start their own businesses. Entrepreneur Egami started her own business when the company she was working for went bankrupt. She buys sundries and apparel from overseas to sell in Japan. She has been running her own business for about ten years. Entrepreneur Fuma is the president of the medical research laboratory where she originally worked as a technician assistant. She has been managing the company for over 27 years.

Defining Success

As stated above, success may be defined as recognition from others, individual achievement, quality of the relationship with clients and number of years in business. All of the Czech entrepreneurs defined success in terms of the number of clients or projects they have and the extent to which the business attracts international clients and customers. The Japanese women also mentioned clients or number of years in business. Several of the Japanese women stated that they did not yet know what success was. In other words, they did not mention individual achievement, although they had been in business for several years. This is consistent with Japanese cultural norms that discourage praise of oneself.

Ana and Frieda talked about important clients from Japan or Russia. Ana, for example, talked about important clients from Russia and Poland

and a network of contacts. Frieda stated, 'I consider what we did for them a big job and also a big success'. She also stated that her experience in the United States contributed to her success by changing her management style and increasing her customer satisfaction. Although Dana had been in business only a short time, she said success for her was that people knew about her business and that her number of clients was increasing. Catarina defined success in terms of both an increase in the number of clients and the long-term relationships with them.

For Beata, success was defined more personally. While she was extremely proud of her business accomplishments, these achievements were tempered by a sense that she was personally unfulfilled. Dana, the owner of the advertising agency, also felt that business success came at personal cost. Although Dana had been in business only a short time, she said success meant that people knew about her business and more clients were attracted to it. Catarina defined success in terms of both increasing the number of clients and working with them on a long-term basis.

Japanese entrepreneur Ando believes that her initial success in business resulted from her ability to be 'ahead of everyone else by half a step'. This insight led her to start a computer company in 1967. In the contemporary world of rapid development and tough competition, however, Ando has found that being ahead just a half a step is not enough to bring success. 'At present', she claims, 'two steps ahead might be better.'

Entrepreneur Ban imports and sells 'general sundries', which she defines as small inexpensive items like key rings, toys and miscellaneous goods sold in fashionable, youth-oriented stores like Tokyu Hands. The current economic slump and the appearance in Japan of discount shops have made business 'difficult', so Ban claims that it is not easy for her to 'know what success is'. She wants to create businesses that allow other entrepreneurs to 'show his or her real ability'. For Ban, success is related to personal fulfillment.

After graduating from university, entrepreneur Chiba found that she 'wanted to do something with others', and so – on a very small scale – she began to circulate a free newspaper produced by volunteers. It was, she affirms, her way of saying 'Here I am!' to society. From these modest beginnings, Chiba moved into new territory. Her strength was her belief that she could do something creative and different: 'I could not win if I did the same things as other people. My strategy was to publish a newspaper for mothers, the first one ever in Japan.' Like Ban, Chiba also thinks that she has not yet succeeded. She believes, however, that her success in the future will grow out of the network of relationships she has created with the women all over Japan and abroad who read her newspaper.

From the beginning of her career, entrepreneur Doi has defined success in terms of helping others and building trust. It has been her lifelong dream to help women 'live independently' by marketing the goods they make at home, such as children's clothing and other handicrafts. In the course of her long career, she has demonstrated her commitment to women by helping them start 'community businesses'. 'Gaining their trust has been one of my successes', Doi believes. Entrepreneurial independence and involvement in a community are Doi's idea of success.

For entrepreneur Egami, success is the challenge of improving both manufacturing processes and workers' general health. The effort to do so also helps her to build solid relationships between herself and the manufacturers in India, China and Korea with whom she makes contracts to produce various textiles and finished goods. 'To see these people [the factory workers in China] smile', she declares, 'was as important as to meet the client's request.' To achieve the smiles and the improved manufacturing processes is a source of joy for Egami. She states, 'That's what business is, isn't it? I hope it is. So I'm waiting for someone who needs me.'

Entrepreneur Fuma is currently the only president of a medical research and manufacturing laboratory in Japan. Lacking a female role model or mentor, she has had to shape her career and forge an executive identity on her own during the 27 years she has run the company. Survival itself is thus one component of her success.

Business- and/or Gender-related Problems

Question 2 addresses the types of business and personal problems faced by female entrepreneurs. As with American entrepreneurs, most of the women interviewed were concerned about how to start a business, where to get the funding, how to find clients or customers, and whom to hire. Many of Czech entrepreneurs had human resources management problems. This may reflect the stresses of coping with a transitional economy that places new emphasis on such factors as individual initiative and the need to reconfigure the employee–employer relationship. Because of their culture and society's attitude toward working women, several of the Japanese women stated that they had a hard time being taken seriously either by their families or by customers.

Czech entrepreneur Ana said she faced many problems every day. However, her greatest concern was finding the right people. In order to maintain high professional standards when dealing with foreign customers, she needed Czech employees with English and German-language skills. People with such skills, however, are in great demand in the Czech Republic. They are difficult to recruit and expensive to maintain. Small businesses find themselves competing with large multinational organizations for the same talent.

Beata was the owner of one of the first private businesses to open in Prague after the revolution. At that time, many Western nations offered a variety of financial and technical support to the 'new capitalists'. As a result, she did not have many problems: 'When I started my business the advantage was that everything was new . . . I benefited from people helping me.'

By comparison, Eva, who just recently started her business, said that she faced bureaucratic barriers and little useful support from Czech government agencies. The international aid that had benefited early entrants into business was no longer available. The location of the various agencies also proved to be a problem for her: 'It takes a lot of time to go from one office to another . . . and I discovered that there is not much government support for small businesses.'

Catarina's problems also involved 'how to start a business, where to find clients and knowing what they want in terms of price and quality'. Frieda needed start-up money and was not sure how to deal with either international competition or the problems of hiring and managing the right people.

Ando has been in business for over 45 years. At the beginning of the interview, she claimed that she did not recall having many problems as a businesswoman, but later she mentioned that she had not been able to borrow money from banks when she was opening her first store during the post-war baby boom. 'Banks didn't lend money at that time', she said. Consequently, like many other women in Japan, Ando was forced to finance her business personally. She also knew little about marketing. Nevertheless, she had determined that she would give up the idea of marriage in order to run her business, so she 'studied very hard' to fill in the gaps in her knowledge. Ando 'never thought it a disadvantage' to be a woman in an industry dominated almost entirely by men. She did, however, feel some discomfort when she joined an organization of both men and women: 'I felt troubled by the presence of the women as I had never been when I was the only woman among all the businessmen.'

At age 28, after quitting her job because she had become pregnant, entrepreneur Ban decided she had some innovative ideas for a new 'niche business' that would allow her to market sundries in Japan. At first, her chief problem was that she knew very little about how to run a business or deal with such issues as taxes. For example she worried that she would not have enough money left after paying her taxes to buy goods. Moreover, as time passed and the growing business demanded more and more of her time, she feared that she was sacrificing her husband and child to the business she had begun for their sake. For extended periods she lived on two hours of sleep per day and 'almost forgot my husband's presence'. Her business was sometimes dismissed by potential clients as nothing more than the amateurish expansion of a 'woman's hobby'. Moreover, in Japan important business relationships are formed after hours in drinking establishments but, as a married woman and mother, she was excluded: 'I could not join in', she explained. Obtaining an adequate loan from a bank was not easy either. When asked by a bank official to identify her assets in order to secure the loan, she replied, 'One child and a car'. The loan subsequently offered by the bank was inadequate, so Ban 'decided to finance my business myself'. A positive result of her decision is that she now has almost no debt. The most serious problems she currently faces are the proliferation of cut-rate shops that have reduced her profits, the difficulty of finding competent employees, and the 'uneasy' business climate in recession-plagued Japan.

Like Ban, entrepreneur Chiba has encountered negative attitudes about her 'newspaper for mothers'. Some people immediately conclude that any 'company of mothers' must be second rate. For instance, when Chiba was running the business from her home, she set aside one room for her own children and those of her co-workers. On one occasion, a client telephoned but was put off by the sound of children in the background and so ended the business relationship. At the same time, she admits that training mothers 'is very hard work' because they are accustomed to being the 'ruler in the home' and so do not quickly adapt to the disciplines of the business world. They also, of course, lack experience and good business sense. Although she attended business school, she feels she has problems explaining her business strategies and tactics. Also like Ban, Chiba did not borrow from banks to finance her business and feels that Japanese banks continue to be reluctant to lend start-up money to women.

When entrepreneur Doi left university and began working in the 1960s, the general expectation was that a young woman would soon leave her job to get married. Instead, Doi left her job to begin her first business enterprise with 'no capital or personal connections'. What she did have was her intelligence, which, as she said to herself at the time, 'I can sell'. Despite her intelligence, Doi encountered resistance when she applied for bank loans because, as she put it, 'bankers make their decisions on the basis of a woman's marital status'. An unmarried woman thus has little chance of getting an adequate loan. Her decision to market women's handicrafts grew out of her own experience of trying to live independently in the face of so many stereotypes about women's roles. She refused to accept the widespread notion that entrepreneur Ban encountered when people characterized the work women do at home as amateurish. Instead, Doi saw that women could 'make money from their hobbies'.

Entrepreneur Egami began her career as an independent business owner when her Japanese employer went bankrupt. Instead of accepting this failure, she transformed it into an opportunity. Realizing that the Chinese manufacturer who produced textiles for the Japanese company would be seriously hurt by the bankruptcy, and because she did not want to see this happen, Egami decided to step in and take over the business of her former employer. As mentioned earlier, the poor state of the Chinese workers' health and the poor quality of the textiles produced by the factory were among the most serious problems she faced in China. On a personal level, Egami admits she has placed burdens on her husband because she is so often absent from home. In addition, some of the men she encountered in her business dealings made inappropriate advances to her. 'It became such a problem psychologically', she admitted, 'that I refused to work with them.' She feels now that she has made her position clear about the proper boundaries of a working relationship and only conducts business 'with people I like personally in China, India, the States and Japan'.

Perhaps because entrepreneur Fuma is the only female president of a company in her industry – medical and biological R&D – she did not experience many problems related to gender discrimination. Like the other female entrepreneurs, however, she had difficulty financing her company because private banks were not willing to lend money. Fortunately, she was able to obtain financial support from government banks and private investors whom she called 'Angels'.

Decision-making and Leadership Styles

The women were asked to describe their decision-making and leadership styles. Although the Czech women are the sole owners of their businesses, most say they consult others when making decisions. Although Ana makes her own decisions, she discusses things with people and said that she has learned the importance of having good staff. Her leadership style is autocratic. Beata is more consultative and stated, 'We discuss and exchange ideas. I love the brainstorming process, but I make the decision.' Catarina is also consultative. For example, she often consults her 28-year-old son before she makes a decision: 'I am not very well educated in management, so whatever I do, I do intuitively. I would like to take some managerial courses, but if the need for decisions arises, I often first think a lot about it and then discuss it with my son. Then we come to a conclusion.'

The entrepreneurs always made final decisions and could be characterized as strong, somewhat autocratic leaders. This leadership style is often prevalent among entrepreneurs, particularly those with relatively small businesses in the early stages of development. Dana consults others only when she is unsure what to do, but she makes the final decisions herself. Eva sometimes discusses or consults with employees; then she chooses what is best for them to do. Frieda is also somewhat autocratic and declared that 'I make all of the decisions'.

In Japan, entrepreneur Ando has made an effort to break down the formality and discomfort that so often exist between the president of a company and her employees. For the last six years, she has given a large birthday cake and a card to each of her employees. She also keeps careful notes on individual employees' 'characteristics' so that she can write personal comments on the cards. The result has been improved relations throughout the company.

Given the difficulty of finding skilled staff, entrepreneur Ban has created a training program to introduce new employees to her company. She has also taken the unusual step of bringing men and women in their forties into the company to benefit from their experience. When it comes to improvements in her company, she says, 'I am always resolute'.

Newspaper publisher Chiba has demonstrated impressive flexibility and creativity in her management of the newspaper for mothers. For example she has extended the reach of the publication by opening a website on the Internet. She has also understood that the economic slump in Japan actually represents an opportunity for women since the 'hard times' have diminished the traditional resistance to their working outside the home. Mothers now have a chance to 'do whatever'. She also recognizes, however, that business requires commitment and discipline. Women have to prove themselves to a skeptical society. 'Therefore', Chiba declares, 'I'm very severe on my employees. I'm a dictatorial president'. She tells the women who come to work for her that they must not be 'dependent' or make excuses for themselves because they are mothers. In the end, Chiba believes that achieving a balance between work and childcare is impossible. One simply does the best one can given the reality that in business one 'has to carry out one's duties. If you don't, the business will not prosper.'

Like Chiba's, Doi's leadership style is flexible and creative. She has been quick to take advantage of changing attitudes and to recognize that as the resistance to women working diminishes, the evaluation of their handicrafts will improve and the market for them will also grow. As a leader, Doi also looks for future trends that will present opportunities to nimble entrepreneurs. She has recognized, for example, that Japanese society is changing in ways that will profoundly alter current ideas about the proper roles for women and men. 'Japanese society', she believes, 'is becoming one in which men and women share the housework, childcare, and care for aged relatives.' These changes will create new needs and new marketing opportunities. Among those she is currently studying is the need for new kinds of housing as the function of traditional homes changes and the population ages. She foresees the growth of businesses that cater to 'group homes' and 'group housing'.

Egami's leadership style might be characterized as 'tough love'. Faced with

serious quality problems and unhealthy workers at the Chinese manufacturing facility, for instance, she attacked both problems head-on. To deal with
the high number of defects, she positioned herself beside the manufacturing
line, a pair of sharp scissors in hand, ready to cut up defects as they appeared.
To improve the workers' health she bought them large quantities of inexpensive seasonal fruits at local markets. She also distributed Japanese medicines
to those workers suffering from bacterial colitis. And when the defects
dropped to the level she had insisted on and the first big order had been
shipped, she invited everyone to dinner, about 70 people in all. 'I invited all
the employees', she said, 'including the woman who worked in the elevator'.

In her commitment to equality and to the welfare of her employees' families, President Fuma resembles Egami. She is a risk-taker, for although her
medical and biological R&D company has the advantage of holding a 90
per cent market share in Japan, she is thinking about entering the much
more competitive international arena. This plan increases the pressure on
her to ensure that her company 'can survive with limited capital and human
resources'.

Impact of Business Education and Training

The four Czech women who participated in the APM business training
program in the US felt that they benefited significantly from the experience.
They felt they had a much better idea of how to run a business; how to
obtain loans; and how to select, train and motivate employees. For
example, when asked about the problems she faced, Beata could not recall
any: 'Right now, I cannot think of any problems. I would say that I studied
a lot and learned. The training helped me to look at the company in
different ways, to see how marketing works, how you should prepare your
offers, what you should discuss with clients.'

Entrepreneur Ando attended a girls' high school after the war, but her
knowledge of business and computers comes from the studying she has
done on her own and from hands-on experience. When asked to comment
of the value of her formal education in terms of running her own business,
Ando declared that there was 'No relationship' between them.

Entrepreneur Ban also has derived her knowledge of business from
hands-on experience and trial and error. She left her salaried position to
start her own company at age 28, but she admits she 'didn't know what a
company was'. Over the ensuing six years, she gradually gained experience
and learned how to be a manager.

As a 'corresponding student', Entrepreneur Chiba earned a degree in
economics at a well-respected university in Tokyo. With three children at
home, it took her ten years to complete the course. She also briefly attended

a business school but, she claims, 'I couldn't understand it at all.' Given her frustrations with business school, she decided it would be better for her to quit and instead start her newspaper business. When asked what training she thinks would be useful to people who are running their own businesses, Chiba replied, 'None. Just do it and learn.'

Entrepreneur Doi studied management at university, but her interest in marketing the handicrafts made by women led her into relatively unknown territory in Japan. As she pointed out, a person interested in starting a business can find information and educational resources in Japan, but the resources available for non-traditional or alternative economic entities, such as 'community businesses' or 'citizen companies', are scarce. Thus she too had to learn how to achieve her goals in the heat of action and not from conventional business education. Egami and Fuma did not comment on the impact of their business education and training on their businesses.

Summary of the Approaches to Entrepreneurship

Results of the analyses of the entrepreneurial process experienced by female entrepreneurs from Japan and the Czech Republic are presented below and summarized in Tables 8.2 through 8.5. Table 8.6 provides a comparison of the two groups.

Table 8.2   Czech entrepreneurs – traits approach[a]

	Ana	Beata	Catarina	Dana	Eva	Frieda
N Achievement	**	*	***			***
Risk-taking		***	***	*		*
Ambiguity		*			*	
Creativity		*		***	***	
Intuition			***	*		
Flexibility	***	*	***	*	***	
N Autonomy		*	*	***	*	*
Self-confidence	**	***				*
Internal LOC		*				
Adaptability		*		*	***	
Dominance		*		*	*	*
Low N Conformity		*		*		
Commitment		*		*		*
Pro-activity		*		*	***	*
Sense of observation	***	*		*		
Sense of humor	*	*	*	*	*	*

Note: a *** = highly descriptive, **descriptive, *somewhat descriptive

Table 8.3   Japanese entrepreneurs – traits approach[a]

	Egami	Fuma	Doi	Ando	Ban	Chiba
N Achievement	*	**	*	*		***
Risk-taking	*	**	***	*	***	***
Ambiguity			*			
Creativity	*		***	***	***	***
Intuition	*		**	**	*	**
Flexibility	*			*	*	***
N Autonomy			*	*	***	*
Self-confidence	**	*	***	**		***
Internal LOC		*				*
Adaptability	**		***	*	**	***
Dominance	**					**
Low N Conformity	**		*	**	**	***
Commitment	***		***	**		**
Pro-activity	***	*	***	***	***	***
Sense of observation		*	**	***	***	***
Sense of humor	*	*	*	*	*	*

Note: [a] *** = highly descriptive, **descriptive, *somewhat descriptive

Table 8.4   Czech entrepreneurs – behavioral approach[a]

	Ana	Beata	Catarina	Dana	Eva	Frieda
Strategic niche	*	*	*	*	*	*
Cash flow	*				*	
Strategic plan	*				*	
Accounting	*				*	
Marketing	*	*	*	*	*	*
Networking	*				*	
Delegating	*	*	*	*	*	*
Sense of humor	*	*	*	*	*	*

Note: [a] *** = highly descriptive, **descriptive, *somewhat descriptive

Table 8.5   Japanese entrepreneurs – behavioral approach[a]

	Egami	Fuma	Doi	Ando	Ban	Chiba
Strategic niche	*	***	*	*	**	
Cash flow		**	*	**	*	*
Strategic plan		**		**		
Accounting				*		
Marketing			*	**		**
Networking	*			***		***
Delegating		*	*		*	***
Sense of humor	*	*	*	*	*	*

Note: [a] *** = highly descriptive, **descriptive, *somewhat descriptive

Table 8.6   Comparison of Czech and Japanese women on the traits and behavioral approaches to entrepreneurship

	Japanese		Czech	
Behavioral approach	# of women	Range	# of women	Range
Strategic niche	4	0–3	6	0–3
Cash flow	5	0–2	2	0–3
Strategic plan	2	0–3	2	0–3
Accounting	1	0–2	2	0–3
Marketing	3	0–3	6	1–3
Networking	5	0–3	3	0–3
Delegating	5	0–3	6	1–3
Traits approach				
N Achievement	1	0–1	4	0–5
Risk-taking	5	0–5	4	0–5
Ambiguity	5	0–3	2	0–1
Creativity	4	0–5	3	0–5
Intuition	4	0–3	2	0–5
Flexibility	5	0–5	5	0–5
N Autonomy	2	0–4	5	0–5
Self-confidence	5	0–5	3	0–5
Internal LOC	2	0–1	1	0–1
Adaptability	5	0–5	3	0–5
Dominance	2	0–3	4	0–1
Low N Conformity	5	0–5	2	0–1
Commitment	5	0–5	3	0–1
Pro-activity	6	0–5	4	0–5
Sense of observation	5	0–5	3	0–5
Sense of humor	6	1–2	6	1–2

Environmental approach

Despite their country's 50-year experiment with communism, two of the Czech women, Ana and Beata, were able to identify role models who owned their own businesses. As Ana explained, 'My grandfather was a wholesaler, and my father has a building company. There were always stories in the family about business and I found it very interesting and tempting.' On the other hand, Dana and Eva felt rejected by the business world. 'In practice', Eva said, 'there is discrimination in the jobs for women. It is difficult for older women to find work.' The impact of these experiences on the Czech women shows that the environmental approach is generally a useful tool for understanding their development as entrepreneurs. On the other hand, neither Catarina nor Frieda had role models, nor did they feel rejected by society, so the environmental model is not applicable to them.

The problem of corporate glass ceilings and other workplace discrimination made some Japanese women feel rejected. In addition, few of the Japanese women identified role models while several felt they were not taken seriously. For example, Ban knew that once she became pregnant, she was expected to give up her job: 'The reason I started a business on my own', Ban explained, 'was that I got pregnant, but I assumed I could still work for a few months. I left my job and started my own business.' Ando also felt that that there was a definite notion of the proper 'marriageable age for women' that pushes them out the company door in their late twenties. She also referred to the widespread problem of sexual discrimination against women in the workplace. Ban criticized male traditions, such as after-work drinking sessions that prevented her from fully participating in work-related discussions. Fuma mentioned the difficulty Japanese women have in being taken seriously as business owners and managers. This bias points to the need to consider cultural differences within the environmental approach.

Traits approach

As can be seen in Table 8.6, each of the items in the traits approach to entrepreneurship was found at least once in one Japanese and one Czech woman. In addition, humor was an important trait exhibited by all the women – but it is not taken into account by this approach. The trait least often associated with these women was an internal locus of control. The Japanese also did not have a very high need for achievement. The traits most often exhibited by these entrepreneurs show them to be risk-taking, flexible, pro-active and in possession of a sense of humor. The Japanese entrepreneurs were self-confident, adaptable, committed and had both a low need for conformity and a strong sense of observation. They were also able to cope well with ambiguity. The Czech women entrepreneurs had a high need for autonomy.

According to Table 8.2, the traits that best describe Ana are flexibility, sense of observation, self-confidence and a high need for achievement. Beata demonstrated high self-confidence and risk-taking traits. Intuition was not a strong point. Every other trait was coded at least once. Catarina had a high need for achievement, risk-taking, intuition and flexibility. Catarina alluded to individuality and autonomy, while none of the other traits were noticeable. Dana was high in creativity and showed a high need for individuality and autonomy. Also noted were risk-taking, intuition, flexibility, an ability to adapt to change, dominance, a low need to conform, commitment, pro-activity and a sense of observation.

Creativity, flexibility, adapting to change and pro-activity were also the traits most characteristic of Eva. She also made reference to tolerance for ambiguity, a high need for individuality and autonomy, and dominance. Finally, Frieda demonstrated a high need for achievement, risk-taking, a high need for individuality and autonomy, self-confidence, dominance, commitment and pro-activity.

Among the Japanese women, Ando was high on creativity, pro-activity and sense of observation traits. Other traits coded by the researchers were intuition, self-confidence, a low need for conformity and commitment. Entrepreneur Ban was high on risk-taking, creativity, self-confidence and sense of observation. Other traits that describe Ban include adaptability and a low need for conformity. Entrepreneur Chiba's traits include a high need for achievement, risk-taking, creativity, self-confidence, adaptability, a low need for conformity, pro-activity and sense of observation. She can also be described as having the traits of intuition, adaptability and commitment.

Entrepreneur Doi was high in the following traits: risk-taking, creativity, self-confidence, commitment, adaptability and pro-activity. She also has some intuition and a sense of observation. Entrepreneur Egami exhibited high pro-active and commitment traits. Other traits that describe Egami are self-confidence, adaptability, dominance and a low need for conformity. Finally, Fuma's traits include high need for achievement and risk-taking.

Behavioral approach
The behaviors listed in the behavioral approach were found at least once for both the Japanese and Czech entrepreneurs. (See Table 8.6.) All of the Czech entrepreneurs had strategic niches, strong marketing skills, delegation skills and humor. Cash flow, networking and delegating were behaviors found for five of the six Japanese women. The lack of business behaviors for the Czech women is probably due to their lack of experience in a capitalistic society. The lack of business behaviors for the Japanese women, such as accounting and strategic planning, is due to inadequate business education and/or inexperience.

Ana and Eva mentioned all of the management skills more than once during the interviews. The skills least mentioned by the Czech women were cash flow management and strategic planning.

In Japan, strategic niche was a behavioral approach identified by all of the entrepreneurs. Cash flow management, while an important issue, was actually viewed in a negative way by the Japanese women who mentioned this behavior. Networking, delegating and humor were also important to all of the Japanese entrepreneurs.

DISCUSSION

All the Czech and Japanese women in this study operated businesses in the service sector. Most of the women started their businesses in the late 1980s or early 1970s, except two Japanese women who have been in business for over 25 years. The women came from large urban areas that present similar obstacles and opportunities to female entrepreneurs in North America (Pellegrino and Reece, 1982). These include where to find start-up capital; how to attract business; and how to hire, train, motivate and retain good employees. A lack of strategic planning is also often seen. This is consistent with research in the United States and Canada (Brush, 1992; Hisrich and Brush, 1987; Schwartz, 1979). A more regional problem is the poor cash flow management skills of the Czech women, which can be explained by the dominance of a Marxist economic system in their country prior to 1989. Many of the Czech women also had problems with human resources. In Japan, on the other hand, it was the lack of formal training and role models that hindered the development of certain entrepreneurial skills. A worldwide problem for women is the reluctance of banks to provide start-up capital. This forces many women to rely on personal and family sources for funds. Inadequate capital is a common cause of business failure among female business owners (Brush, 1992).

The women interviewed in the Czech Republic were well educated. Most of them had master's degrees. The impact of the American training program was also significant. By shadowing entrepreneurs in the United States, the four Czech women who participated in the training program gained a better understanding of basic business principles and developed more useful skills than the women who did not receive the training. For example, they learned how to run a business more effectively; how to obtain loans; and how to select, train and motivate employees. The significant contribution of small businesses to economic growth is another reason why the success of women entrepreneurs is so important. Governments should both make it easier for women to borrow money and provide assistance along the lines of the Small Business Administration in the US. Business skills training programs would be beneficial to all entrepreneurs, whether female or male, in transition economies.

In Japan, two of the six women had attended universities to study business or economics, but neither of them felt that their studies had provided the skills they needed to run a business. On the other hand, all the women clearly believed that they learned most about owning and managing a business from the hands-on experience.

Some of the Czech women expressed frustration with managing people, but those women who participated in the training program were more successful than those who did not. However, in economies that have not historically encouraged worker empowerment, there is a need to teach state-of-the-art human resources principles and practices. Changing outmoded attitudes and behaviors is always a slow process, and learning new ways of thinking about the roles and responsibilities of employees and employers takes time and effort. Significant change requires consistent actions on the part of business owners.

Interestingly, none of the Czech women felt that gender was a significant barrier to success. While they did say that their business involvement placed stress on relationships with family and friends, gender did not play a significant part in the way they were treated by financial institutions, customers or suppliers. Indeed, more than one respondent felt that being a woman was helpful to her business. On the other hand, all the Japanese women mentioned gender as an issue. To be a woman in Japan makes it much more difficult to get a bank loan, create a network, have a drink with male colleagues or clients, or do business with men. For those women who had families the problems of balancing work and family life were considerable. The women also had to struggle against stereotypes about working women and about the quality of businesses operated by women.

For the Japanese women, success took a wide variety of forms from intuition and foresight to personal fulfillment and independence. Like their Czech counterparts, the Japanese women may be characterized as strong, independent and autocratic leaders. Most of them made business decisions themselves (except for Fuma, who worked with a team of people). In general, the Japanese female entrepreneurs make a point of hiring women and try to adapt the work environment for them in terms of childcare and family matters. Ban also hires older people: 'I have recently hired three people in their 40s, including men', she said, 'because I though it would have a good effect both inside and outside the company.'

The Czech women interviewed in this study are not very different from entrepreneurs in North America or other Central and Eastern European countries (Hisrich and Fulop, 1994; McCarthy *et al.*, 1997) based on the traits, environmental and behavioral approaches. Entrepreneurs in the Czech Republic face many of the same challenges as other women entrepreneurs, such as managing people and delegating authority (McCarthy *et al.*, 1997).

This exploratory study, like all research, has its limitations. The sample is small and focuses primarily on women in service industries. The data are enriched, however, by comparing women in two very different countries and cultures. The study is also strengthened because of the diverse training and skills that the women interviewed brought to their entrepreneurial projects.

Future research may examine how women compare to male entrepreneurs in the same businesses, how women entrepreneurs fare over a longer time frame, and how Czech and Japanese entrepreneurs compare with those from other Central European or Asian countries. Finally, this chapter provides support for the development of a universal model of entrepreneurship. The traits, environmental and behavioral approaches used in North America seem to adequately describe these women small-business owners in the Czech Republic and in Japan. This is consistent with other research results showing that people in the similar professions (for example, engineers and nurses) have more similarities than differences across cultures (Baba *et al.*, 1998; Lituchy and Kittireungcharn, 1998). This may be true of entrepreneurs as well. The researchers, however, believe that the traits model was missing an important trait: humor. In several studies, for example, humor has been related to successful leadership, fruitful negotiations and decreased stress. Furthermore, the behavioral approach is missing general business/management skills, general human resources skills and communication skills.

IMPLICATIONS AND RECOMMENDATIONS

The women in this study faced the same challenges and difficulties as women entrepreneurs in the United States (Pellegrino and Reece, 1982). Delegating and managing people were important concerns for all the women. A more regional problem is the poor cash flow management skills of the Czech women, which can be explained by the dominance of a Marxist or communist economic system in these countries prior to 1989. In Japan, it was the lack of business skills training and lack of role models that hindered the women from developing entrepreneurial skills. This research, which should be extended to other countries, has particularly important implications for training women entrepreneurs in developing economies. Assistance by developed-country governments or international organizations can make a notable difference in the success or failure of women's businesses. The training program provided by USAID to the Czech women entrepreneurs provides a model of success.

Gender-based bias is widespread and takes many forms, such as glass ceilings, unfair promotion and retention policies, contemptuous attitudes toward women's skills and accomplishments, inadequate access to capital, sexual harassment and demeaning job requirements. Awareness of these problems is the first step toward moderating and ultimately eliminating them. Future research on women entrepreneurs can contribute to an understanding of discriminatory practices, necessary skills and effective strategies. Understanding is, in turn, the royal road to reform and business success. Mentoring, privately and publicly funded training programs, and support networks created by and for businesswomen are also key elements in the reform and learning process.

Just as small business has been a significant engine of growth in the West, so have small businesses managed by women in Central and Eastern European countries contributed to economic growth and stability. As Japan continues to restructure and more and more small and medium-sized enterprises come into existence, women may have a greater role in their country's economic reform. The significance of small businesses to the economic growth of these countries is another reason why the success of women entrepreneurs is so important. These successful women will then be important mentors, role models and advisors to other women considering starting their own businesses.

REFERENCES

Baba, V.V., B.L. Galperin and T.R. Lituchy (1998), 'Work and depression: a study of nurses in the Caribbean international', *Journal of Nursing Studies*, 2: 163–84.

Birley, S., C. Moss and P. Saunders (1987), 'Do women entrepreneurs require different training?', *American Journal of Small Business*, 12: 27–35.

Brush, C.G. (1992), 'Research on women business owners: past trends, a new perspective and future directions', *Entrepreneurship: Theory and Practice*, 16 (4): 5–30.

Buttner, E.M. (1997), 'Women's organizational exodus to entrepreneurship: self-reported motivations and correlates with success', *Journal of Small Business Management*, 35(1): 34–47.

Buttner, E.H. and B. Rosen (1988), 'Bank loan officers' perceptions of the characteristics of men, women, and successful entrepreneurs', *Journal of Business Venturing*, 3(3): 249–58.

Capowski, G.S. (1992) 'Be your own boss? Millions of women get down to business', *Management Review*, 81: 24–30.

Chandler, S. and K. Murphy (1994) 'Women Entrepreneurs: they're Forming Small Business at Twice the Rate of Men', *Business Week (Special Report)*, 18 April, 104–10.

Economist (1996), 340 (7978), 10 August, 13.

Esters, S. (1997), 'Conning studies female entrepreneurs', *National Underwriter*, 101: 47.

Godfrey, J. (1995), 'What's good for women is good for the country', *Vital Speeches of the Day*, 61: 538–44.

Graham, D. and L. Duncan (1995), 'Law's new entrepreneurs', *ABA Journal*, 81: 54–60.

Hisrich, R.D. and C.G. Brush (1983), 'The woman entrepreneur: implications of family, education and occupational experience', *Frontiers in Entrepreneurs Research*, Wellesley, MA: Babson College, pp. 255–70.

Hisrich, R.D. and C.G. Brush (1987), 'Women entrepreneurs: a longitudinal study', *Frontiers in Entrepreneurs Research*, Wellesley, MA: Babson College, pp. 187–9.

Hisrich, R.D. and G. Fulop (1994), 'The role of women entrepreneurs in Hungary's transition economy', *International Studies of Management and Organization*, 24: 100–13.

Hofstede, G. (1991), *Cultures and Organizations: Software of the Mind*, London: McGraw-Hill.

Hofstede, G. (1993), 'Cultural constraints in management theories', *The Academy of Management Executive*, 7 (1): 81–95.

Ibrahim, A. Bakr (1990), *Entrepreneurship and Small Business Management: Text, Readings, and Cases*, Dubuque, IA: Kendall/Hunt Pub. Co.

Ibrahim, A. Bakr (1994), *Family Business Management: Concepts and Practice*. Dubuque, IA: Kendall/Hunt Pub. Co.

Ibrahim, A.B. and J. R. Goodwin (1986), 'Perceived causes of success in small business', *American Journal of Small Business*, 12: 11–25.

Knight, G. (2000), 'Entrepreneurship and marketing strategy: the SME under globalization', *Journal of International Marketing*, 8: 12–32.

Lituchy, T. and N. Kittireungcharn (1998), 'The impact of satisfaction and commitment on turnover intentions: Thai public sector engineers', *World Congress of Sociology Proceedings*, 46: 185–90.

McCarthy, D.J., S.M. Puffer and A.I. Naumov (1997), 'Case Study – Olga Kirova: a Russian entrepreneur's quality leadership', *International Journal of Organizational Analysis*, 5 (3): 267–90.

Miles, M. and A. Huberman (1984), *Qualitative Data Analysis: A Sourcebook of New Methods*, Newbury Park, CA: Sage.

Nakada, G. (2000), 'The big sell,' *Asian Business*, 36: 14–15.

OECD (1986), *Local Initiatives for Employment Creation*, Paris: OECD, p. 6.

Pellegrino, E.T. and B.L. Reece (1982), 'Perceived formative and operational problems encountered by female entrepreneurs in retail and service firms', *Journal of Small Business Management*, 20: 15–24.

Schein, V., R. Mueller, T. Lituchy and J. Liu (1996), 'Think manager – think male: a global phenomenon?', *Journal of Organizational Behavior*, 17: 33–41.

Schwartz, E.B. (1979), 'Entrepreneurship: a new female frontier', *Journal of Contemporary Business*, 47–76.

Silvestri and Lukasiewicz (1987), 'A look at occupational employment trends to the year 2000', *Monthly Labor Review*, 110(9), 463.

Steinhoff, P. and K. Tanaka (1998), 'Women managers in Japan', in N. Adler and D. Izraeli (eds), *Women in Management Worldwide*, New York: Sharpe.

Stoner, C.R., R.I. Hartman and R. Arora (1990), 'Work–home role conflict in female owners of small businesses: an exploratory study', *Journal of Small Business Management*, 28(1): 30–38.

Waddell, F.T. (1982), 'Factors affecting choice, satisfaction and success in the female self-employed', *Journal of Vocational Behavior*, 23: 294–304.

Yin, R. (1984), *Case Study Research: Design and Methods*, Beverly Hills, CA: Sage.

PART 3

Emerging Dimensions of Management Policy

9. Toward a transnational techno-culture: an empirical investigation of knowledge management

Leo-Paul Dana, Len Korot and George Tovstiga

INTRODUCTION

Even before globalization affected society at large, the elite of one country often mixed with the elite of another. Although the peasantry of England had little – if any – contact with that of the Continent, the royalty corresponded with, intermingled with, and even married with the aristocracy in Europe. Take Victoria and Albert, for instance. The Queen of England was married to an individual who was born in a different country than she, and whose mother-tongue was German. While the English commoner had little in common with any Prussian, Victoria and Albert shared a regal culture that transcended national boundaries. She had more in common with her German-speaking husband than with the working class of East London or the herder of the Highlands. What we see is that, in different countries, there was an elite that shared less with the masses of their home country than with the elite of other countries. In other words, the elite shared a transnational culture that transcended national boundaries.

In today's world, the traditional factors of production have given way to knowledge as the driving force behind wealth creation. There is a new transnational elite, based on knowledge. We recall that the royal family of Elizabethan England had more in common with that of Spain than with English-speaking serfs. Along the same lines, we note that the MBA graduate in Spain shares more with the MBA graduate in England than with the sheep farmer in the Pyrenees (Dana, 2000).

The objective of this chapter is to show that in the knowledge-intensive high-technology sectors there exists an intercontinental techno-culture that transcends national boundaries. Focusing on knowledge-intensive high-technology sectors, Silicon Valley was an obvious setting in which to start our investigation. Since we wanted to test across continents as well as across nations, the Netherlands seemed to be an appropriate choice to represent Europe. In Asia, we identified Singapore as having an important knowledge-intensive, high-technology sector. Hence, we set out to examine knowledge management in these three contexts.

Understandably, there is growing questioning about how companies manage knowledge, i.e., what management practices they employ to exploit their knowledge. This is in part fueled by recognition that knowledge is central to the success of business in the digital economy. It is further fueled by a growing interest among investors in the measurement and valuation of intellectual capital and the representation of this value in the balance sheet of the enterprise (Roos *et al.*, 1997). There is also a recognition that much of an organization's intellectual capital is in a tacit – that is, people-embodied – form, rather than in explicit form (Birchall and Tovstiga, 2000), and this leaves firms at risk if key personnel are attracted elsewhere. Another challenge that taxes firms, in many economies, is a skills shortage in key areas of technology development; there is a need to find mechanisms for retaining access to a pool of motivated talent.

There is, in the comparative management literature, a continuing debate between those who advocate 'convergence' and those who advocate 'divergence'. In a prescient statement, the convergence perspective was clearly stated by Richman and Farmer (1965):

> As the general similarity of men everywhere is recognized, and as managerial and technological necessity presses all types of culture toward a common road, nations everywhere become more similar; the logic of technology and management will lead all to the same general position.

By sharp contrast to the view of Richman and Farmer, the strongest and most visible advocates of the divergent position are Hofstede (1981; 1991; 2001) and Laurent (1983). In his landmark work with IBM, Hofstede found significant cultural differences among the 53 national subsidiaries represented in his study; those differences were reflected in four major dimensions: Power Distance, Individualism vs Collectivism, Masculinity vs Femininity, and Uncertainty Avoidance. Based on his research with INSEAD Executive Development students, André Laurent (1983) concluded:

> Deep-seated managerial assumptions are strongly shaped by national cultures and appear quite insensitive to the more transient culture of organizations . . . There is no such thing as Management with a capital M. The art of managing and organizing has no homeland.

The premise of our study of high-technology, knowledge-intensive firms is a convergent one, i.e., as we look at international entrepreneurship, we see high-technology, knowledge-intensive organizations as the vanguard of a new, networked, global economy that is rapidly erasing national and cultural boundaries. To test this premise, we have studied knowledge management practices within knowledge-intensive firms located in three major regions of knowledge: Silicon Valley, the Netherlands, and Singapore. We pose the following research propositions:

(1) Knowledge management practices and the cultural beliefs, values and behavioral norms of the study organizations will be more akin than dissimilar, regardless of national context.
(2) Leading-edge firms, those that strongly identify with Network Age cultural assumptions, will differ significantly from laggard firms, still firmly entrenched in Industrial Age assumptions and practices.

CONCEPTUAL FRAMEWORK

A recurrent theme in current management thinking is how to build sustainable competitive advantage in a boundaryless, volatile, innovation-driven marketplace. As technology propels us ever more rapidly and deeply into the Network Age, the need for identifying organizational practices and culture that characterize successful entrepreneurial firms becomes urgent. The key to establishing competitive leadership is how these ventures will manage their knowledge-based intangible assets. There is growing recognition that real competitive advantage lies in what the organization knows and how quickly it can access and apply that knowledge. People-embodied knowledge has become the only meaningful resource in a networked world, irrevocably replacing Industrial Age factors of production such as labor, capital and land (Drucker, 1993).

> When we talk about the new economy, we're talking about a world in which people work with their brains instead of their hands . . . A world in which innovation is more important than mass production. A world in which investment buys new concepts or the means to create them, rather than new machines. A world in which rapid change is a constant. A world so different its emergence can only be described as a revolution. (Browning and Reiss, 1998)

Amidon (1997) pointed out that the knowledge-intensive organization is more appropriately viewed from the perspective of a strategic business network (SBN) rather than the traditional strategic business unit (SBU).

In this chapter, we contrast the Industrial Age with the Network Age, as illustrated in Table 9.1 below. The Network Age has several unique features. For one, it has at its root the notion of connectivity. Kelly (1997) made the point that the grand irony of our times is that the era of computers is over; that all of the major consequences of standalone computers have manifested themselves. In contrast, all of the most promising techno-logical developments now emerging are mainly due to communications between computers. Connectivity and reach are the key drivers behind many of the emerging business opportunities and models. In this environ-ment wealth is gained not from perfecting the known, but by imperfectly seizing the unknown, and as Kelly pointed out, the ideal environment for cultivating the unknown is to nurture the flexibility, nimbleness and agility of networks.

Table 9.1   Contrasting economic phases

	Industrial Age	**Network Age**
EXTERNAL ENVIRONMENT	• Static, predictable, linear	• Fluid, global, unpredictable, complex
WORK PROCESSES	• 'Scientific management' focused on efficiency	• Focused on effectiveness
ORGANIZATIONAL STRUCTURE	• Linear, hierarchical, functionally differentiated	• Networked, organic, flexible; chaotic; emergent
DECISION-MAKING	• Top-down, command-and-control	• By diverse, self-managing teams
KNOWLEDGE	• Restricted to management and 'experts', emphasis is on 'explicit' knowledge	• Universally shared, emphasis is on 'tacit' knowledge
KNOWLEDGE WORKERS	• Specialized, segmented; prevalent attitude: 'knowledge is power'	• Knowledge is collectively held – members of the organization are multi-faceted, always learning
ORGANIZATIONAL LEARNING	• 'Single-loop', underlying assumptions rarely challenged; no tolerance for experimentation; failed attempts at innovation are punished	• 'Double-loop', underlying assumptions always challenged; experimentation is constantly encouraged, failure is essential to learning

Another important aspect of the Network Age is its implications for the organizational structure of entrepreneurial firms. Imparato and Harari (1994) suggested that, in the Network Age, technologies, markets, and competitors are in a state of perpetual flux. Consequently, the Network Age organization has to focus constantly on emerging technological innovations and short-lived market opportunities. Relentlessly connecting and extending reach is at the root of the Network Age, as is the drive to augment, amplify, enhance and extend relationships and communication between all beings and all objects. The Network Age has had an immense impact on the organization. We are beginning to see the emergence of so-called *fluid-network* organizations – organizations featuring permeable boundaries, minimal rules and flexible architectures (Maira, 1998). The Network Age demands that any firm must be fast on its feet and act quickly as new developments and opportunities unfold, constantly balancing structure and process in order to sustain the flow of innovation. We observe the following major distinctions between the Industrial Age and the Network Age.

Knowledge in Techno-culture

Knowledge, Pederson (1998) pointed out, can be described as the integration of ideas, experience, intuition, skill, and lessons learned, that has the potential to create value for all stakeholders of a firm. Value is created through knowledge by providing a more informed basis for decision-making and action. Nonaka and Takeuchi (1995) extended the notion of knowledge in the firm and defined two realms of knowledge: *explicit* and *tacit*.

Explicit knowledge is easily identifiable, easy to articulate, capture and share. It is most readily apparent, but forms only the tip of a knowledge iceberg. It resides in the heads of people and therefore consists predominantly of intuition, insight, perception and beliefs and to a great extent is experiential. Tacit knowledge is deeply imbedded in the culture of the firm and is therefore elusive, difficult to capture and even more difficult to transfer. Of the two, tacit knowledge carries the greater value. It is a key determinant of competitiveness and forms the basis of exceptional performance.

Managing knowledge in the Network Age is a truly multidimensional challenge. It requires simultaneous management of four inextricably linked domains, as illustrated in Figure 9.1: culture, content, process and infrastructure, all of which have a tacit as well as an explicit dimension. In Figure 9.1, the solid domains indicate our estimation of the explicit knowledge portion; the open domains the tacit knowledge for each of the four dimensions (Birchall and Tovstiga, 1999; Chait, 1998).

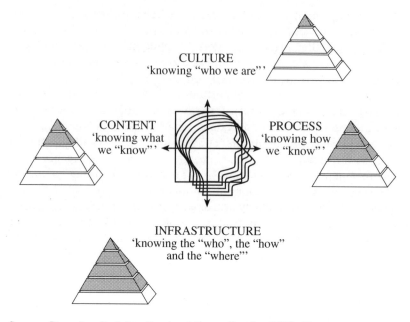

Source: Dana, Leo-Paul, Len Korot and George Tovstiga (2001), 'Convergence vs. Divergence', *Journal of Enterprising Culture*, 9 (1): 7–20.

Figure 9.1   Organizational knowledge domains

Knowledge Culture, or *'Knowing Who We Are'*

It is in this domain that the values, beliefs and behavioral norms are played out. It is the most elusive domain but is the prime determinant in the success of knowledge management. It is here that we find the cutting distinction between Industrial Age and Network Age enterprises. With reference to Schein's (1992) three levels, culture ranges from the highly explicit, visible organizational structures and procedures ('artifacts') to those highly tacit, largely out-of-awareness, deeply imprinted core beliefs that guide an individual's behavior.

Knowledge Content, or *'Knowing What We Know'*

This domain comprises the firm's stock of strategically relevant knowledge, both explicit and tacit. It exists in the firm in the form of:

● experiential knowledge – highly tacit, derived from previous experience and often difficult to articulate;

- formal knowledge – refined, documented, highly explicit in nature; and
- emerging knowledge – both tacit and explicit, emerging at the interface of highly innovative and cross-disciplinary interactions in the firm such as new product development projects.

Knowledge Infrastructure, or *'Knowing the "How" and the "Where"'*

This domain encompasses all functional elements in the firm that support and facilitate the management of knowledge. Information and communication technology is one such element. For many organizations, knowledge management stops here. To our understanding, however, knowledge infrastructure involves much more; it includes the carriers of knowledge such as cross-functional, cross-national project teams. Fluid processes (Maira, 1998) and flexible teams ensure the rapid transfer of knowledge across complex and shifting internal and external organizational boundaries.

Knowledge Process, or *'Knowing How We Know'*

A firm's knowledge process domain incorporates how knowledge is created, converted, transferred, applied and ultimately discarded. Nonaka and Takeuchi (1995) identified four key knowledge conversion modes or processes: 'socialization' (tacit to tacit), 'internalization' (explicit to tacit), 'externalization' (tacit to explicit) and 'combination' (explicit to explicit). Knowledge processes can also involve roles played by knowledge workers in the firm (Tovstiga, 1999).

RELATED CONCEPTS

Knowledge Creation

One of the more comprehensive conceptual frameworks for knowledge creation and conversion is that of Nonaka and Takeuchi (1995) and Von Krogh *et al.*, (2000). The authors describe how knowledge-intensive organizations, when innovating in response to a changing environment, create new knowledge. Knowledge creation occurs as a result of the spiral interaction between tacit and explicit modes at different points within the organization. The key is in the externalization process that mobilizes and converts tacit knowledge. When shared across the organization, this newly created knowledge contributes to increased learning in the organization. Knowledge, the authors assert, cannot be managed; at best, the organization can manage appropriate enabling conditions for knowledge creation. Nonaka and Takeuchi's theory forms a major building block for the instrument used in this study.

Comparative Management

In the voluminous literature and research published in the field of comparative management, the most visible and used work is that done by Geert Hofstede. In his landmark cross-national study of IBM, Hofstede (1981) identifies four dimensions that differentiated national cultures: Power Distance, Individualism vs Collectivism, Masculinity vs Femininity, and Uncertainty Avoidance. Based on their work with Asian organizations, Hofstede and Bond (1988) have added Long-term Orientation as a fifth dimension. Hofstede's framework continues to drive a number of comparative management studies and serves as a prime support for the divergent viewpoint – i.e., that national culture differences override similarities in management thinking and processes.

Ulijn and Kumar (1999) reviewed the comparative management literature in pursuit of the question: how can cultures respect each other, learn from each other and co-operate effectively, for instance, in business and technology? In the broad spectrum of communication, language and national culture studies summarized by that study, the underlying premise is that of divergence.

In contrast, Korot (1989) pursued the hypothesis that there is a high-technology culture that transcends national identity. The original research was based on a survey of 17 high-tech start-ups in Ireland, the UK and France. The survey instrument corresponds to Schein's (1992) definition of organizational culture and assessed respondents' perceptions of the effectiveness of their organization in dealing with the issues of external adaptation and internal integration. The study concluded that convergence existed among the corporate cultures of these diverse enterprises. The addition of Silicon Valley technology start-ups to the study sample confirmed the findings of the earlier study leading to an organizational profile that characterizes techno-cultures.

Knowledge Worker Profiling

It is the knowledge worker who is critical to effective knowledge management. In his study of knowledge creation/conversion processes and the contributions of knowledge workers to each of the knowledge processes, Tovstiga (1999) concluded that the knowledge worker's role is really a hybrid and flexible composite of competencies and attributes distributed across boundary-dissolving communities of knowledge practices. These often informal, loosely structured communities are the essence of cross-national convergence of knowledge management practices.

CULTURAL AND COMMERCIAL CONTEXT

Silicon Valley

In a small area – 35 miles long and 10 miles wide – south of San Francisco, once heavily agricultural, lies the most concentrated source of technological innovation in the world. From a modest start in a small Palo Alto garage, two young engineers, Bill Hewlett and David Packard, created the Silicon Valley's first entrepreneurial venture. With his invention of the transistor at Bell Labs, William Shockley returned to his home town of Palo Alto in 1955, and launched Shockley Semiconductor Laboratories which, in turn, spun off entrepreneurs who created hundreds of new technology-driven companies.

Fueled by an extraordinary fusion of technical talent, imagination and capital, unhampered by the traditional management constraints of the Industrial Age, the Valley continues to set the pace for globally driven entrepreneurship. Over a three-year period, more than 3,000 new ventures have been launched, supported by billions of dollars of venture capital. There are now over 7,500 technology companies crammed into this narrow corridor. What accounts for this unique center of the evolving Network Age?

- Sheer density, providing access to a deep, constantly refreshed, pool of talent
- Constant transfer of knowledge, both tacit and explicit, through informal and formal forums and through the constant movement of people from company to company
- An advanced, broad networked infrastructure
- A regional culture that amply rewards innovation and risk-taking and accepts failure as a natural consequence of experimentation
- A global perspective in which product marketing and manufacturing know no geographical boundaries
- Young knowledge workers driven by the opportunity to be on the frontier of innovation and by the possibility of making lots of money
- An abundance of venture capital.

It's a perpetual motion machine which is accelerating daily. The venture business and Silicon Valley entrepreneurship have always been incredibly intense businesses, which move at the speed of light. New company formation is occurring faster than at any time in its history. (*San Jose Mercury News*, 2000)

Silicon Valley has, in the span of a few decades, moved from being dry, sleepy patches of fruit orchards and vegetables to becoming the mind and soul of the Network Age, spawning international entrepreneurship at an unprecedented pace. As a measure of its impact, if Silicon Valley were a nation, it would now rank among the world's 12 largest economies.

The Netherlands

For a small country with a small population, the Netherlands has a powerful and large economy. It ranks as the world's sixth largest exporting country and the sixth largest source of investment; its gross domestic product is the 14th largest in the world. The Netherlands has become a hub of European commerce. Its location as the gateway to the European continent, its expertise in international trade, one of the world's most advanced telecommunications infrastructure, and its educated multilingual workforce make it an attractive beachhead for multinational companies seeking to expand business to the European continent.

On one hand, we find a deliberate move on the part of the Ministry of Economics to actively encourage technological innovation. A wide range of subsidies open to all companies in the Netherlands, regardless of the owners' nationality, and generous support for small and medium-sized companies through a network of 18 Innovation Centers attest to a deliberate national policy for promoting the growth of new enterprises. Indeed, many people think that recent economic reforms in the Netherlands offer a successful half-way house between Anglo-American free markets and continental European welfare states. It has even been given a name: the *polder-model*. Economic editors of most international newspapers have praised the economic performance in the *polder* behind the dykes. The *New York Times* wrote about 'the third way'. The German weekly *Wirtschaftswoche* wrote about 'our sturdy neighbor'. The German *Die Zeit* has alluded to the 'Dutch Cure'.

Our own observations, based on our research in a wide range of firms in the Netherlands, suggest a somewhat differentiated reality in many of the Dutch firms we studied. We found a prevailing attitude and mode of thinking that (still) adhered primarily to that West European type of capitalism known as the Rhineland model – a largely regulated market economy with a comprehensive system of social security. We also observed numerous remnants of the Industrial Age. In the Rhineland model, the welfare state is combined with a so-called 'consultation economy'. It is a consensus model. Participants (known as 'stakeholders' rather than 'shareholders') try to achieve a harmony across a broad spectrum of interests. The primary goal is not the maximization of short-term profits for the benefit of the shareholders. Rather, the main concern is a sustainable, stable and continuous economic growth. How does the Rhineland model manifest itself in the day-to-day situation in Dutch firms?

- First, there is a prevailing lack of competition. Dutch legislation on competition is relatively lax, shown by the fact that consumer goods are approximately 20 per cent more expensive in the Netherlands than, for example, in the United States, according to a 1997 McKinsey study.
- Second, we find that rigid labor-market regulations characteristic of the Rhineland model, determined by collective bargaining agreements, including those pertaining to working hours, hiring and firing, lead to severe restrictions in the sourcing of young and fresh knowledge talent in small innovative enterprises. In the OECD Jobs Study of 1995, the Netherlands scored 4 points on a scale from 0 (over-regulation) to 10 (very little regulation), in contrast to 7 for the United States.
- Finally, the Rhineland model sets the stage for an essentially unattractive climate for setting up new companies in what are, or rather should be, fast-growing sectors. Strict regulation drives up labor costs. This hurts small firms especially. A recent international comparison of administration costs in eight countries (including Germany and the United States) showed that the costs of hiring the first employee are highest in the Netherlands.

Singapore

Only 646 square kilometers in area, Singapore is home to almost 100,000 entrepreneurs (Dana, 1999). Early entrepreneurs in Singapore were middlemen in the international trade of spices between Indonesia and Europe. In 1819, Sir Thomas Stamford Raffles, Lieutenant-Governor of Bencoolen, selected Singapore as a base for the British East India Company. He paid for permission to create a free port, and Singapore became part of the Straits Settlements. In 1867, the Straits Settlements became a Crown Colony, and in 1869, the inauguration of the Suez Canal made Singapore an important node along the route from England to Australia; this made Singapore a distribution hub for international trade. The British promoted commerce, and this attracted entrepreneurs to Singapore. Based in Singapore, Teochew merchants (originally from Guang Dong Province) dominated the trading price across Asia.

Singapore became an independent republic in 1965. Until 1985, it relied on foreign multinationals to industrialize the economy. Then, a recession prompted the State to focus efforts on promoting entrepreneurship. In 1985, B.G. Lee Hsien Loong (then Acting Minister of Trade and Industry, as well as Chairman of the Committee on Small Enterprise Policy) introduced the Small Enterprise Bureau of Singapore. This was a single agency to create schemes for entrepreneurs and to provide a one-stop service for small enterprises. At the time, $100 million was set aside for the promotion of Singaporean entrepreneurs.

In 1993, Senior Minister Lee Kuan Yew declared, 'we can enthuse a younger generation with the thrill and the rewards of building an external dimension to Singapore. We can and we will spread our wings into the region and then the wider world.' The State would soon promote the internationalization of Singapore firms. In 1995, the Singapore Productivity and Standards Board was created. It undertook to promote entrepreneurship, and to help enterprises expand.

The Economic Development Board set up the 'Local Industry Upgrading Programme' to foster ties between multinationals and small-scale suppliers of parts and services in Singapore. The Economic Development Board also administers 'Going Regional Grants' including the Malaysia in Singapore Third Country Investment Feasibility Study Fund. The purpose of this program is to encourage Singaporean firms to internationalize. As well, the Economic Development Board administers the Singapore–Australia Business Alliance Forum Joint Feasibility Study Fund to encourage the participation of Singaporeans in joint ventures. The Business Development Scheme assists Singaporean entrepreneurs to identify opportunities abroad. As the domestic market becomes increasingly saturated, it becomes increasingly important to look abroad.

METHODOLOGY: PROFILING ORGANIZATIONS

Survey Instrument

The diagnostic instrument for gathering the research data of this study, the organizational Knowledge Practices Survey (KPS) tool, was originally developed by Tovstiga and Korot (2001) to help understand cultural practices and processes in knowledge-intensive firms. The survey tool has been used in Europe, in the Middle East and in the Far East, as well as in Silicon Valley. It is a benchmarking tool that establishes a momentary 'fingerprint' or cultural and practices profile of the organization relating to how knowledge is dealt with in the firm. The underlying premise is that knowledge plays a dominant role in knowledge-intensive firms. The KPS queries organizational knowledge practices in four domains: knowledge culture, content, processes and infrastructure. For this study, a total of 69 firms was selected from our research carried out in was Silicon Valley, in the Netherlands, and in Singapore. A random sampling of employees at all levels of the surveyed companies was asked to rate their organizations on 21 performance indicators reflecting specific organizational practices in those four major domains of organizational knowledge.

- *Knowledge culture* addresses organizational learning practices, attitude toward experimentation, patterns of participation within the firm, attitudes toward openness and trust, and organizational structure.
- *Knowledge content* seeks to establish where knowledge resides in the firm, how new knowledge is sourced, how available knowledge is disseminated and patterns and modes of knowledge flow.
- *Knowledge process* addresses the firm's strategy process, its learning process and the area of performance gap management.
- *Knowledge infrastructure* examines practices relating to access to key knowledge, sharing of knowledge, degree of interpersonal networking and knowledge metrics.

Research Sampling

The survey data for this study were collected from a random sampling of managers and technical professionals in 69 knowledge-intensive organizations: 30 Silicon Valley enterprises, 8 Dutch enterprises and 31 Singapore enterprises. Surveys were distributed to each of the 69 organizations by the researchers directly, or by internal research assistants. The average return rate was 60 per cent.

The firms that were studied in each of the three regions included firms from a broad cross-section of industry sectors and firm sizes. The study sample included both regional-specific start-ups as well as established multinationals. The survey was translated and back-translated in the native language, although English was the version chosen by the majority of companies. For managers and technical professionals in high-technology companies around the globe, English and 'technotalk' are rapidly becoming universal.

Employees of the surveyed companies were asked to rate their perceptions of: (1) the extent to which the specific practice described in the survey tool describes the organization's current level of practice with respect to that particular practice; and (2) the importance the organization places on the particular practice. The ratings are then plotted on web-like maps, which provide a visual sense of the relative levels of performance of companies. Plot points on the outer rings of the web indicate high scores while those closer to the center indicate low scores (see, for example, Figure 9.2 below).

RESEARCH PROPOSITIONS

For the purposes of the analysis, key questions and their outcomes on the basis of the KPS survey were selected to examine and measure the key constructs of our study. These, in turn, focus on certain key practices that we have found particularly illuminating in our previous work. The three key practices selected to measure our propositions were chosen from a total of 21 practices as described earlier. They relate to (1) how experimentation is dealt with in the firms studied, (2) level of knowledge sharing, and (3) mode of decision-making. In our previous research findings, we have consistently found that these three practices differentiate most clearly between traditional 'command-and-control' (Industrial Age) organizations we have studied and those that are clearly moving toward the Network Age organization. These three practices uniquely distinguish the entrepreneurial character of the leading-edge Network Age firm and have therefore been singled out for the purpose of comparative analysis. Nonetheless, it is important that they also be considered in the context of the overall pattern that emerges when all 21 practices are examined (shown in Figures 9.2, 9.3 and 9.4 below).

The basic unit of analysis and comparison we use is the innovative, entrepreneurial firm; we do not distinguish here between start-up and established; large and small. In addition to the general research propositions, specific sub-propositions will test assumptions about some of the cultural differences identified in Hofstede's (1981; 1991; 2001) work.

P1: There will be no significant difference in the key knowledge management practices of the study companies, regardless of national context, i.e. Singapore vs Silicon Valley vs the Netherlands.

In innovative, entrepreneurial firms, regardless of national context

P1a: Experimentation is encouraged, supported and facilitated
(Hofstede's 'Uncertainty Avoidance').
P1b: Knowledge is collectively shared, not retained by individuals
(Hofstede's 'Collectivism vs Individualism').
P1c: Employees at every level are collectively involved in decision-making
(Hofstede's 'Power Distance').

Operational definitions (i.e., of key practices examined and analyzed for measurement of research proposition)

P1: Comparison of the mean scores on both *Current* and *Importance*, of all items for the three regions.
P1a: Comparisons of the mean scores on item 7 (Experimentation)
P1b: Comparisons of the mean scores on item 1 (Knowledge Residency)
P1c: Comparisons of the mean scores on item 8 (Participation in Decision-making)

RESEARCH FINDINGS

Figures 9.2, 9.3 and 9.4 show comparisons of perceived current levels of practice and perceived importance of these for each of the three regions studied. The overall results for Singapore indicate high congruence between importance and current practice with only a slight gap between Knowledge

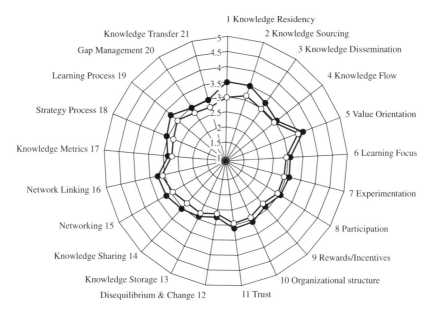

Note: Current practice = ○; Perceived importance = ●

Figure 9.2   Comparison of Singapore firms (current practice versus perceived importance)

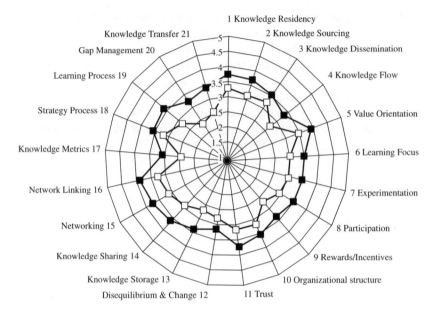

Note: Current practice = □; Perceived importance = ■

*Figure 9.3   Comparison of Silicon Valley firms (current practice versus
           perceived importance)*

Residency and Knowledge Sourcing. However, the overall level for both
current practice and importance is only average, hovering around 3.0.
These results, when compared to the other two regions, suggest that the
expectations of Singapore knowledge workers are relatively lower than
those of the Silicon Valley and the Netherlands. We can speculate that
Singapore respondents, largely Chinese and Malay, are accustomed to and
more comfortable with hierarchical, 'power distance' management norms
and thus less demanding of more empowering management practices than
either their Silicon Valley or Dutch peers.

   The overall results for Silicon Valley indicate significant gaps between
importance and current practice on a number of knowledge management
practices. The overall level for current practice, similar to Singapore, is near
3.0, indicating an average degree of satisfaction. The overall level for
importance is close to 4.0, indicating a need for improved practices in virtually all areas. So, even though Silicon Valley is considered in the forefront
of the Network Age, the knowledge workers sampled in this study feel that
the knowledge management practices in their firms can be significantly
improved. Based on interviews with a number of Silicon Valley profession-

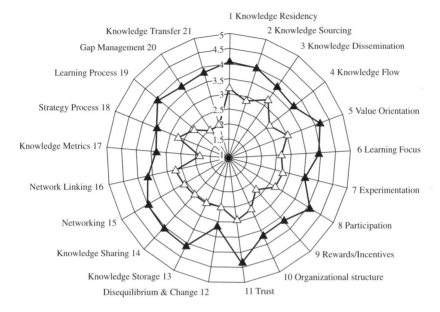

Note: Current practice = △; Perceived importance = ▲

Figure 9.4   Comparison of Dutch firms (current practice versus perceived importance)

als, the authors speculate that the shortfall in knowledge management practices reflects the extraordinary time and task pressures placed on all firms as they strive to remain competitive in the dynamic, swiftly changing arena of high-technology innovation described in the previous section on commercial and cultural context.

The Dutch firms show the most dramatic gap between current practice and importance, reflecting very strong dissatisfaction by the respondents with all of the knowledge management practices by their firms. Current practice level is below both the Singapore and Silicon Valley samples and the importance level is above both other regions. This dramatic gap, in the view of the authors, reflects the persistence of the 'Rhineland model'. Based on our interviews, these Dutch knowledge workers are clearly aware of the sharpened competitive forces in the Network Age, but are deeply frustrated by management they regard as relics of the Industrial Age, unwilling to give up the comfort and predictability afforded historically in the Dutch business and government cultures.

Lessons

Figure 9.5 shows a comparison of the three regions' disposition toward current practice and perceived importance of the practice. Examining our specific research proposition, we find a mixed picture:

P2: There is no significant difference among the three regions in that to a similar degree, experimentation is actively encouraged; knowledge is collectively shared and decision-making is collective.

Thus, these results provide us with evidence supporting our hypothesis that knowledge management practices and the cultural beliefs, values and behavioral norms of firms will be more akin than dissimilar, regardless of national context. We do find some variation in the degree to which firms in the three regions differentiate between perceived current practice and importance of that practice, as shown in Figure 9.5. We find key selected knowledge practices positioned similarly with respect to one another – on the lines representing perceived importance versus current performance – on a relative scale, despite distinct regional 'colorings' (represented by the varying slopes of the lines). For Silicon Valley, there is a perceptible gap between current practice and importance; for the Netherlands, a very significant gap exists between current practice and importance; while for

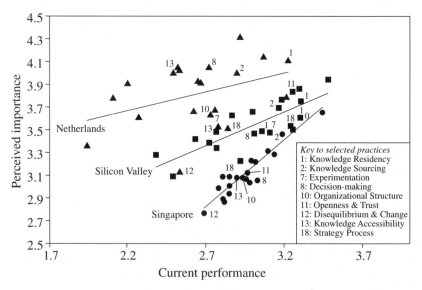

Figure 9.5　Comparison (perceived importance versus current performance) of the three regions

Singapore the gap is almost negligible. We attribute these regional 'color-ings' to national cultural attributes.

For example, we find all firms' disposition toward the practice 'Disequilibrium & Change' (#12) consistently positioned in a way that sug-gests a relatively low perceived importance, regardless of national context. 'Disequilibrium & Change' relates to fluctuations deliberately introduced into the organization in order to promote the breakdown of routines, habits and cognitive frameworks (Nonaka an Takeuchi, 1995). Fluctuations of this type constitute an interruption of the organization's habitual, comfort-able state of being and therefore provide a good pretext for reconsidering fundamental thinking and for questioning basic assumptions and presup-positions.

Fluctuations of this type demand higher levels of social interaction through dialogue and exchange of ideas. A continuous process of disequilib-rium and change, involving the process of questioning and reconsidering existing premises by individual members of the organization, thereby nur-tures the creation of new organizational knowledge. Needless to point out, fluctuations of this type demand that members of the organization have the ability to reflect upon their actions. Without reflection, disequilibrium and change leads to destructive chaos. Nonetheless, we have consistently found organizations – regardless of performance level, cultural makeup or geo-graphic location – to be ill at ease with this very important practice dimension.

We are currently focusing on collecting and isolating KPS data from a sample of technology-based, entrepreneurial firms characterized as leading edge within their industry. Our preliminary results indicate a much higher level of congruence, both in terms of current practice and importance of knowledge management practices than in the broad sample of knowledge-driven companies represented in this study.

IMPLICATIONS

We observe that rapidly changing competitive environments have encour-aged many companies to change toward a form of organization that fits our profile of the Network Age enterprise. A distinguishing feature of the Network Age enterprise is its intrinsic entrepreneurial character that man-ifests itself in key organizational knowledge practices relating to organiza-tional knowledge culture, processes, content and infrastructure. This chapter reports on the outcome of our field research in which we set out to study the performance profiles of firms in three geographic regions in these key knowledge practice areas.

Our research provides evidence that innovative, entrepreneurial firms, no matter where they are located, tend to exhibit organizational knowledge practices that correlate with our profile of the Network Age firm. That is to say, our research provides evidence supporting our proposition that knowledge management practices and the cultural beliefs, values and behavioral norms of innovative, entrepreneurial firms will be more akin than dissimilar, regardless of national context. Key Network Age practices that were found to be common to leading-edge firms in all regions included: (1) experimentation is actively encouraged; (2) knowledge is collectively shared, and (3) decision-making is collective.

Furthermore, leading-edge firms were found to have a structure that is flexible and self-adapting, possessing the ability to evolve and thrive amidst constant and unpredictable change. Nimbleness and agility, we found in our work, correlated closely with a high degree of change-readiness. Generally, these firms have done away with cumbersome political, top-down, command-and-control corporate cultures. In their place, open, non-hierarchical, team-driven, knowledge-sharing, innovative and rapid response cultures have emerged. Nimbleness and responsiveness are of paramount importance. A member of one of the organizations studied used the following animal metaphor to describe his organization: 'A leopard – nimble, fast, quick, smart, compassionate, competitive, shrewd.' In its extreme form, this has brought forth small, fast-changing, amoebae-like clusters within firms that come together to get a job done and then break apart, only to reconfigure in a different form around another project.

The implications of our findings for international entrepreneurship are significant: regardless of national context or setting, innovative, entrepreneurial firms appear to share a set of attributes that we ascribe to the Network Age. These attributes are intimately linked to the organizational cultural makeup of the firm and the way in which it manages its most important resource, people-embodied knowledge, and not to its national setting. The key challenge to management, therefore, lies in understanding the key drivers and enablers of the organization's knowledge. The authors suggest that management attention should focus on organizational knowledge in the four realms culture, processes, content and infrastructure.

Our final conclusion, a familiar one in the literature, is that much more work needs to be done to fully comprehend the impact that this revolutionary Network Age is having on management and culture. Historical and cultural influences, as we see in Singapore and the Netherlands, still constrain organizations from achieving optimum knowledge management. And even within that vanguard center of innovation and change, Silicon Valley, firms are still in transition from Industrial Age practices toward the open, boundaryless, non-hierarchical, continual learning organization required in the twenty-first century.

REFERENCES

Amidon, Debra M. (1997), *Innovation Strategy for the Knowledge Economy: The Keen Awakening*, Boston: Butterworth–Heinemann.

Birchall, David W. and George Tovstiga (1999), 'The strategic potential of a firm's knowledge portfolio', *Journal of General Management*, 25 (1): 1–16.

Browning, John and Spencer Reiss (1998), 'Encyclopedia of the new economy', *Wired*, March.

Chait, Laurence P. (1998), 'Creating a successful knowledge management system', *Prism*, Second Quarter: 83.

Dana, Leo-Paul (1999), *Entrepreneurship in Pacific Asia: Past Present & Future*, Singapore, London and Hong Kong: World Scientific.

Dana, Leo-Paul (2000), 'Sheep farm in the Pyrenees', in Ken Miller and Roger Layton, *Fundamentals of Marketing* (4th edn), Roseville: McGraw-Hill Australia, pp. 335–8.

Drucker, Peter (1993), *Post-Capitalist Society*, Boston: Butterworth–Heinemann.

Hofstede, Geert H. (1981), *Culture's Consequences: International Differences in Work-related Values*, Newbury Park, CA: Sage.

Hofstede, Geert H. (1991), *Cultures and Organizations: Software of the Mind*, London: McGraw-Hill.

Hofstede, Geert H. (2001), *Culture's Consequences: Comparing Values, Behaviors, Institutions and Organizations Across Nations*, Newbury Park, CA: Sage.

Hofstede, Geert H. and Michael Harris Bond (1988), 'Confucius & economic growth: new trends in culture's consequences', *Organizational Dynamics*, 16 (4): 4–21.

Imparato, Nicholas and Oren Harari (1994), *Jumping the Curve: Innovation and Strategic Choice in an Age of Transition*, San Francisco, CA: Jossey-Bass.

Kelly, Kevin (1997), 'New rules for the new economy', *Wired*, September.

Korot, Len (1989), 'Technoculture: leading edge to European integration or an organizational anomaly?', *Proceedings of the 1989 Annual Conference*, European International Business Association.

Laurent, André (1983), 'A cultural diversity of Western conceptions of management', *International Studies of Management and Organization*, 13: 75–96.

Maira, Arun N. (1998), 'Connecting across boundaries: the fluid-network organization', *Prism*, First Quarter Issue.

Nonaka, Ikujiro and Hirotaka Takeuchi (1995), *The Knowledge Creating Company*, New York: Oxford University Press.

Pederson, Paul O. (1998), Contribution in *Knowledge Management Review*, 1 (March/April).

Richman, Barry M. and Richard N. Farmer (1965), *Comparative Management and Economic Progress*, Homewood, IL: Jossey-Bass.

Roos, Johan, Goran Roos, Nicola Carlo Dragonetti and Leif Edvinsson (1997), *Intellectual Capital: Navigating the New Business Landscape*, London: Macmillan.

San Jose Mercury News (2000), 'Venture capitalists open gates on record-breaking torrent of money', 13 February.

Schein, Edgar H. (1992), *Organizational Culture and Leadership*, San Francisco, CA: Jossey-Bass.

Tovstiga, George (1999), 'Profiling the knowledge worker in the knowledge-intensive organization: emerging roles', *International Journal of Technology Management*, 18 (5/6/7/8): 731–44.

Tovstiga, George and Len Korot (2001), 'Knowledge-driven organizational change: a framework', *International Journal of Entrepreneurship and Innovation Management*, 1 (1): 22–33.

Ulijn, Jan and Rajesh Kumar (1999), 'Technical communication in a multicultural world: how to make it an asset in managing international businesses, lessons for Europe and Asia for the 21st Century', in Peter J. Hager and Howard Jeffrey Scheiber (eds), *Managing Global Communication in Science and Technology*, New York: John Wiley & Sons, pp. 319–48.

Von Krogh, Georg, Kazuo Ichijo and Ikujiro Nonaka (2000), *Enabling Knowledge Creation*, New York: Oxford University Press.

10. E-commerce and the internationalization of SMEs

Kittinoot Chulikavit and Jerman Rose

INTRODUCTION

Small and medium-sized enterprises (SMEs) play an important role in most of the economies of the world. In the last decade researchers have increasingly been interested in how SMEs contribute to economic growth and development (Rovere, 1996; von Potobsky, 1992). While the term 'SME' is widespread, there is no generally agreed definition that isolates this type of organization (Yusof and Aspinwall, 2000; von Potobsky, 1992). A variety of definitions for SMEs can be seen among different countries (von Potobsky, 1992), industries and government agencies (Yusof and Aspinwall, 2000). Some researchers have defined SMEs on quantitative criteria while some others have used qualitative criteria (von Potobsky, 1992). Quantitative criteria involve factors such as: sales figures, social assets, number of employees, number of customers, value of the equipment, capital investment, production, levels of energy consumption, and so on. But because these quantitative limits differ from country to country, even something so apparently concrete as a quantitative limit causes misunderstandings. Qualitative criteria, on the other hand, are related to behavioral attributes such as how SMEs are run, how decisions are made, how authority is given, and so on.

Since it is the behavior of SMEs that is key to the relationship between emerging electronic commerce and export behavior, we will focus on some of the established qualitative descriptions of SMEs. Using this approach, we have in mind firms exhibiting production flexibility, adaptability to changing markets (von Potobsky, 1992), ownership, independence (O'Farrell and Hitchins, 1988), niche-taking, innovativeness, rapidity of decision-making, production simplicity, less effectiveness of information and communication management, and working motivation (Rovere, 1996). SMEs' most significant constraints are limitations of internal resources such as financial, human, information and management resources (Yusof and Aspinwall, 2000; Buckley, 1989; Erramilli and D'Souza, 1993).

The number of SMEs going international has increased recently (Coviello and Martin, 1999; Coviello and McAuley, 1999; Erramilli and D'Souza, 1993; Bonaccorsi, 1992). Research has been conducted on the internationalization process in SMEs (Jones, 1999; Coviello and Martin, 1999; Coviello and McAuley, 1999; Bonaccorsi, 1992; Wolff and Pett, 2000; Reuber and Fischer, 1997; Naidu and Prasad, 1994). Among the topics explored are the competitive advantages of SMEs, choices of entry mode, and SMEs' international constraints.

Some researchers such as Bonaccorsi (1992) have argued that SMEs' size provides SMEs flexibility to enter and exit foreign markets more easily than larger firms. Size also allows internal information and communications activities to flow more effectively (Rovere, 1996; Yusof and Aspinwall, 2000; Liesch and Knight, 1999). Innovativeness is another characteristic of SMEs (Yusof and Aspinwall, 2000). This advantage gives SMEs the ability to develop (Rangone, 1999) or continually improve products or processes. In addition, SMEs are often more customer oriented and quicker to adapt to new technologies (Mascarenhas, 1996) because cumbersome management levels do not exist within the organizations (Liesch and Knight, 1999; Yusof and Aspinwall, 2000).

The recent emergence of the resource-based theory of the firm is useful in this context because it suggests that whether a firm can be competitive in its business environment depends on how its internal resources can differentiate the firm from its competitors (Rangone, 1999). In other words, how firms make use of their internal resources is more important than the quantity of internal resources the firms have. SMEs are by definition resource limited and many have already succeeded in the competitive environment. One area where SMEs can overcome resource constraints is the way they have become successful in entry to foreign markets. This used to be very difficult for SMEs.

Internationalization and SMEs

How firms enter foreign markets has been discussed by many researchers. Johanson and Vahlne (1977) suggested that firms follow a foreign entry pattern from exporting their products through local distributors at the beginning, then trying to have licensing agreements when they feel more comfortable, followed by foreign direct investment (FDI) at the final stage (Fina and Rugman, 1996). Furthermore, Bonaccorsi (1992) explains that there is a general agreement among researchers that 'small firms may grow in the domestic market and avoid undertaking a risky activity like exporting, while large firms have to export if they are to increase their sales' (p. 606). However, this finding has been found not to be true for all types of firms, especially small firms, by many researchers, such as Bonaccorsi (1992), Oviatt and McDougall (1994), and Wolff and Pett (2000).

In recent years, a significant number of SMEs have become involved in international business (Wright, 1999; Etemad and Wright, forthcoming). Some even export to foreign markets immediately after founding their businesses (Oviatt and McDougall, 1994; McDougall *et al.*, 1994). Sometimes the motivation for such firms is small or limited domestic markets for high-technology or highly specialized products (Bonaccorsi, 1992). For most SMEs exporting has become the alternative of choice for entry mode and internationalization (Leonidou and Katsikeas, 1996).

SMEs' International Constraints

As noted above, SMEs commonly have limited internal resources. Firms with resource constraints have traditionally been unable to engage in international activities. Limitations in financial, human or management resources all impact the ability to be competitive in an international market. For example, limited financial resources can lead to slow investment in new products and processes (Yusof and Aspinwall, 2000). Human resource is also one of the most critical internal resources that international firms should have in place (Welch and Luostarinen, 1988; Lorange, 1986). Management resource, which is part of human resource, is considered to be very important, especially at the beginning of exporting when firms need decision-makers or managers with foreign experience, education and language training (Reid, 1981; Miesenbock, 1988; Oviatt and McDougall, 1994; Reuber and Fischer, 1997).

Above all, some researchers (Liesch and Knight, 1999) see information and knowledge as the most important resources for SME internationalization. Although SMEs usually lack international information and knowledge resources, the recent developments facilitate SMEs' acquisition of information and knowledge more effectively (Liesch and Knight, 1999).

Exporting: SMEs' Choice of Entry Mode

Export is 'the international, marketing-related decisions and activities of internationally active firms' (Shoham, 1998, p. 60). Firms will export their products or services by themselves directly or through agents or distributors to their foreign customers in foreign countries without having any control of foreign operations (Shoham, 1998). One of the main reasons for SMEs to choose exporting as their primary mode of entry to foreign markets is that exporting can work very well with SMEs' characteristics of flexibility with minimum resource investment (Young *et al.*, 1989).

According to the stage theory of internationalization, a small firm will pass through developmental stages, in which the firm will gain more experience and confidence (Wolff and Pett, 2000). However, resource-based theory (Barney, 1991) suggests that small firms do not always have to complete the stages. Some firms sell their products internationally from the time they start their businesses (Oviatt and McDougall, 1994; McDougall *et al.*, 1994). This shorter process is made possible in part by advanced communications and information management (Oviatt and McDougall, 1994).

What impact does the emergence of new business models caused by the growth of the Internet have on this picture of SME internationalization through export? We will now turn to this issue.

ELECTRONIC COMMERCE

Electronic commerce (e-commerce) over the Internet has been used actively for less than ten years, and its exponential growth has generated tremendous impacts on the business environment. Broadly defined, e-commerce is any form of economic activity conducted via electronic connections (Wigand, 1997). Many researchers, such as Zwass (1996) and Applegate *et al.* (1996), have pointed out that e-commerce involves buying and selling products or services, transferring information and conducting other business activities over telecommunications networks. While researchers view e-commerce broadly as a wide range of telecommunications applications, common usage considers '[e]-commerce as simply buying and selling goods over the Internet' (Riggins and Rhee, 1998, p. 90).

E-commerce is the application of information and communication technology for electronically conducting business transactions in order to achieve a business goal (Wigand, 1997). For the purpose of this chapter, e-commerce is viewed as transactions conducted over the Internet because the Internet is at the cutting edge of today's e-commerce activities and appears to offer a reasonable and accessible alternative for SMEs to conduct such business. Responding to this accessibility, many firms have created websites on the Internet and expect to develop new customer and business relationships (Barua *et al.*, 1997) while simultaneously maintaining current relationships.

E-commerce: SMEs' Aid to Internationalization

Although it is still early for definitive conclusions, there is evidence that the Internet has provided opportunities for SMEs, which usually have limited internal resources, to conduct business with customers, suppliers and partners globally (Etemad and Wright, 1999). There is also evidence that the Internet helps SMEs enter foreign markets with lower costs and more effective business processes than other means of internationalization (Kleindl, 2000).

Early studies indicate that e-commerce offers some advantages to SMEs. One advantage is the lowering of costs for information, advertising and promotion, catalog, and market research; while increasing image and public recognition quickly (Hamill and Gregory, 1997; Turban *et al.*, 2000). At the same time the Internet allows SMEs to reach global and niche markets more easily and quickly (Alba *et al.*, 1997; Kleindl, 2000; Turban *et al.*, 2000).

Nevertheless, there are some limitations for SMEs as well. SMEs are likely to lack advanced information systems necessary to generate complete and effective business transaction processes. They also may lack necessary human resources to make full use of the Internet (Turban *et al.*, 2000).

From the internationalization perspective, e-commerce helps firms expand their markets worldwide. By means of the Internet, firms can penetrate into new international markets, present the details of their product information and corporate profiles, and offer effective interactive customer services. They can deal more effectively with customer orders, complaints and queries (Lituchy and Rail, 2000). There are indications that e-commerce gives SMEs the opportunity to reach foreign markets very rapidly with low transaction costs (Hamill and Gregory, 1997; Lituchy and Rail, 2000) in spite of the limitations. Issues related to Internet accessibility, language and translation, local government interference, culture and currency differences, international agreements and regulations, buyer and seller identification, trust and security, and financial aspects such as electronic payment systems are still impediments that simply having a website will not solve (Samiee, 1998; Turban *et al.*, 2000).

E-COMMERCE EXAMPLES FROM THAILAND

A review of the literature shows that SMEs have characteristics that enable them to internationalize even with limited internal resources. Recent studies are suggesting that e-commerce can help SMEs boost their export performance and facilitate internationalization. In order to test the boundaries of the relationship between e-commerce and SME export, we conducted interviews with four Thai firms to help identify directions for further research. The information from the four firms is presented as exploratory case studies or preludes, which are analyzed in order to develop the most appropriate propositions (Yin, 1993).

The four interviewed firms are all located in Chiangmai, Thailand, the home of many manufacturing and exporting handicraft SMEs. Table 10.1 summarizes the main characteristics of each of the four firms. These four firms can be quantitatively categorized as SMEs based on the number of employees. Each firm has fewer than 200 employees. In addition, each of the four firms possesses major qualitative characteristics of SMEs. For instance, they all are managed by single owners who make all business decisions within very short periods of time due to short decision processes. Because of their less complex and more flexible production processes, the firms produce customized products as requested as well as standardized products. Even with their standardized products, the firms always change the products' styles to satisfy changing customer needs and wants and also introduce new products to their niche markets.

All of the firms are manufacturing and exporting firms that have attempted to use e-commerce within the past five years to expand their markets internationally. All of the firms' products fall into the handicraft category. The products are delicate jewelry, clothing products, mulberry-paper products and scented candles. We found that two of these firms (Firms A and B) have experienced some difficulty in conducting e-commerce. As might be expected, this led them to minimize their e-commerce activity. The other two firms (Firms C and D) have been very successful using e-commerce as their main medium to connect with their current foreign customers and attract new customers. These firms' sales increased between 30 per cent and 50 per cent after they launched their own websites.

The subject firms used their websites primarily as a form of advertising. The initial response seemed very positive, as more and more potential customers sent requests for product information. The two firms (Firms A and B) that found e-commerce problematic were asked for product samples and catalogs by potential customers more often than the others (Firms C and D), due in significant part to the types of products, custom jewelry and clothing. Their products are so complex and customized that the product pictures available on their websites do not sufficiently show the products. As a result, they had to bear large sample and catalog costs and mailing expenses. Finally, they learned through experience that most of those who requested information never ordered their products. So the expense of sending materials was not balanced by an increase in sales.

On the other hand the successful firms (Firms C and D), whose products seem to be more standardized than the first two (Firms A and B), have received fewer requests for their product samples and catalogs than the first two firms did. The information provided on their websites, such as product pictures and sizes, answers most of potential customers' questions. When samples or catalogs are requested, the firms send them only to those cus-

Table 10.1 Summary of the main characteristics of the interviewed firms

Characteristics	Firm A	Firm B	Firm C	Firm D
Types of businesses	Manufacturing and exporting	Manufacturing and exporting	Manufacturing and exporting	Manufacturing and exporting
Types of products	Delicate jewelry	Clothing products	Mulberry-paper products	Scented candles
Number of employees	50	200	150	50
Ownership	Single owner	Single owner	Single owner	Single owner
Percentage of sales increase due to e-commerce	Less than 5	Less than 5	30	30–50
E-commerce communication	Via the firm's web developer	Via the firm's web developer	Via the firm's private e-mail address	Via the firm's private e-mail address
Degree of owner involvement	Low	Low	High	High
Owner's perspective on e-commerce	Costly promotion	Costly promotion	Effective communication and promotion	Effective communication and promotion

tomers with high potential to buy. Moreover, these two firms (Firms C and D) have pursued a high-quality differentiation strategy via their websites. One of the firms has found this strategy very effective. It can sell its products at higher prices compared to competitors. The other found it could increase its sales volume by encouraging Internet customers to compare prices among many suppliers.

We also found that the firms' management teams have had significant influences on the firms' attitudes toward e-commerce. The first two firms' (Firms A and B) management teams seem to have quickly lost their enthusiasm for e-commerce as soon as problems appeared. While their lack of enthusiasm in the face of failure may be expected, their lack of willingness to investigate the sources of their failure may indicate that their expectations may have been too high. Management commitment is essential to any new operational initiative. E-commerce is new, and management must be willing to learn and adjust as it would when testing any other new approach.

The managing director of one of the successful firms (Firms C and D), on the other hand, is committed to developing this tool and believes that doing business via the Internet has helped ease communication, maintenance of long-term customer relationships, and is getting more new customers at very low costs. The management team of the other successful firm considers e-commerce an effective marketing tool that can help the firm advertise its products worldwide.

To be successful in e-commerce, the management team has to have not only enough understanding of how e-commerce works and its costs and benefits, but also positive expectations of its outcome. Furthermore, international skills and experiences, including English language, understanding of cultural differences, and international marketing, are still required for the management team. Both of the successful firms (Firms C and D) have management teams with international skills and experience who can communicate with foreign customers directly. As a result, decision-making and communication processes are usually short and fast.

E-COMMERCE AS AN AID TO SME EXPORT

We learned from our interviews that e-commerce is a double-edged sword, with both advantages and disadvantages for SMEs.

To be successful in exporting their products to foreign markets by means of e-commerce, SMEs not only need to know how to utilize e-commerce effectively but also have to be innovative and flexible in a continually changing environment (Kleindl, 2000).

Since the Internet offers consumers more choices of suppliers (Barua *et al.*, 1997), the extent to which suppliers have to compete with each other is very severe. Therefore, although e-commerce is beneficial to SMEs to some extent, SMEs have to exploit their unique advantages.

It will help us to formulate research questions regarding the development of SME exporting if we can develop or identify a conceptual framework that will fit the emerging interaction of e-commerce and SMEs. Therefore, the framework developed for this chapter (see Figure 10.1) is the combination of the suggestions from the resource-based view of a firm; the SME studies by Namiki (1988), Wolff and Pett (2000), and Julien *et al.*, (1997); many critical recommendations by SME researchers, such as McDougall *et al.*, (1994), Oviatt and McDougall (1994), Reuber and Fischer (1997), and so on; significant findings from the exploratory case studies from Thailand; and finally recent literature in the e-commerce and Internet studies.

Nobuaki Namiki (1988) developed such a framework for competitive strategy in export markets shown above, which provides a useful base for examining issues of e-commerce and SME exporting. The framework has been adopted and supported by other researchers such as Wolff and Pett (2000). In their study of 157 small firms in a midwestern state of the United States, Wolff and Pett (2000) found that their SME competitive patterns of export activity are consistent with Namiki's patterns. Moreover, the research

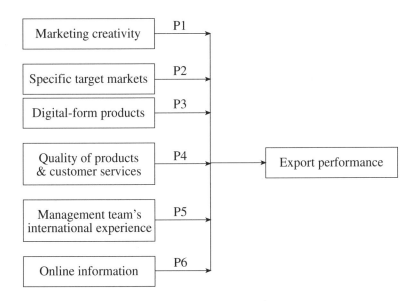

Figure 10.1   Conceptual framework for successfully utilizing e-commerce to increase SMEs' export performance

results from case studies of 20 Canadian small and medium-sized manufacturing exporters conducted by Julien *et al.* (1997) have reflected Namiki's exporting patterns. According to Namiki (1988), to be successful in exporting their products, SMEs should possess capabilities in four different categories as follows.

First, a small or medium-sized firm must have marketing differentiation of pricing, brand, distribution relationships, advertising, and marketing innovation (Namiki, 1988; Wolff and Pett, 2000). This pattern is consistent with the resource-based theory of the firm, which suggests that the assets and capabilities of a firm would provide the firm its marketing advantages (Day, 1994). In this case, the assets would include advertising, promotions, brand image, and location and channel advantages while the capabilities consist of pricing, customer service capabilities, innovation, and product development (Day, 1994). In recent research conducted by Moen (1999), it was found that price competitiveness was one of the specific competitive advantages for SMEs. Furthermore, marketing leadership, which includes innovative marketing techniques and careful control of distribution channels, can help SMEs build effective foundations for their objectives, decisions and actions (Knight, 2000).

The capabilities of the Internet and web management have challenged firms to attract their customers with price and brand differentiation, such as ready comparison of the same product with different prices from different suppliers (Barua *et al.*, 1997) and to offer their customers effective distribution channels such as home delivery (Kleindl, 2000) and very effective advertising with useful information (Kleindl, 2000; Lituchy and Rail, 2000; Barua *et al.*, 1997). Marketing creativity would be utilizing established marketing approaches in a new way or in a new context. Firm D from the above case studies has successfully increased its e-commerce sales by using the advantage of ready price comparison mechanism provided by the Internet system. As a result, the first proposition is given as:

Proposition 1: The more marketing creativity an SME has, the more likely it will be able to utilize e-commerce to increase its export performance.

The second pattern involves marketing new or specialty products and a broad range of products to specific target groups (Namiki, 1988). With limited resources, SMEs can take advantage of developing product uniqueness or technologically sophisticated niche products for niche markets (Moen, 1999) if the limited resources include human capital resources of experience, intelligence, and insight of individual managers and workers that can identify suitable and valuable niche markets for their firms and bring the firms sustained competitive advantage, which is explained by the resource based theory (Barney, 1991). Both product and market selection strategies are major export marketing strategies (Kleinschmidt and Cooper, 1984). According to Knight (2000), international SMEs that focus on niche markets and new industries possess the fastest growth rate. The Internet system allows sellers to reach and offer their specific products or services to specific groups of consumers via a direct linkage (Barua *et al.*, 1997; Wigand, 1997) while it also enables sellers to offer a variety of their products to targeted customers via search engines. Both successful interviewed firms (Firms C and D) have carefully designed their products for some specific target markets. For example, most of Firm C's products have the Western styles while Firm D's products are stylish and fashionable. Moreover, the owners of both firms have realized how search engines can help advertise their websites and bring them to their target markets. Therefore:

Proposition 2: The more specific target markets an SME has, the more likely it will be able to utilize e-commerce to increase its export performance.

The third pattern involves differentiation and innovation through higher-technological products and new product development to non-specific potential customers (Namiki, 1988). According to Day (1994), a firm has to possess distinctive capabilities, such as new product development and continuous quality improvement for high-technology products, to deliver value to customers. These distinctive capabilities are necessarily not easy to imitate by the firm's competitors in order for its competitive advantages to be sustained. SMEs, which possess unique knowledge and skills in some specific areas, often introduce breakthrough products and innovations to the markets (Wolff and Pett, 2000). In addition, SMEs' advantages of flexibility, speed and advantage-seeking behavior have provided them the opportunities for new product development and entrepreneurship (Karagozoglu and Lindell, 1998).

Producers or suppliers of innovative or highly targeted technological products that can easily be produced and stored in digital-form products, such as graphic art and design, information, audio or video recordings, software, and so on, can deliver their samples or products online (Kleindl, 2000; Turban *et al.*, 2000). Additionally, customers who seek specialty and innovative products, and who are familiar with Internet technology, may be more comfortable using the Internet. While our exploratory case studies, which were conducted in the handicraft industry, do not offer evidence to support this proposition, good practical examples can be drawn from the well-known success of Indian information technology businesses. It has been agreed that one major reason that enabled India to become competitive in the software industry is that 'software can be digitized and therefore moved back and forth between [suppliers and customers in] different locations instantaneously through telecommunication links' (Kapur and Ramamurti, 2001, pp. 25–6). Accordingly:

Proposition 3: The more an SME's products can be put in digital form, the more likely it will be able to utilize e-commerce to increase its export performance.

The last pattern emphasizes a product-oriented strategy, which includes high quality of products and customer services (Namiki, 1988). Again, with the distinctive capabilities of human resources of a firm, the firm can provide higher quality of products and customer services than its competitors by whom the quality level cannot be matched easily (Day, 1994). SMEs with focused expertise are able to concentrate on improving the quality of their products and customer services to satisfy their specific customers' needs more effectively than competitors (Wolff and Pett, 2000). Specifically, Julien *et al.* (1997) found that the importance of product quality has been realized by all Canadian SMEs in their study.

Internet business users have been interested in using the Internet to provide information about the quality of their products and improve their customer services. Online forums have allowed firms' representatives and potential customers, outside experts and consumers, previous customers and potential customers, to exchange product information including the quality of products to each other (Turban *et al.*, 2000). Moreover, customers can communicate with suppliers in real time via electronic mail (Lituchy and Rail, 2000; Barua *et al.*, 1997) when they have product questions and problems, or need some advice. The Internet allows customers to place their orders online and wait for the orders to be delivered at home (Kleindl, 2000). Firms C and D of the exploratory case studies whose websites provide all necessary product information in detail always answer additional questions that customers ask via electronic mail as soon as they receive the mail by the owners who can communicate in English very well. On the other hand, Firms A and B present very little information about their products on their websites, and all customer electronic mails are handled by their web developers. Examples of quality-related product information and customer services can be offered easily with almost no costs on the Internet. Hence:

Proposition 4: The higher quality of products and customer services an SME has, the more likely it will be able to utilize e-commerce to increase its export performance.

In addition to Namiki's (1988) framework for competitive strategy in export markets, we suggest a critically important addition. Many researchers, such as Reuber and Fischer (1997), McDougall *et al.* (1994), and Oviatt and McDougall (1994), have argued that the degree of SME management team's international experience has a positive relationship with SME international abilities. The study of SMEs in the Canadian software products industry by Reuber and Fischer (1997) shows that internationally experienced management teams, which can be seen as the firm-specific human resources from the resource-based point of view, lead SMEs to engage more in international activities such as having more foreign strategic partners and seeking foreign sales within a shorter period after opening their businesses.

Furthermore, since an increasing number of firms develop their own websites, the competitive advantage of a firm is not having its own website, but having appropriate skills and knowledge to make better use of its website than its competitors (Samiee, 1998). Business strategy and a vision from top management are parts of e-commerce development (Turban *et al.*, 2000). Because of the limitation of internal resources, an SME management team is likely to have to be directly involved in the e-commerce activity of the firm. Since this is the case it is perhaps even more important for SMEs that undertake to facilitate export activity using the Internet to have internationally experienced management. Firm C may be the best example for this investigation. The firm's website and all its content were created and have been updated by its managing director/owner, who is an American and has international experience. In addition, Firm D's Thai owner, who has significant international experience, plays an important role in creating and updating its website. As a result, both websites provide information in a more professional and international way. Therefore:

Proposition 5: The higher capabilities to transfer the management team's international experience to its e-commerce activity an SME has, the more likely it will be able to utilize e-commerce to increase its performance.

Finally, information acquisition and collection have become a key factor for the success of exporting SMEs (Julien *et al.*, 1997). Insufficient information to support their internationalization process can create a barrier for SMEs to expand their markets overseas (Cafferata and Mensi,

1995; Mahone, Jr and Choudhury, 1995). A study of Korean small and medium-sized manufacturing firms, for example, showed that information available for the firms had the most significant impact on export decision-making (Weaver and Pak, 1990).

The Internet contains a tremendous number of information sources for firms to search for or update their current information about competitors and their products, new regulations or policies of related organizations, relevant industry news update, and so on. More specifically, the Internet has provided SMEs opportunities to acquire necessary information for developing their export plans and export strategies (Yeoh, 2000). Internet users can receive information in some specific areas through e-mail free of charge or with little fee (Turban *et al.*, 2000). Moreover, firms can obtain informal feedback related to their own or competitors' products and services from chat rooms and message boards, as well as their incoming e-mails. Since all four interviewed firms are located in Thailand, which has a less effective traditional communications system than other more developed countries, the Internet has become their most useful communications system. They use it to acquire and collect the information about their foreign competitors, markets, potential customers and other business information including electronic-mail feedback. Therefore:

Proposition 6: The higher capabilities to gain access to online information an SME has, the more likely it will be able to utilize e-commerce to increase its export performance.

CONCLUSIONS

The discussion by Wolff and Pett (2000) that 'With . . . improved international communication and information networks, many small firms are pressed to compete in international markets' (p. 35) implies the SMEs will be challenged by changing position in global competition. Even though many SMEs have no intention to internationalize, they are unavoidably put into the global market. E-commerce may be the tool to help some SMEs compete on an international basis.

E-commerce can help SMEs not only to expand their markets but also to survive within the changing business environment. According to the suggestion by Turban *et al.* (2000) that '[t]he major advantage of EC is the ability to do business anytime and from anywhere and do it rapidly at a reasonable cost' (p. 445), e-commerce seems very suitable to the characteristics of SMEs in the global environment. However, whether SMEs can utilize e-commerce effectively depends in part on their individual characteristics, such as type of business, products and services, target customers, and their available resources, especially management resource.

Future empirical work is suggested to test the propositions. More research should be conducted on how an SME with limited knowledge of e-commerce could be able to take advantage of it, whether e-commerce affects network development of SMEs, what SMEs' marketing plans would be appropriate for their e-commerce, and so on. E-commerce is in its infancy, even though it is growing rapidly. Recent developments in technology, such as automatic translation software, promise to reduce some of the old barriers to international communication. Other barriers, such as government regulation and taxes, will continue to challenge SMEs. We found in our interviews that the role of management attitude and experience remains a key factor in success. E-commerce is a tool like any other that requires knowledgeable managers for proper application. The strategic adaptability stream of research could be enriched by investigations of the role of e-commerce in adapting to change.

IMPLICATIONS FOR MANAGEMENT

The findings from both conceptual research and the studied cases suggest that e-commerce can be very helpful to many but not all SMEs. Many SMEs have experienced difficulties in dealing with e-commerce. Some of them have finally stopped conducting e-commerce and gone back to managing their businesses in traditional ways. For SMEs that have limited internal resources, suitable competitive strategies that enable them to make full use of their unique characteristics and the benefits of e-commerce will help them succeed in global markets.

The studied cases also imply another critical aspect of conducting e-commerce, namely the SME management team's e-commerce experience. The SME management teams have to understand how the strengths of e-commerce can help them expand their markets internationally and also recognize the limitations of e-commerce as their challenges. Many SME management teams have stopped supporting e-commerce because they have not seen the actual benefits but only its obstacles. Moreover, utilizing e-commerce to expand its markets internationally requires an SME to have a qualified management team that possesses necessary international skills and knowledge such as foreign languages (at least English), international experience and culture differences.

REFERENCES

Alba, Joseph, John Lynch, Barton Weitz, Chris Janiszewski, Richard Lutz, Alan Sawyer and Stacy Wood (1997), 'Interactive home shopping: Consumer, retailer, and manufacturer incentives to participate in electronic marketplaces', *Journal of Marketing*, 61 (3): 38–53.

Applegate, L.M., C.W. Holsapple, R. Kalakota, F.J. Radermacher and A.B. Whinston (1996), 'Electronic commerce: Building blocks of new business opportunity', *Journal of Organizational Computing and Electronic Commerce*, 6 (1): 1–10.

Barney, Jay B. (1991), 'Firm resources and sustained competitive advantage', *Journal of Management*, 17 (1): 99–120.

Barua, Anitesh, Sury Ravindran and Andrew B. Whinston (1997), 'Efficient selection of suppliers over the Internet', *Journal of Management Information Systems*, 13 (4): 117–37.

Bonaccorsi, Andrea (1992), 'On the relationship between firm size and export intensity', *Journal of International Business Studies*, 23 (4): 605–35.

Buckley, Peter J. (1989), 'Foreign direct investment by small and medium-sized enterprises: The theoretical background', *Small Business Economics*, 1 (2): 89–100.

Cafferata, Roberto and Riccardo Mensi (1995), 'The role of information in the internationalization of SMEs: A typological approach', *International Small Business Journal*, 13 (3): 35–46.

Coviello, Nicole E. and Andrew McAuley (1999), 'Internationalisation and the smaller firm: A review of contemporary empirical research', *Management International Review*, 39 (3): 223–56.

Coviello, Nicole E. and Kristina A.-M. Martin (1999), 'Internationalization of service SMEs: An integrated perspective from the engineering consulting sector', *Journal of International Marketing*, 7 (4): 42–66.

Day, George S. (1994), 'The capabilities of market-driven organizations', *Journal of Marketing*, 58 (4): 37–52.

Erramilli, M. Krishna and Derrick E. D'Souza (1993), 'Venturing into foreign markets: The case of the small service firm', *Entrepreneurship Theory and Practice*, 17 (4): 29–41.

Etemad, Hamid and Richard W. Wright (1999), 'Internationalization of SMEs: Management responses to a changing environment', *Journal of International Marketing*, 7 (4): 4–10.

Etemad, Hamid and Richard W. Wright (forthcoming), *International Entrepreneurship in Small and Medium Size Enterprises*, Cheltenham, UK and Northampton, MA: Edward Elgar Publishing.

Fina, Erminio and Alan M. Rugman (1996), 'A test of internalization theory and internationalization theory: The Upjohn Company', *Management International Review*, 36 (3): 199–213.

Hamill, Jim and Karl Gregory (1997), 'Internet marketing in the internationalisation of UK SMEs', *Journal of Marketing Management*, 13 (1–3): 9–28.

Johanson, Jan and Jan-Erik Vahlne (1977), 'The internationalization process of the firm: A model of knowledge development and increasing foreign commitments', *Journal of International Business Studies*, 8 (1): 23–32.

Jones, Marian V. (1999), 'The internationalization of small high-technology firms', *Journal of International Marketing*, 7 (4): 15–41.

Julien, Pierre-Andre, Andre Joyal, Laurent Deshaies and Charles Ramangalahy (1997), 'A typology of strategic behaviour among small and medium-sized exporting businesses. A case study', *International Small Business Journal*, 15 (2): 33–50.

Kapur, Devesh and Ravi Ramamurti (2001), 'India's emerging competitive advantage in services', *The Academy of Management Executive*, 15 (2): 20–33.

Karagozoglu, Necmi and Martin Lindell (1998), 'Internationalization of small and medium sized technology-based firms: An exploratory study', *Journal of Small Business Management*, 36 (1): 44–59.

Kleindl, Brad (2000), 'Competitive dynamics and new business models for SMEs in the virtual marketplace', *Journal of Developmental Entrepreneurship*, 5 (1): 73–85.

Kleinschmidt, E.J. and R.G. Cooper (1984), 'A typology of export strategy applied to the export performance of industrial firms', in E. Kaynak (ed.), *International Marketing Management*, New York: Praeger, pp. 217–31.

Knight, Gary (2000), 'Entrepreneurship and marketing strategy: The SME under globalization', *Journal of International Marketing*, 8 (2): 12–32.

Leonidou, Leonidas C. and Constantine S. Katsikeas (1996), 'The export development process: An integrative review of empirical models', *Journal of International Business Studies*, 27 (3): 517–51.

Liesch, Peter W. and Gary A. Knight (1999), 'Information internalization and hurdle rates in small and medium enterprise internationalization', *Journal of International Business Studies*, 30 (2): 383–94.

Lituchy, Terri R. and Anny Rail (2000), 'Bed and breakfasts, small inns, and the Internet: The impact of technology on the globalization of small businesses', *Journal of International Marketing*, 8 (2), 86–97.

Lorange, P. (1986), 'Human resource management in multinational cooperative ventures', *Human Resource Management*, 25 (1): 133–48.

Mahone, Jr, Charlie E. and Pravat K. Choudhury (1995), 'Small and medium sized manufacturers and traders', *Multinational Business Review*, 3 (2): 17–26.

Mascarenhas, B. (1996), 'The founding of specialist firms in a global fragmenting industry', *Journal of International Business Studies*, 27 (1): 27–42.

McDougall, Patricia Phillips, Scott Shane and Benjamin M. Oviatt (1994), 'Explaining the formation of international new ventures: The limits of theories from international business research', *Journal of Business Venturing*, 9 (6): 469–87.

Miesenbock, Kurt J. (1988), 'Small business and exporting: A literature review', *International Small Business Journal*, 6 (2): 42–61.

Moen, Oystein (1999), 'The relationship between firm size, competitive advantages and export performance revisited', *International Small Business Journal*, 18 (1): 53–72.

Naidu, G.M. and V. Kanti Prasad (1994), 'Predictors of export strategy and performance of small- and medium-sized firms', *Journal of Business Research*, 31 (1/2): 107–15.

Namiki, Nobuaki (1988), 'Export strategy for small business', *Journal of Small Business Management*, 26 (2): 32–7.

O'Farrell, Patrick N. and P.W.N. Hitchins (1988), 'Alternative theories of small firm growth: A critical review', *Environment and Planning*, 20 (10): 365–83.

Oviatt, Benjamin M. and Patricia Phillips McDougall (1994), 'Toward a theory of international new ventures', *Journal of International Business Studies*, 25 (1): 45–64.

Rangone, Andrea (1999), 'A resource-based approach to strategy analysis in small–medium sized enterprises', *Small Business Economics*, 12 (3): 233–48.

Reid, S.D. (1981), 'The decision-maker and export entry and expansion', *Journal of International Business Studies*, 12 (2): 101–12.

Reuber, A. Rebecca and Eileen Fischer (1997), 'The influence of the management team's international experience on the internationalization behaviors of SMEs', *Journal of International Business Studies*, 28 (4): 807–25.

Riggins, Frederick J. and Hyeun-Suk Rhee (1998), 'Toward a unified view of electronic commerce', *Communications of the ACM*, 41 (10): 88–95.

Rovere, Renata Lebre La (1996), 'IT diffusion in small and medium-sized enterprises: Elements for policy definition', *Information Technology for Development*, 7 (4): 169–81.

Samiee, Saeed (1998), 'Exporting and the Internet: A conceptual perspective', *International Marketing Review*, 15 (5): 413–26.

Shoham, Aviv (1998), 'Export performance: A conceptualization and empirical assessment', *Journal of International Marketing*, 6 (3): 59–81.

Turban, Efraim, Jae Lee, David King and H. Michael Chung (eds) (2000), *Electronic Commerce: A Managerial Perspective*, Englewood Cliffs, NJ: Prentice Hall.

von Potobsky, Geraldo (1992), 'Small and medium-sized enterprises and labour law', *International Labour Review*, 131 (6): 601–28.

Weaver, K.M. and J. Pak (1990), 'Export behaviour and attitudes of small and medium-sized Korean manufacturing firms', *International Small Business Journal*, 8 (4): 58–70.

Welch, Lawrence S. and Reijo Luostarinen (1988), 'Internationalization: Evolution of a concept', *Journal of General Management*, 14 (2): 34–55.

Wigand, Rolf T. (1997), 'Electronic commerce: Definition, theory, and context', *Information Society*, 13 (1): 1–16.

Wolff, James A. and Timothy L. Pett (2000), 'Internationalization of small firms: An examination of export competitive patterns, firm size, and export performance', *Journal of Small Business Management*, 38 (2): 34–47.

Wright, R.W. (1999), *Globalization and Emerging Businesses: Strategies for the 21st Century*, Greenwich, CT: JAI Press.

Yeoh, Poh-Lin (2000), 'Information acquisition activities: A study of global start-up exporting companies', *Journal of International Marketing*, 8 (3): 36–60.

Yin, Robert K. (ed.) (1993), *Applications of Case Study Research*, California, CA: Sage Publications.

Young, Stephen, James Hamill, Colin Wheeler and J. Richard Davies (eds) (1989), *International Market Entry and Development*, Englewood Cliffs, NJ: Prentice Hall.

Yusof, Sha'ri Mohd and Elaine Aspinwall (2000), 'Total quality management implementation frameworks: Comparison and review', *Total Quality Management*, 11 (3): 281–94.

Zwass, V. (1996), 'Electronic commerce: Structures and issues', *International Journal of Electronic Commerce*, 1 (1): 3–23.

11. Managing relations: the essence of international entrepreneurship

Hamid Etemad*

INTRODUCTION

Competition in international markets was traditionally the realm of large companies, with smaller businesses remaining local or regional. The global competitive environment has changed dramatically. The drivers of globalization are removing the barriers which segmented the competitive environments of small and large firms. Firms of all sizes are beginning to share the same competitive space (Etemad, 1999; Dana *et al.* 2000 and 2001). As a consequence, it is increasingly difficult for independent, small firms to thrive on their own unless they become internationally competitive – whether they actually enter the international markets or not.

As smaller firms are increasingly forced to compete in the new global arena, new forms of internationalization are devised and utilized. They cover a wide range: collaborative networks, strategic alliances, integrated outsourcing, etc., some of which are rival models to the operations of multinational enterprises (MNEs). Such new arrangements are used by newly internationalizing competitors to compete in the global marketplace with others, including MNEs. However, neither traditional internationalization models nor theories of entrepreneurship can adequately explain them. These new models of international business involvement require a new, or modified, approach to explain them as they rely on different kinds of relations, capabilities and skills. Paramount among them is the ability to manage such inter-firm relationships.

The primary objective of this chapter is to demonstrate that internationalization is increasingly based on the management of an enterprise's commercial, industrial, personal and even political interactions – i.e., simply, *relations*, regardless of size – with associates and stakeholders. The context of these relations changes, as partnering firms grow in size and their objectives

* The author is grateful to Professor Richard Wright for his constructive comments on earlier versions and also for editorial correction of this paper.

and strategies evolve from relatively simple, localized and largely personal relationships to ones of much greater complexity and scope, requiring a much higher degree of formalization, and institutionalization, than before. Similarly, the partnership's competitors grow within their own evolutionary paths, adding to the complexities of the environment impacting inter-relations. We posit that managing such relations remains the essence of entrepreneurial endeavor for growth and survival in today's global competitive arena. Those who succeed in managing their relations with their associates, partners and stakeholders for *higher mutual benefits than each could manage independently* will become more competitive and stand higher growth prospects in the highly competitive marketplace. We suggest the word *synergy*[1] to embody the emphasis on higher efficiency and effectiveness due to co-operation among partners. For the purposes of this chapter, we use the concept of synergy to refer to co-operation between firms (at least two) joining forces in order to obtain certain mutual objectives not easily achievable by each member in isolation, or to accomplish an outcome jointly much more effectively than individually. The context for the concept is primarily one of effective management for increased competitiveness.

As switching costs disrupt collaborative arrangements, tax joint outcomes, strain productivity and reduce partners' co-operative potentials, partnership-related characteristics, including trust, reliance on the partner's loyalty, and stability in the relationship, become necessary for achieving higher mutual benefits over time. We suggest the word *symbiosis*[2] to convey the concept. The primary emphasis here is on what is necessary for a strong and stable partnership to endure, including attributes such as trust, reliance or dependence and undivided loyalty. Furthermore, we propose the combined concepts of *symbiotic synergy*, or its mirror image concept of *synergistic symbiosis*, to exemplify the higher efficiencies (or outcomes) associated with highly dependent (or co-dependent) relations. Logically, relations based on symbiotic synergy should be able to achieve higher competitiveness and thus withstand higher competitive pressures, enabling the partnership to achieve sustained internationalization over time.

This chapter reviews the literature on the international growth of larger international enterprise in order to illustrate that managing relationships has been the essence underlying the internationalization process for growing firms. It then proceeds to illustrate that the nature of such relationships, especially between *smaller growing* and *larger* firms, have much in common with those in the larger enterprises (e.g., MNEs) and exhibit aspects of symbiotic synergy. Using several illustrative case examples, this chapter illustrates how a well-managed partnership, regardless of potential size differentials, can obtain the maximum outcome possible. Discussion and conclusions of this new perspective are presented at the end.

Stated briefly, the basic premise of this chapter is that the key requisite for success in today's rapidly internationalizing business arena is the ability to manage relationships with others exceptionally well, in order to achieve the higher degrees of symbiotic synergy needed to sustain global competitiveness.

INTERNATIONAL EXPANSION THEORIES OF THE LARGE FIRM

Theories of the multinational enterprise have evolved along two main streams. One, emanating mainly from the work of Hymer, posits that an internal, or proprietary, advantage(s) enables the firm to overcome the handicaps of operating in new and distant markets. The other, known broadly as the 'Scandinavian school' or 'stages model', focuses more on the process of internationalization as the firm gains experience and evolves gradually over time, from a purely domestic operation into an integrated multinational corporate system. Both of these approaches view the firm as essentially a self-contained unit, with little reference to networking, partnership and/or external relationships. However, on a closer examination, both of these approaches can be seen as predicated on the effective development and management of relationships, although mainly internal to the MNE.

Hymer's 'proprietary advantages', which allow the firm to overcome the obstacles of distance and 'foreignness', are based essentially on the linkages between subsidiaries and the parent company. It is the parent–subsidiary relations, governed by ownership and direct control, which set the overseas subsidiary apart from local competitors. As for the firm evolving through 'stages' of progressively fuller overseas involvement, it is in fact the accumulated experiential and economic resources of an elaborate network of relationships, among the parent company and affiliates, including subsidiaries, that gives the network an advantage over the local competitors. These theories are further examined below.

THEORETICAL PERSPECTIVES ON INTERNATIONALIZATION OF LARGE ENTERPRISES

The modern theory of internationalization goes back to the early seventies, when Stephen Hymer (1976) first questioned the reasons for the existence and the growth of multinational enterprises. As Hymer saw it, MNEs with foreign direct investments abroad should be at a competitive disadvantage in foreign markets, due to the additional costs and risks of remote operations in the host nations, and would suffer from 'foreignness' in those environments. He concluded that MNEs must possess certain *intrinsic advantage(s)* not available to their domestic counterparts in the host country, thus giving them a competitive edge. Consider, for example, a typical subsidiary of a globally integrated MNE. Its *relationship-based* privileges include access to technical and support staff at the MNE's headquarters, R&D, developments in the parent and other sister-subsidiaries, and the possibility of cross-subsidization of products and markets.

This exclusive, or privileged, access to a much larger and richer pool of resources through the subsidiary's special relationship with the rest of the MNE's corporate system – i.e., the headquarters in conjunction with the sister-subsidiary system – is a powerful proprietary advantage not readily available to domestic firms, regardless of their size. Local competitors, lacking such relations, cannot benefit from the associated access to complementary resources (beyond their own) at privileged prices. They are thus at a relative disadvantage. Hymer argued that it was the impact of such advantage(s) which distinguished MNEs from other firms, thus enabling MNEs to overcome the handicap of 'foreignness', and to survive and prosper in the diverse host market environments within which they operate. Unfortunately, Hymer approached these advantages in purely economic and comparative-advantage terms. He did not question the underlying reasons giving a subsidiary such real advantage, nor examine it from another perspective in order to identify the true nature of the advantage.

Recent scholars have extended Hymer's pioneering work. Following the original work of Coase (1937), Buckley and Casson (1976) formulated 'Internalization Theory'. It focused on the MNE's attempt to control the 'internal market' of its sister-subsidiary system. This focus was further developed and popularized by Rugman (1979 and 1982). Williamson's (1975 and 1981) 'Transaction Cost Theory' elaborated on the transaction cost aspects of internalization. He viewed MNEs' 'internal market' as an internal hierarchy, substituting for international open markets, providing for the system's required resources at internally set and fiat prices. These developments culminated in the formulation of Dunning's 'Eclectic Theory' of MNEs (1977; 1980; and 1988).

However insightful, none of the above scholars probed the real essence of the MNE's 'advantage'. Retrospectively, Hymer, and other scholars following him, could have easily reformulated the advantage in terms of a set of *privileged relations*, which would provide access to the required economic resources. Theoretically, the hierarchical powers emanating from the MNE's direct ownership of its subsidiaries govern an elaborate and integrated system of rights and privileges, including access to resources accumulated elsewhere in the system. It is this set of formal, internal relationships which constitutes the essence of the traditional MNE's proprietary advantage. Such privileged relations empower local subsidiaries to acquire the necessary resources at privileged prices to compete against national firms.

Other scholars have sought to explain internationalization in terms of its *process*. Johanson and Vahlne (1977 and 1990), Johanson and Weidersheim-Paul (1975), Cavusgil (1980 and 1982), and Cavusgil *et al.* (1979), among others in this school, advocated a longitudinal progression of internationalization, in stages, starting with simple exporting (Bilkey, 1978) to familiar markets with a short 'psychic distance' (Stöttinger and Schlegelmilch, 1998), and evolving over time into more involved and fuller 'stages' of internationalization (Bilkey and Tesar, 1977; Cavusgil and Nevin, 1981, Cavusgil and Kirpalani, 1993; Cavusgil, 1984). Such stage-wise progression provided for accumulation of experiential knowledge (Erikson *et al.*, 1997) in the MNE system. This, in turn, enabled the internationalizing enterprise to draw upon them in order to gain a more equal footing in host markets initially foreign to the enterprise.

Scholars of this school maintained that internationalizing enterprises would expand to less risky markets (e.g., those with shorter psychic distance from home) in the earlier stages of their internationalization. As they gained experience and knowledge over time, enabling them to overcome the disadvantage of foreignness, they expanded further to other markets, while relying on the rest of the system and drawing on the accumulated knowledge in the entire enterprise. As a direct result of its expanding portfolio of experientially accumulated knowledge and the economic efficiencies associated with them, a subsidiary would eventually shed its foreignness and operate very much like the local firms with which it would compete. Beyond the accumulated experiential knowledge and resources, this conceptual approach did not attribute a comparative, or competitive, advantage to MNE operations as Hymer had previously envisioned. If anything, it characterized a typical subsidiary operation as one of initial disadvantage (concurring with Hymer on this point), the burden of which had to be controlled – through the mode of entry and careful selection of markets – and overcome with time. Although the limitations of this perspective are pointed out elsewhere (see, for example, Leonidou and Katsikeas, 1996; McDougall *et al.*, 1994; Oviatt and McDougall, 1994 and 1997; Knight and Cavusgil, 1996), these theories are neither confirmatory nor contradictory to the perspective of this chapter's thesis as they viewed learning and experimentation processes instrumental to international expansion without exploring the actual essence underlying them.

THE ESSENCE OF 'SPECIAL RELATIONSHIPS'

The discussion above illustrates that relationships of one form or another have always been at the core of competitiveness. The literature on small business/entrepreneurship points out, however, that networks of relationships need not necessarily be 'internalized' or controlled by direct ownership and internal hierarchies to be effective. What we are witnessing today is a shift from traditional forms of collaboration, in which the locus of control lies in formal control through ownership, to newer forms of collaboration in which mutual control emanates from interdependence and mutuality of benefit. This represents a departure from the past tradition. In the newly emerging competitive paradigm, the unit of competition is no longer the individual firm; but rather, networks of firms collaborating interdependently for higher mutual benefit than their respective independent operations. In this network-centered system, SMEs can specialize in a set of capabilities, competencies, knowledge and skills much needed by the network (resembling symbiotic relations) in order to generate higher benefits both to themselves and to their network partners than either could by operating independently. Each member of such networks – often regardless of size – would specialize in a different part of the value chain, which may be located in different parts of the world.

It seems evident from the theoretical discussion above that *special, or privileged, relationships* capture the essence of internationalization both for internationalizing SMEs and for MNEs. The two words – 'special' and 'relationships' – merit further elaboration. It is commonly accepted that the nature of the relationships between the subsidiary and the parent company is complementary and thus synergistic. A typical relationship between a subsidiary and the headquarters is clearly symbiotic as well, with the headquarters usually dominating. A typically young subsidiary would not survive the competitive and sustained attacks of the large national firms if the umbilical cord to headquarters were to be severed (especially in the earlier stages of a young subsidiary's life). Such clearly symbiotic relations are consistent with Hymer's original observation. However, the exact nature of the dependence, and the degree of accrued mutual benefit associated with a relationship, can vary widely over time. For example, the relationship between a highly specialized subsidiary and its headquarters may remain interdependent (in terms of specialized functions located partly in the subsidiary and partly in the headquarters or in the rest of the system), without the headquarters necessarily dominating. What may have begun as a largely one-way dependence may evolve over time toward indispensable two-way interdependence, in which neither party dominates the other. Some relations evolve even further into a reverse dependency as both firms learn to rely on each other fully as they specialize in certain aspects (related to their respective locally based advantage) and eliminate redundancy.

While Hymer allowed implicitly for the pool of the resources of the MNE system to nurture the young subsidiary to survive in foreign, and possibly hostile, environments, he did not explicitly formulate the mechanism for the transfer of the advantage from one member in the MNE system to the other. However, his followers did. For example, 'Internalization Theory' (Buckley and Casson, 1976) can be viewed as an internal mechanism for acquiring and distributing advantage within the internal market(s) of the MNE's sister-subsidiary system. Dunning's (1977, 1980 and 1988) insightful contribution is in his decomposition of the *source of the advantage*: firm (or ownership)-specific advantages, intrinsic to the parent corporate system, and location-specific advantage, inherent in a geographic location such as a particular host country). Dunning (1980 and 1988) combined *o*wnership, *l*ocation and *i*nternalization advantages to constitute his OLI theory of foreign direct investment. The MNE's system as a whole can be then viewed as a clearing-house for the internal allocation of specific advantages or resources. The internal market mechanism acted as a hierarchical clearing-house (Williamson, 1975 and 1981) for the allocation of supply and demand for resources on the basis of privileged relations, as discussed earlier. The internally optimal allocation of all resources supported the firm's growth and global expansion.

The examples of Fuji–Xerox, and of IBM-Japan, further illustrate such relationships and how they evolve over time. They demonstrate how symbiotic and synergistic relations can emerge in the parent–subsidiary system of established multinationals (Yoshino and Rangan, 1995; Gomes-Casseres, 1996). Neither Fuji–Xerox nor IBM-Japan could have stood up to their Japanese competitors at the outset without the strong support of the parent firm(s). Nor could the parent companies – Xerox and IBM – have later survived the onslaught of intense global competition without the help of their Japanese affiliates, as these subsidiaries grew and developed their own competitive arsenals. The nature of these relationships evolved and transformed over time. The initial uni-directional flow of knowledge – from headquarters to subsidiaries – actually reversed itself to aid the 'disadvantaged' parents later on. For example, Fuji–Xerox, which started with a license for xerography from one of its parents, Xerox, now holds more patents than the rest of the Xerox family combined; and it collects more royalties and license fees than its parent companies (Gomes-Casseres, 1996, p. 22). The essence of these special relations – based initially on a strict hierarchical control and one-way dominance by parent companies through equity ownership and contractual control – evolved into *interdependence*, or *co-dependence*, in which the parties manage their relations for ever-higher mutual benefits (Gomes-Casseres, 1996, 22–9).

The special relationships described above are by no means unique. Relations between Yamatake–Honeywell and Honeywell, Hewlett and Packard (HP) and Yokogawa–HP, Fujitsu and Amdahl, IBM and Toshiba (Gomes-Casseres, 1996, pp. 70–80), and also between Ford and Mazda, and Motorola and Toshiba (Yoshino and Rangan, 1995, pp. 25–40), to name a few, are similar in nature. The communitarian orientation of Japan's culture (Lodge and Vogel, 1987, pp. 154–5) may have accentuated the particular attention paid by corporate Japan to their partnerships (Wright, 1989) in the early stages of internationalization. However, such cultural arguments cannot be invoked in the later stages of internationalization, where Japanese subsidiaries became as competitive as their parents. Although the recent scholarly developments in strategic alliances would have acknowledged the individual components of what we have articulated as special relations – comprising attributes such as 'symbiosis' (Dana *et al.*, 2000; Etemad *et al.*, 2001), 'synergy' (Etemad, 1999), 'co-destiny' (Gomes-Casseres, 1996, p. 26), 'co-evolution and co-dependence' (Acs and Yeung, 1999) – the totality and the essence of such relations have remained elusive to most scholars.

Similar to these older arrangements, the recent successful business developments highlight the critical value of such special relations to international growth of *non-hierarchically oriented partnerships* as well. We present, below, very brief case studies of three fast-growing and highly dynamic enterprises, from different industries. Each began as a small start-up, then grew internationally at unprecedented rates: in fact, each compressed its full growth cycle, from birth to a global giant, into less than a decade. We suggest that they are variants of a newly emerging paradigm of rapid internationalization of start-up firms, based largely on partnership in non-hierarchical networks and careful management of special relationships.

EXAMPLES OF THE EMERGING PARADIGM

Sun Microsystems

Although a multi-billion-dollar company today, Sun Microsystems ('Sun') began as a small but highly entrepreneurial start-up in the 1970s. It still competes as vigorously and as entrepreneurially in work-stations and network devices as it did much earlier in its life. Sun is still growing rapidly, and its rate of return on investment has been well above industry standards.

Sun has managed to avoid several waves of technological upheaval in the industry by its reliance on a network of relationships with other firms. For example, in a major technological shift, from CISC-based to RISC-based central processing (CPU) chips, Sun entered into an alliance with an equally progressive start-up, called MIPS, spearheading the development of a RISC-based CPU chip. Sun became one of MIPS' early supporters and nurtured it through its collaborative relations. This allowed MIPS to leverage its partnership with Sun, sign up others, and enlarge its own circle of alliances. When MIPS was eventually acquired by Silicon Graphics, it was at the hub of some 140 alliances with world-class electronics firms, such as Olivetti, Nixdorf, Kubota, Prime, Samsung, Siemens, Toshiba, and many others, while Sun had launched the development of its own RISC-based CPU chip and its associated web of alliances. The initial co-learning within the MIPS alliance allowed Sun to design and produce its own RISC chip, later called SPARC®, without much loss of time and resources, which gave it an early entry and strong point of differentiation from others in the slowly emerging work-station industry founded on RISC-based CPU chips.

The product and marketing strategy of Sun is remarkably entrepreneurial. The massive network of partnerships with its suppliers enables Sun to rely on its partners for much of the 'commodity' components – components not used as a basis of differentiation for Sun, although still proprietary to Sun – for its work-stations (Strauss and Frost, 2001, pp. 190–91). In turn, this frees Sun to concentrate on introducing a continuous progression of innovative features that further differentiate Sun's work-stations from others and keep it ahead of the industry, where Moore's law reduces product life cycles at ever faster rates.

The important fact about Sun is that it does not manufacture most components of its products (Strauss and Frost, 2001, pp. 151–2). Even those parts potentially vital to differentiating Sun from others are made partly by Sun and partly by Sun's partners, as Sun can rely on the undivided loyalty of its partners. Naturally, these relationships have become much stronger and more complex than those in a typical strategic alliance: Sun conducts the R&D, develops the technology and transfers it to its partner(s). The partnership then begins the process of learning how to improve manufacturing processes to near perfection for achieving the highest possible quality and yield through joint experimentation. This is done mainly by the partner and with Sun's full support. This highly co-operative and interdependent management is a key to the success and prosperity of both Sun and its partners. In the process, however, Sun has become as dependent on its partners as they are on Sun. The relations, between Sun and manufacturing partners manifest features of symbiotic synergy as defined and presented earlier.

Sun recognized early on that a long-term, interdependent and symbiotic partnership cannot be managed through the customary *formal* methods (such as *competitive bidding, contract administrations and litigation*); nor even through the customary *informal* methods (such as implicit *financial penalties, withholding financial incentives, not sharing technological improvement, etc.*) or excluding partners from certain shared activities more valued to them than to Sun. Sun developed its own persuasive method of building higher dependencies by strengthening partners' need to maintain their special relations with Sun. Sun's system for managing such delicate and involved symbiotic partnerships, called the 'Score Card,' has become legendary in the industry (Holloway, 1996).

A critical factor is that Sun actually 'invests' in relationships with its partners through teaching, training and nurturing them on the mutual aspects of their relations, which in turn enables Sun to demand loyalty combined with quality performance for its high technical standards. An example of such practices is in the manufacturing of parts vital to Sun's differentiation strategy. The differentiating features, shared with partners, are the bloodline of the company's existence. While highly proprietary information must be shared with partners, there is a recognition that any breach or disclosure of technical information, design features, manufacturing processes and quality standards, or even compromise in the tacit aspects of the relations, could be highly damaging to Sun's long-term prospects. However, with Sun's long-term success, its partners prosper on a sustained basis. Without a *complete* commitment from Sun to its strategically valuable supplier partners, those partners might not remain as loyal and might seek greener pastures with Sun's competitors. Conversely, without the partners' full faith in and loyalty to Sun, Sun could not focus on improving the few differentiating elements, or new features, pivotal to its prosperity, if not to its survival. These arrangements, based on extreme dependence in the Sun's partnership system, have evolved over time. They have become the partnership standard to which the rest of the industry aspires. They exemplify the pattern of management practices that we have, in this chapter, termed as managing *special relations for symbiotic synergy*.

Millennium Pharmaceuticals

Marc Levin, the co-founder and CEO of Millennium Pharmaceuticals, calls it a 'bio-pharmaceutical company of the future' (Champion, 2001, p. 115). Founded by Levin and Raji Kucherlapati in 1993, Millennium Pharmaceuticals ('Millennium') now enjoys one of the highest growth rates of any Fortune 500 company, and has experienced the highest growth rate in the industry over the entire eight years of its life. By 1999, Millennium's revenues surpassed $1.5 billion and its market valuation was nearly $1 billion. The world's largest pharmaceutical companies, including Bayer

AG, Eli Lilly, Hoffmann–LaRoche, Lundberg and Monsanto, are now among its impressive list of partners (Thomke, 2001; Watkins, 1999). How did Millennium become a billion-dollar company in one of the most regulated, time-pressured, capital-intensive and intellectual-property-intensive industries in the world, in less than ten years?[3] It accomplished its meteoric growth largely by managing its relations methodically as a hub in a web of strategic partnerships, which is now spread all over the world.

Millennium's strategy of partnerships with members of the pharmaceutical industry was designed to be as symbiotic and synergistic as possible from the outset. A typical relationship is complex and multilevel. At one level, Millennium would heavily rely on partners to provide it with financing for further development, while partners would depend on Millennium for technology-based improvement in their joint drug discovery process. Neither member could achieve the expected progress without the other. Arguably, Millennium would not survive beyond the initial years without its partners as it did not have its own independent revenues or other source of funds.

At another level, in its highly entrepreneurial and progressive environment, Millennium nurtured and flourished its entrepreneurially oriented scientists, whose innovations and discoveries made faster drug discoveries possible, at a pace which stunned the industry. Cognizant of this complexity, partners provided the resources to nurture Millennium's truly innovative scientists and their innovative products and processes, which in turn allowed Millennium to deliver unique scientific results to its partners. These results hold the key to amassing a portfolio of new pharmaceutical products in record times. With such arsenals, partners were empowered to assemble potent portfolios of drugs for fighting non-partners within the industry.

Could Millennium have grown as fast as it did and gained its current international stature and presence without partnerships? In the absence of a clear alternative strategy for growth from start-up to multi-billion dollars in record time, the answer is probably no. The management of strategic alliances in the pharmaceutical industry seems to have taken a form and a direction which are distinctly Millennium's. Can Millennium continue to grow and prosper? Although the dynamics of larger and more complex firms rule against the continuation of previous growth rates, industry analysts did not expect Millennium to reach even its current size. Millennium's stated objectives are simple, yet very challenging: although Millennium remakes itself every 12 months (Champion, 2001, p. 115), it must deliver sustained benefits to its partners. The word 'partner' is central here. To Millennium and its partners, it implies a trusting, if not symbiotic, reliance on one another for potentially synergistic outcomes.

Without the necessary support, generated by downstream activities of others, to make its upstream activities possible in their shared value chain, Millennium's growth model would not have succeeded. Millennium still needs its partners' support to go on; and without Millennium's technology platform, its partners would be unable to meet the competitive challenges from within and the outside the industry. Simply stated, the partnership saves time and resources and generates potent solutions in an industry where payoffs associated with both time and resources are in the range of multi-billion dollars and risks of failure are equally substantive.

Siebel Systems

Siebel Systems ('Siebel') is in the software industry, competing head-on with the likes of Oracle and Microsoft. When a company like Microsoft sells a software package through the extensive worldwide channels of distribution for electronics, the independent channel member is unlikely to net more than 15 per cent on a Microsoft product. In contrast, when Siebel sells, or licenses, its highly sought-after Customer-Relation-Management (CRM) software platform and e-business systems to, and through, its worldwide network of strategic alliances, it receives no more than 15 per cent of the final billings. Its meteoric growth rate and revenues, from a start-up in July 1993, are no less impressive than those of Millennium Pharmaceuticals or Sun Microsystems: its revenues topped $1.8 billion in the year 2000, and its growth rate during the seven years since its birth has exceeded all expectations (Sull, 2001).

Siebel's initial business model was anchored in partnership: Siebel would extend its upstream technological services to support the local partner's downstream activities: marketing and local market support. Siebel Systems would produce and support its CRM software as a powerful, diverse and general-purpose platform for the local consulting partner to license, install, upgrade, customize to local customer requirements, and service them on an ongoing basis. Without a partnership-based model, such a wide and ambitious range of value-adding services would be impossible to achieve for a typical start-up independently. Likewise, the possibility of an independent global presence in such a service-intensive industry would be equally remote.

The crown jewel in this partnership strategy was Siebel's early partnership with Andersen Consulting (renamed Accenture in 2001). Accenture adopted Siebel's CRM program as the platform for its worldwide CRM-related consulting, which gave Siebel an instantaneous worldwide presence. Accenture also agreed to support further development of Siebel's CRM, which in turn gave Accenture a highly competitive arsenal for its worldwide CRM-related consulting, complemented with an equally attractive share of the proceeds.

Accenture's downstream activities enhanced and supported the fast evolution of the software program with the wealth of feedback from its customers worldwide. Access to such feedback, experience and contacts, although through partners, was critical to the fast evolution of Siebel's CRM. It also made Siebel an instantaneous household name in the field. Siebel became a 'born global' in a highly concentrated industry dominated by large, well-established firms such as Oracle, Peoples Soft, SAP and others.

Had it not been for Accenture's early support, partnership and a worldwide launch, Siebel would likely have remained an undiscovered and obscure start-up for some time. Without Siebel's CRM platform, and later its business system, Accenture would probably not have achieved its current worldwide leadership position in CRM and e-business-related services. This platform served as the perfect weapon in Accenture's re-engineering arsenal for re-organizing its client's worldwide businesses facing the onslaught of e-commerce-driven competitive attacks, especially on the supply chain automation side (i.e., the business-to-business side of the value chain). It is evident that these partnership relations have been based on high co-dependence and have become very satisfying for all parties. Simply stated, neither of the partners could have done as impressively as they did in the past short while without their special relation with the other.

Where will Siebel go on from here? Siebel is determined to build on its business model based on a high degree of *interdependence – resembling symbiotic partnership* – that has evolved from its successful early partnership with Accenture. It functions now as the central hub in a web of more than 700 other smaller strategic partnerships with consulting houses worldwide, which have also adopted Siebel's as their respective CRM platform. These partners rely on Siebel's continuously updated CRM software to assist them with solving a host of customer-related problems for their respective business clients as they emerge and evolve. Similarly, an ongoing re-engineering of business processes, based on its constantly updated CRM platform, is in continual progress. This is a true multi-level 'creative destruction' based on equally 'innovative combinations' (Schumpeter, 1911/1934 and 1947) not tried, or even conceived of, before.

Siebel's relations with its local consulting partners at one level complement those of the consulting partners with their clients at the next level. As clients are continuously evolving, their respective feedback loop (from business clients to Siebel through the local consulting partners) and Siebel's subsequent feed-forward loop (Siebel's upgrades for solving clients' more demanding problems through the local partner) constantly update respective capabilities. The end result of each feedback and feed-forward cycle is that Siebel's subsequent CRM and e-business platforms are further updated and are more powerful than previously. As a direct result, partners are equally empowered to attack more complex problems. All of these relations have a one-to-one quality (the essence of CRM) and are, in the truest sense, very special relations. Again, the word 'special' attains a richer and stronger meaning not experienced before. The noteworthy point is that Siebel exemplifies CRM: it treats *each* of its local consulting partners as if it depends on each of them for its survival (i.e., *symbiotically*). It solicits their downstream feedback in return for solutions to their particular problems much more effectively than they could do on their own (i.e., *synergistically*). This in turn sets the tone for each of the local consulting partners to extend similar attention and service to their respective clients and treat them as 'special' as they could make them. This maximizes the mutual and collective benefits for all concerned.

The lessons of the above theoretical discussion followed by examination of the cases are summarized and presented in Table 11.1. This table underscores a wide contrast between the kinds of relations implied in the traditional models of internationalization, and those of the newly emerging one reviewed in this chapter.

DISCUSSION

The cases of Millennium, Siebel and Sun indicate that the nature of relations in partnerships may evolve over time, becoming progressively fuller. In each case the relationships evolved from simpler and more formal involvement to more complex and fuller partnerships. In Millennium's case, for example, collaboration started with a high-technology platform as an upstream activity in the value chain of a partner. It expanded quickly to fuller involvements with a few partners and eventually progressed to sharing the risks, benefits, and ownership of jointly developed drugs (a downstream activity). This resulted in a significant and rapid downstream expansion for Millennium in the pharmaceutical's customary value chain.

From a conventional perspective, movement of an independent firm – upstream or downstream – would put the company in direct and head-on competition with other firms in those activities, including partners. The pharmaceutical industry, populated with large, well-established and integrated firms, has traditionally set relatively high entry barriers for newcomers. Logically, competition between the new small entrant and the large established firms would be ferocious, especially in the early stages of an independent entrant's life cycle, when the firm is relatively feeble and lacks the necessary reserves to provide it with a temporary life-support system. This would have been the case with Millennium; however, by belonging to a family of partnerships with special and privileged relations, Millennium

Table 11.1 Selected characteristics of the conventional model and the emerging partnership-based paradigm

States/components:	Conventional model	Partnership-based paradigm
Basis of value proposition	Differentiation: based on small to moderate scale and much larger specialization and scope economies	Lower cost and higher quality: based on much larger scale economies
Nature of value	Mostly objective upper bound: market	Mostly subjective lower bound: market
Firm's strategic value	Close to market valuation (revenue-based)	Based on strategic value of one partner to the partners' value chains (value-chain-based)
Nature of relations in the supply chain	Adversarial	Co-operative and co-operative (e.g., strategic alliances and other collaborative arrangements)
Nature of competition	Avoidance and low mobility due to barriers (legal and cultural)	Participation in free, open, international markets (e.g., highly competitive, deregulated, and with high mobility)
Nature of the competitive game	Closer to zero-sum	Closer to constant- or increasing-sum

becomes stronger in the newly emerging partnership-based paradigm. Millennium's migration downstream was actually supported by partners as its participation in, and contribution to, the collaborative network of partnerships grew. Millennium's expansion can therefore be viewed as an accumulation of expanded capabilities for partnership, more threatening to non-members than to partners. From this perspective, the partnership can be supportive and protective of a new and innovative member as the young member strives to become stronger and aims for even higher mutual benefits for the partnership as a whole.

On the contentious issue of control through acquisition and ownership when a partner is becoming more successful, the above cases are also instructive. The larger partners could have acquired the smaller growing partners, especially in the early stages of their life cycles. Consider Millennium, for example. Each of Millennium's large partners, including Hoffmann–LaRoche and Eli Lilly, could have easily acquired, controlled and operated Millennium as a subsidiary, especially in the earlier days, when Millennium's revenues and capitalization were relatively small. From a conventional viewpoint, it remains very puzzling why they did not.

Viewed from the perspectives of partnerships and special relationships presented in this chapter, the risks and costs of such acquisitions outweigh their potential benefits. Even a passive acquisition would have certainly exposed the acquiring company to additional risks without many incremental benefits; and possibly resulted in reduced benefits as compared to partnership-based collaboration. The concept of extreme co-dependence, or symbiosis, is capable of providing partners with most, if not all, associated features of ownership without the risks associated with ownership and control. Furthermore, the acquisition would give the acquirer not much beyond control, which could be even counter-productive in highly entrepreneurially oriented companies, such as Millennium. When such companies are taken over or acquired, there is a real risk of losing their entrepreneurially oriented pool of scientists to other companies. Similarly, the substantive risks and fears that Millennium's extraordinary entrepreneurial spirit might have drowned in the sea of the acquirer's corporate culture may have also played a significant role in the partners' decision against a take-over of Millennium. The synergic value of Millennium's strategic relations with all other partners would have been lost as well. The pivotal position of Millennium, at the hub of its web of alliances and partnerships, made its mutual relationships highly valued to partners, as it provided each partner with much more than what it invested in Millennium financially and more than it could accomplish independently, without Millennium. The cases of Siebel and Sun further confirm the above discussion.

CONCLUSION

The theoretical examination, together with the cases studies discussed in this chapter, suggest that a new *modus operandi*, or even a new paradigm, is emerging. This newly emerging paradigm is typified by new partnership arrangements based on interdependence as opposed to control by owner-ship, hierarchy or a dominant partner. This chapter documented that even the dominant and entrenched champions of the traditional model (e.g., IBM) have slowly migrated to, and embraced, the newly emerging model. IBM, for example, is presently involved in a massive number of strategic partnerships. The independent, self-sufficiency, ownership and control pre-occupations of the past are gradually replaced with partnership-based col-laboration with trusted and loyal, yet interdependent, partners (as the case of Sun Microsystems, for example, demonstrates). In contrast to *internaliza-tion*, well-managed and *externalized* relations are gaining stronger currency.

The Old and the Emerging Paradigms

In the old paradigm, SMEs grew systematically, experientially and sequen-tially over time to become larger, multi-product and multi-location opera-tions, and consequently MNEs. The concept of 'born globals' – small firms that internationalize at the start, or soon after they are created (Cavusgil, 1994; Knight and Cavusgil, 1996; McDougall *et al.*, 1994; Oviatt and McDougall, 1994 and 1997) – did not exist and could not be easily explained.

In the emerging paradigm, SMEs can become global enterprises at birth, as the case of Siebel Systems demonstrated. Siebel's non-exclusive partner-ship with Andersen Consulting/Accenture early in its existence gave it a global presence. In a fast progression, Siebel expanded its global reach to more than 700 other local partners by providing them with a CRM and e-business platforms to regenerate their respective consulting services, while emphasizing extreme co-dependence and synergy in their multi-level partnerships.

Millennium Pharmaceuticals, on the other hand, grew rapidly by lever-aging its high-technology drug discovery platform in different product lines and industries, using its capabilities to save time and expense for its part-ners to further leverage its partner-based relations. In a short time Millennium reached close to world-scale operations. Implicit in all of the above enterprises' fast growth and internationalization, partnership was a pivotal part of their business model and an integral part of their strategy from the outset. Retrospectively, their respective strategies were imple-mented without deviation from those early conceptions.

Similarly, companies solidly anchored in the old paradigm, including IBM, General Motors and others, who refused to conduct business through any form of partnership for some time, have changed course. When competitors began to capitalize on the efficiencies associated with symbiotic and synergistic relations and became much more competitive than enterprises still stuck in the old paradigm, the hard competitive lessons were driven home. The ferocious competitive pressures of the open international marketplace forced such older companies to make the choice: adopt the new paradigm rapidly or perish slowly. IBM, for example, currently manages some 20,000 active alliances and partnerships.

Our conclusion is that there is a convincing volume of evidence lending much stronger support to the partnership-based paradigm than to the traditional one. The emerging paradigm is leading to superior performance as partners learn to pool resources, learn from one another, amass experiential knowledge at a faster rate, and thus manage their collective relations for achieving much higher mutual benefits and increasing competitiveness than the traditional model.

ENDNOTES

1. 'Synergy' is defined as the combined action or operation of at least two entities, such as those of muscles, nerves, etc., to be more efficient and effective than the sum total actions of all entities, each acting in isolation. For example, when the combined effect of two or more drugs is more potent than the action of each separately, the word 'synergy' is invoked.
2. 'Symbiosis' is defined as the living together in intimate association, or even close union, of two dissimilar organisms. Ordinarily, it is used for cases where the association *of at least two entities* is advantageous, or often necessary, to one or both, and not harmful to either.
3. A typical drug development process takes $500 million and 15 years. These figures are simple proxies for the high capital and intellectual capital intensities present in this industry, unmatched by others.

REFERENCES

Acs, Zoltan and Bernard Yeung (1999), 'Entrepreneurial discovery and the Global Economy', *Global Focus*, 11 (3): 63–72.
Bilkey, W.J. (1978), 'An Attempted Integration of the Literature on the Export Behavior of Firms', *Journal of International Business Studies*, 9 (1), Spring/Summer: 33–46.
Bilkey, W.J. and G. Tesar (1977), 'The Export Behavior of Smaller Sized Wisconsin Manufacturing Firms', *Journal of International Business Studies*, 8 (1), Spring/Summer: 93–8.
Buckley, Peter J. and Mark Casson (1976), *The Future of the Multinational Enterprise*, London: Macmillan.

Cavusgil, S. Tamer (1980). 'On the Internationalisation of Firms', *European Research*, 8.

Cavusgil, S.T. (1982). 'Some observations on the relevance of critical variables for internationalization stages', in M. Czinkota and G. Tesar (eds), *Export Management: An International Context*. New York: Praeger, pp. 276–85.

Cavusgil, S.T. (1984), 'Differences Among Exporting Firms Based on Their Degree of Internationalization', *Journal of Business Research*, 12 (2): 195–208.

Cavusgil, S.T. (1994), 'Born Globals: A Quiet Revolution Among Australian Exporters', *Journal of International Marketing Research*, 2 (3): Editorial Note.

Cavusgil, S.T., W.J. Bilkey and G. Tesar (1979), 'A Note on the Export Behavior of Firms', *Journal of International Business Studies*, 10 (1), Spring/Summer: 91–7.

Cavusgil, S.T. and V. Kirpalani (1993), 'Introducing Products into Export Markets: Success Factors', *Journal of Business Research*, 27 (1): 1–15.

Cavusgil, S.T. and R.J. Nevin (1981), 'International Determinants of Export Marketing Behavior', *Journal of Marketing Research*, 28: 114–19.

Champion, David (2001), 'Mastering The Value Chain: An Interview with Mark Levin of Millennium Pharmaceuticals', *Harvard Business Review*, June: 109–15.

Coase, R.H. (1937), 'The Nature of Firm', *Economica*, 4: 386–465

Dana, Leo-Paul, H. Etemad and R. Wright (2000), 'The Global Reach of Symbiotic Networks', *Journal of Euromarketing*, September: 1–16.

Dana, Leo-Paul, H. Etemad and R. Wright (2001), ' Symbiotic Interdependence', in Dianne Welsh and Ilan Alon (eds), *International Franchising in Emerging Markets*, Riverwoods, IL: CCH Publishing, pp. 119–29.

Dunning, John H. (1977), 'Trade, Location of Economic Activity and MNE: A Search For An Eclectic Approach', in the *International Allocation of Economic Activity: Proceedings of A Nobel Symposium Held at Stockholm*, London: Macmillan, pp. 395–418.

Dunning, J.H. (1980), 'Toward an Eclectic Theory of International Production: Empirical Tests', *Journal of International Business Studies*, 11 (1): 9–31.

Dunning, J.H. (1988), 'The Eclectic Paradigm of International Production: A Restatement and Some Possible Extensions', *Journal of International Business Studies*, 19 (1): 1–31.

Eriksson, K., J. Johanson, A. Majkgard and D. Sharma (1997), 'Experiential knowledge and cost in the internationalisation process', *Journal of International Business Studies*, 28 (2): 337–60.

Etemad, Hamid (1999), 'Globalization and Small and Medium-Sized Enterprises: Search for Potent Strategies', *Global Focus* (formerly *Business and Contemporary World*), 11 (3), Summer: 85–105.

Etemad, Hamid, Richard Wright and L.P Dana (2001), 'Symbiotic International business Networks: Collaboration Between Small and large Firms', *Thunderbird International Business Review*, 43 (4), August: 481–500.

Gomes-Casseres, Benjamin (1996), 'Alliance Strategies of Small Firms', *Small Business Economics*, 9(1): 33–44.

Holloway, Charles A. (1996), 'Supplier Management at Sun Microsystems (A)', Stanford University Graduate School of Business, Palo Alto, CA.

Hymer, Stephan (1976), International *Operations of National Firms: A Study of Direct Foreign Investment*, Cambridge, MA: MIT Press.

Johanson, J. and J.E. Vahlne (1977), 'The Internationalization Process of the Firm – Four Swedish case studies', *Journal of Management Studies*, 12 (3): 305–22.

Johanson, Jan and Jan-Erik Vahlne (1990), 'The Mechanism of International-
ization', *International Marketing Review*, 7(4): 11–24.
Johanson, Jan and Finn Wiedersheim-Paul (1975), 'The Internationalization of the
Firm: Four Swedish Cases', *Journal of International Management Studies*, 12 (3),
October: 36–64.
Knight, Gary A. and S. Tamer Cavusgil (1996), 'The Born Global Firm', in S.
Tamer Cavusgil and Tage Koed Masden (eds), *Advances in International
Marketing* 8, Greenwich, CT: JAI.
Leonidou, L.C. and C.S. Katsikeas (1996), 'The Export Development Process',
Journal of International Business Studies 27 (3): 517–51.
Lodge, George and Ezra Vogel (eds) (1987), *Ideology And Competitiveness*, Boston,
MA: Harvard Business School Press.
McDougall, P., S. Shane and B. Oviatt (1994), 'Explaining The Formation
International New Ventures: The Limit of Theories From International Business
Research', *Journal of Business Venturing*, 9 (4): 469–87.
Oviatt, B. and P. McDougall (1994), 'Toward A Theory of International New
Ventures', *Journal of International Business Studies*, 25 (1): 45–64.
Oviatt, Benjamin Milton and Patricia McDougall (1997), 'Challenges for
Internationalization Process Theory', *Management International Review*, 37 (2):
85–99.
Rugman, A.M. (1979), *International Diversification and the Multinational Enter-
prise*, Lexington, MA: Lexington Books.
Rugman, A.M. (1982), *New Theories of Multinationals*, London: Croom Helm.
Schumpeter, Joseph Allois (1911), *Theorie der wirtschaftlichen Entwicklung*,
Munich and Leipzig: Dunker und Humblot; translated (1934) by R. Opie, *The
Theory of Economic Development*, Cambridge, MA: Harvard University Press.
Schumpeter, J. (1947), 'The Creative Response in Economic History', *Journal of
Economic History* 7, November: 149–59.
Stöttinger, B. and B. Schlegelmilch (1998), 'Explaining export development through
psychic distance: enlightening or elusive?', *International Marketing Review*, 15
(5): 357–72.
Strauss, Judy and Raymond Frost (2001), *E-Marketing*, Upper Saddle, NJ:
Prentice-Hall.
Sull, Donald (2001), 'Siebel Systems: Partnering to Scale', Boston, MA: Harvard
Business School Publishing.
Thomke, Stefan (2001), 'Millennium Pharmaceuticals, Inc. (A)', Boston, MA:
Harvard Business School Publishing.
Watkins, Michael (1999), 'Strategic Deal-Making at Millennium', Boston, MA:
Harvard Business School Publishing.
Williamson, O.E. (1975), *Markets and Hierarchies: Analysis and Anti-Trust
Implications*, New York: Free Press.
Williamson, O. (1981), 'The Economics of Organization: The Transaction Cost
Approach', *American Journal of Sociology*, 87: 548–77.
Wright, Richard W. (1989), 'Networking, Japanese Style', *Business Quarterly*, 54
(2), Autumn: 20–4.
Yoshino, Michael and V.S. Rangan (1995), *Strategic Alliances: An Entrepreneurial
Approach to Globalization*, Boston, MA: Harvard Business School Press.

Index